T0383201

PHOENIX
without the ashes
Achieving Organizational Excellence
through Common Sense Management

PHOENIX
without the ashes
Achieving Organizational Excellence
through Common Sense Management

Gary English, Ph.D.

S^t_L

St. Lucie Press
Boca Raton   Boston   London   New York   Washington, D.C.

Library of Congress Cataloging-in-Publication Data

English, Gary
    Phoenix without the ashes : achieving organizational excellence
through common sense management / by Gary English
       p. cm.
    Includes bibliographical references and index.
    ISBN 1-57444-219-8 (alk. paper)
    1. Industrial management — United States. 2. Total quality
management — United States. 3. Teams in the workplace — Training of —
United States. I. Title
HD70.U5E55   1998
658.4'013—dc21
                                                                           98-16304
                                                                                CIP

© 1998 by CRC Press

No claim to original U.S. Government works
International Standard Book Number 1-57444-219-8
Library of Congress Card Number 98-16304
Printed in the United States of America 1 2 3 4 5 6 7 8 9 0
Printed on acid-free paper

Introduction

One might think, from the near hysterical calls for managerial revolution and organizational destruction in numerous books on management and quality, that American management has not budged from the bad ol' days when the Japanese where eating our lunch. In some cases that is true, but those operations are either rapidly changing or disappearing. In truth, an ubiquitous quality revolution continues to sweep the country. It may be called different things, but the major thrust is the same — improve the internal operation of an organization and its ability to be effective in whatever market it must strive.

Revolution and frustration

While the focus of most literature seems to be on the major companies, there are tens of thousands of organizations all over the U.S. undergoing efforts at quality improvement. Like the major corporations, school districts, community banks, trade associations, government agencies, small businesses, and local facilities of large companies across the country have some improvement program underway. Working with them are thousands of consultants. All of this has created a major industry in itself, what might be called a "management quality industry".

While this is an evolutionary development, the pace, depth and dispersion of change by American management may well be seen, in the telescoping hindsight of history, as truly a revolution in American management. America is, once again, becoming a preeminent world management model.

Still, amidst all of its success there seems to be much disenchantment and dismay about much of the effort, even as it seems to be working. People are concerned about a tendency for the progress to unravel, for the disruption and pain to be too much, even counterproductive, and for management to feel its control slipping or that its cost-benefit is not quite right. There seems to be a tendency to pursue one technique after another in the hope that the next one will somehow be the magic potion. Terms like "flavor of the month" and "management by best seller" are suggestive of the cynicism and skepticism that has crept in.

Management wonders if the improvement efforts are really improving the bottom line or why others, such as middle managers and employees, "can't get with the program". In the bowels of many organizations and "successful" programs are employees who are frustrated at the difference between what management says and what may seem to be management's cruel and mindless actions.

Looking for root cause

This book attempts to explore why many of these new ideas, though logical, plausible and promising, so often seem to go awry in application. Problems in management improvement efforts have been noted and discussed in many articles and books, and are a common topic of conversation among managers and employees everywhere. In most every exploration, the chief reasons for failure in improvement efforts are (1) a reluctance by management to undertake improvement efforts initially and (2) getting them to stay the course until the program pays off.

These "reasons," however, are not root causes, i.e., the significant factors that drive the actions of managers. In keeping with the quality strategy, this book attempts to look behind the obvious and understand the "why's" of management actions and failures. It looks at the hidden aspects and forces that tend to frustrate, if not defeat, efforts at improvement. By analyzing some of the less visible underlying factors, as well as some of the commonly held management precepts, I have attempted to suggest what managers can do to really change their organizations and operations without the costs, disruption, and uncertainty that seem to accompany so many change efforts. It is only by understanding the causes of things that one can really manage them.

While I have tried to write with simple clarity, the topics explored in this book are profound, such as the relationship between language and thought or systems and motivation. Still, the topics of language, thought, systems, and motivation are, to me, critical factors that determine organizational outcomes. Finally, these factors are integrally related such that anyone can significantly influence the outcome of management actions. When all this is assembled, the reader will be challenged. Still, these are the factors that must be understood if one is to "know what you are about" and manage organizations with true quality assurance and optimal efficiency.

I don't believe that the problem stems from management's stupidity, laziness, or lack of concern about quality and improvement. While there are certainly some cases of that, most managers I have worked with are smart, work hard, and care a great deal about what they do. Most of them do the best they can given their understanding of the circumstances in which they work. That, however, is the key — to understand better the real-life circumstances of management and how that improved understanding can be employed for more effective management results.

A qualifier of this confidence in America's managers is that I refer only to those who are concerned about optimizing their operations. Certainly, in a capitalist society stock values are important, but if some managers have regard only for portfolio management, with operational matters being a necessary inconvenience, this book is not for them. It is for the managers who seek to optimize shareholder value by optimizing the value-adding abilities of their organizations.

Managing change

Organizational change is one of life's inevitabilities. The models used to manage change, however, are not self-effecting. Whatever the compelling virtues of any model, the future reality of an organization is a function of its present realities. Probably no example is quite so evident of this as the several Latin American countries, such as Brazil and Mexico, that used the American constitutional model to form their own "United States". The "model" was stellar, but the results of its use have had decidedly different historical results.

While good models can provide valuable understanding and guidance for change, the critical factor in managing change and quality improvement is less the model than of management's understanding of their own organization and how it works. Thus, it is not for managers to be experts on all the latest models and techniques, there being so many coming so fast that no one really is. To truly manage, however, they must understand the basic forces and factors of organizations that drive, effect, and define change. With that understanding, models and techniques become part of the inventory of a manager's tool box, to be used as appropriate with some skill to be developed as needed. Without such understanding, managing change becomes more akin to groping in the dark.

Even though there is a great deal of snake oil on the market, the great bulk of today's management thought is quite solid, even brilliant. It is bold for me, I admit, to attempt to see beyond what they have already provided. If I have succeeded, perhaps it is because I have a better view from their shoulders. While I may take issue with some of them, it is not to argue against them but to put their thinking into what I consider a better perspective, to broaden their context so that managers might understand and employ more effectively their new concepts and recommended techniques.

Part I discusses the nature of common sense and of quality as a condition of organizational excellence. Part II explores the nature of organization, human behavior, and the factors that can undermine and thwart efforts at quality improvement. Part III attempts to suggest how management might approach improving organizational quality using ordinary methods but using them from a different perspective suggested by modern knowledge and thought.

The points offered in this book are counter to many popular trends. For example, the book argues that common sense, not stylized technique, is the key to effective organizational management. It argues that routine is the very essence of an organization, not its nemesis. It defines the primary role of an organization as translating the grand purpose of its mission into practical work and discusses the management role and tools for this. The book also argues for the value, indeed inevitability, of incremental change, albeit strategically controlled.

Finally, the book argues that no one quality approach, whether reengineering, TQM, teams, etc. is adequate in itself. Rather, a variety of techniques are required if the effort is to be significantly and lastingly effective. A practical, overarching model for managers in their efforts, one that will "makes sense" throughout the organization, is that of "organizational rationality".

The author

Gary English, Ph.D., is a consultant in organizational performance, applying behavioral systems and technologies to operational improvement. His numerous clients have included manufacturers, chemical plants, agricultural operations, and nonprofit and governmental agencies. He has served on the faculties of several colleges and universities, teaching management and communications.

Dr. English has managed several national and regional operations, serving primarily as a turnaround executive for organizations in trouble. His articles on management and organizational communications have appeared in such journals as *Management Review, Quality Digest, Training & Development, Journal of Commercial Lending,* and *Public Administration Review.* In his work, Dr. English combines the perspective of a behavioral and social scientist with the workplace reality of a practicing executive.

Acknowledgments

A number of people have been helpful in developing this book through their advice and encouragement. These include Nancy Bullen, Jim Fink, Bill Wheeler, and my daughter, Rebecca, who made sure that it was understandable to at least one second grade teacher. My friend, Horst Max, lent his talents to some illustrations. Especially, I appreciate the trust that my clients have had in me, allowing me access to their operations and to my many colleagues who over the years have taught me much.

Contents

Part I. Common sense and the search for improvement

Chapter one. Making sense of modern management 3
Pressure for change 4
Waiting for the Phoenix 6
Fallacy of the clean slate 7
Confusion in the cornucopia 8
Snake oil and silver bullets 9
Not a passing phase 10
Mixed reviews 11
Promises and pitfalls 13
Need for a strategic rudder 14
Search for rationality 15
Search for easy answers 16
Strategic rationality 17
Invitation to argue 18
Endnotes 18

Chapter two. Common sense and organizational excellence 21
Management sense and management science 22
Science has it easy 22
Contours of common sense 23
Management styles 24
Whole-minded approach 25
Situational common sense 27
Measures of common sense 27
Experience, instruction, and inference 28
Common sense and individual style 29
Organizational knowledge 29
Quality as organizational excellence 30
Endnotes 31

Chapter three. The modern challenge of increasing complexity 33
The challenge of complexity 33
Chaos and the difficulty of knowing 35

Complexity and control 37
Search for elegance 37
Elegance vs. simplism 38
Elegant control 39
Endnotes 40

Chapter four. Excellent knowledge and organizational rationality 41
Shade tree management 42
Lessons from experience 43
Conceptual learning 43
Organizational knowledge 44
Essence of organizational being 45
Organizational irrationality 47
Organizational common sense 47
Amoeba-like organization 49
Managing knowledge 50
Beyond amoeba 51
Parochial vs. management control 52
Converting parochial into management control 53
Necessity of open dialog 54
Talk but no walk 56
Establishing organizational rationality 57
The *Dilbert* factor 58
Endnotes 59

Part II. Paradoxes and problems in management perspective

Chapter five. The paradox of language 63
Language and thought 63
Undermining common sense 64
Acceptable is okay 65
"Okay" becomes "excellent" 66
Us and them 67
Creating organizational classes 68
Price of separation 69
In other words 70
Enabling the organization 71
Winning performance 72
Between success and failure 73
Endnotes 74

Chapter six. American management ideology 75
Ideological lens 76
Adaptive thinking 77
Rational reframing 78
The right questions 79
Low and high context cultures 80
Weakness through strength 81

The irony of success 83
Newton vs. Einstein 84
From Aristotle 85
... to the Peter Principle 86
Endnotes 89

Chapter seven. Authority and control 91
Search for truth 91
Pressure to prevent 92
Pressure to produce 93
Blind faith in "bossism" 93
The bad habits of "bossism" 94
Need for modern controls 95
Paradox of overcontrol 96
The Soviet model 98
Rule-basing and bureaucracy 99
Leadership and control 100
Endnotes 102

Chapter eight. Decision making and work-process rationality 103
The decision stream 104
Decisions as translation 105
Inevitability of multiple outcomes 105
Lack of excellent knowledge 106
Decision as creative process 107
Creating realities 108
Gaining the favor of chance 110
Dialog of reality 111
Rational organizational decisions 112
Rational is as rational does 113
When discipline fails 113
Endnotes 115

Part III. Structural impediments to improvement

Chapter nine. Budgeting and organizational rationality 119
Management knowledge vs. accounting 120
Cost vs. waste management 120
Irrationality of cost-basing 121
Blind hope 123
Irrational incentives 124
Budget and control 125
Activity-based costing 126
Integrative budgeting 127
Paying for performance 128
Free enterprise ideology 129
Ownership and frugality 130
Budgeting as knowledge 131
Endnotes 132

Chapter ten. Framing the organization 133
Looking and seeing 133
Misplaced expertise 135
Primitive models 136
Models and management 137
Finding the organization 138
Social and technical systems 139
Management focus 141
Three basic errors 141
Endnotes 143

Chapter eleven. Routine as rut and groove 145
Routine not the problem 146
Paradox of routine 146
Poor routines and poor perspectives 148
Resistance to change 148
The invisible paradigm 149
When good routines go bad 151
Inherent resistance to change 152
Camels and straws 153
Inherent dynamic of change 154
Endnotes 156

Chapter twelve. Hierarchy and organizational learning 157
The new hierarchy 158
Hierarchy of knowledge 158
Clash of paradigms 160
Muddle in the middle 161
Built-in contentions 161
Role of middle management 162
Creating the blend of knowledge 163
Middle management alternatives 164
Inherent diversity of opinions 165
Translation and organizational change 166
Need for new concepts of hierarchy 168
Performance-based design 169
Endnotes 170

Part IV. Management, leadership, and organizational performance

Chapter thirteen. Leadership, coaching, and quality 175
Leadership style and all that 175
What leaders must do 177
Honesty first 178
Honest demands 179
Coaching to win 180
Price of power 182
Responsibility and power 183
Endnotes 185

Chapter fourteen. Leadership and motivation 187
Elements of motivation 188
Management and leadership 189
Translation and common sense 190
The centrality of purpose 191
Purpose and priorities... 192
Organizational common sense 193
Organizational quality as discipline 194
Purpose and common sense rationality 196
Quality and managerial leadership 197
Endnotes 198

Chapter fifteen. Common sense management 199
Priorities and urgencies 200
Centrifugal and centripetal forces 201
Natural elegance 202
Common sense, rationality, and purpose.. 203
Common sense and the aspects of enterprise 204
Emotion and rationality 207
Endnotes 209

Part V. Creating organizational excellence

Chapter sixteen. Strategies for change 213
Goodness of fit 213
Keeping fit 215
Stability and flexibility 216
Incremental approach 218
Strategic incrementalism 219
Incremental holographs 220
Using what you have 221
Incremental advantage 222
Endnotes 224

Chapter seventeen. Quality and organizational rationality 225
An unclear picture 226
Search for a better way... 227
Start where you are... 228
Establishing organizational rationality 229
Marks and measures of rationality 230
 Clear purpose... 231
 Benefit of customer focus 231
 Plan as translator 232
 Best available data and analysis... 234
 Best tools and craftsmanship 235
 Performance-based systems 237
 Managerial control 238
Endnotes 239

Chapter eighteen. The quest for quality 241
Making it happen 241
Actions and reactions 242
The being of doing 243
The keystone system 245
Effective performance management 247
Preparing for modern management 248
Organizational Rationality Audit Syllabus 248
Endnotes 252

Index 253

Part I

Common sense and the search for improvement

Chapter one: Making sense of modern management
Why do good ideas seem to cause as many problems as they solve?
The pressures of today's operating environment have pushed every major corporation, along with thousands of smaller companies, plants, and nonprofit agencies and governmental agencies, into organizational change and quality improvement programs. These programs have been wildly successful, terrible failures, or somewhere in between, depending on who is speaking. The difference seems to be less the techniques themselves than management's use of them.

Chapter two: Common sense and organizational quality
Why common sense is both simply unavoidable and as complex as human behavior itself
For whatever reason, many management gurus tend to condemn common sense. Common sense, however, is what managers use to do their jobs. Using common sense is not the same as being unthinking, but rather is employing the human faculties of finding purpose, imagining, analyzing, and getting emotionally energized. The reality of quality is to be found in people's abilities to use their common sense to achieve excellence, not in some particular technique.

Chapter three: The modern challenge of increasing complexity
Why things keep getting more confusing until we reach a new level of understanding
While every job at some point relies on knowledge of that particular activity, organizational effort also requires knowledge of the organization's larger purpose, the work of others in the organization, and how one's work fits in. Moreover, successful strategies require some understanding and appreciation of the particular work required to carry out those strategies. When different knowledges are appropriate and properly blended such that all work is optimized, an organization can be said to have "excellent knowledge" and is capable of achieving organizational quality.

Chapter four: Excellent knowledge and organizational rationality
What is the nature of organizational knowledge and how does it relate to organizational action?
An organization learns through communication with itself, such that all employees can learn, share knowledge, and work together for optimal organizational success. This allows the organization to become highly adaptive and make timely, effective responses to the market and operating environment.

chapter one

Making sense of modern management

Why do good ideas seem to cause as many problems as they solve?

> *From its ashes came forth another phoenix, either*
> *perfect or at first in the shape of a white grub.*
> ∽Tacitus

The division executive vice president was still in a state of stunned disbelief. Only a few weeks before, the CEO had announced to corporate top management that they were beginning to change at the speed of light, that there would be continuously shifting paradigms, that they were going to reinvent the corporation, and the process would be never ending. The company had already downsized. His division had already lost many of his most experienced middle and front line managers and more were to go.

The executive ranks were being thinned, and several senior executives were already gone. The division executive sat atop the finest facility of its kind in the world, but the world market was changing to a different kind of product, and he must adapt, albeit with reduced staff capability. The CEO prophesied that there would be a lot of pain, but in the end a leaner, meaner, and stronger organization would emerge "like a Phoenix from the ashes."

As I listened to this string of buzz words, I studied the executive to see if he was giving me a parody of modern management self-improvement techniques, but he was quite serious. His goal was now to keep things going for a couple of years so that he could retire before he himself got caught up in the conflagration. Six months later, one of the corporation's primary subsidiaries filed for Chapter 11. Several months later, the company's CEO was obliged to step down.

Welcome to life in modern corporate America. This executive was not with one of the companies that seem to be written about in the articles and books on management, but it is probably more representative of the thousands of corporations, facilities, and public agencies that have gone through, and continue to attempt, improvement efforts. Their faith and efforts have often brought more pain than productivity, more quarrels than quality. If we miss their stories, we miss the real management history of our times.

Pressure for change

It is frequently in the newspapers, but it is not news: Today's organizational skippers must navigate through perilous and often uncharted seas of rising costs, narrowing margins, new technologies, changing employee attitudes, resurgent labor unions, and a never-ending swell of new competitors.[1] Unlike the captains of old, however, modern managers do not suffer from a lack of navigational charts. To the contrary, there are daily warnings of newly discovered threats from rocks and shoals, coupled with new notions on how to get to the land of productive workers and happy customers. These are the solicitations of the purveyors of the quality movement, sometimes called gurus, and they are many and varied.

Unfortunately for managers, selecting from among the many competing "quality" approaches can be as challenging as the business environment itself. Even if the choice is clear, managers have the practical problem of implementing large-scale change without losing control over their organizations. The pressures to improve and the continuing flows of new change schemes have created a conundrum for modern managers that will not go away. Managers are trying hard to find ways to improve and to make their ideas work. The sale of business books has more than doubled during the past 10 years, and fees to consultants have more than tripled during the same period.[2]

The quality movement can point to clear and eminent successes. Motorola, which has reached a new standard in reducing errors, increased its profits by reducing cycle times and strengthened its position as a significant force in the international market. Another example is Canadian Airlines, which increased its customer service ratings from dead last to first in just a few years through improved quality of operation and service. On a smaller scale, Velcro, after going through its quality program, reduced the number of quality control staff from 23 to 12. Moreover, the logic of quality is compelling. It just makes sense to prevent problems rather than trying to fix them after they have become too frequent or big to ignore, to plug the leak rather than increase the bailing, to pull the rope (process) rather than trying to push it.

Deming, Juran, and Crosby estimate that 85% of productivity problems are in the system and can be remedied. Proponents of cycle-time management argue that "as many as 90% of the existing activities are nonessential and can be eliminated."[3] Further," Crosby argues, "quality is free" in that improvements in process essentially allow you to get your money's worth from what one already is paying. Research continues to confirm the value of system-oriented management. A recent study of errors in medication, which kill 18,000 and injure more than a million patients annually and are the primary cause of medical malpractice, resulted not from poor individual effort but from systems that require flawless performance by everyone, a foolish expectation. A study of banking operations found that 50% of operating costs supported error-prone procedures.[4]

It is trendy to characterize American management as reluctant to try new ways. While there certainly are some such managers, the evidence is overwhelming that organization leaders are trying most anything that looks promising. Part of the confusion is that "quality" itself can mean almost any improvement change from ISO 9000 to calling supervisors "coaches". One estimate is that almost $2 billion have been spent during the past 10 years on quality programs. AT&T is reported to have spent more than $347 million for consulting and research services in 1993.[5] What has been spent through indirect costs, such as employee work time in meetings, is difficult to imagine.

In their efforts to find ways to improve, modern managers have studied the lessons of Sun Tzu, Alexander the Great, Attila the Hun, and other unlikely ancients. They have climbed trees and fallen backwards into waiting hands and played countless workshop games and simulations. The new notions are being tried through acts of faith and a commitment of money that any revivalist preacher would envy. It has been estimated that 75% of managers are trying some new approaches, and companies, on the average, are trying 12 new techniques. So many new things are being tried that some companies have established positions for managing the new efforts, and management literature is now turning to finding ways that these various approaches can fit together.[6]

The ancient Egyptian scholar who was concerned that "everyone is writing books" would certainly be alarmed at the flood of management advice being published today. Any visit to some bookstores finds the shelves in the management section groaning under the weight of advice. Early in this century, Frederick Taylor developed "scientific management", and the Hawthorne studies at Westinghouse discovered a group psychology in the workplace. In recent years, the pace of change and flurry of new ideas have, in management as in most areas of American life, been dizzying and telescopic. It seems just yesterday that management was quoting the gospel of the "Peter Principle" and Tom Peters' *Search for Excellence*. Now, these seem almost quaint in the face of reengineering, cycle-time management, activities-based management, quality-function development, self-directed teams, ISO 9000, work process mapping, and a torrent of new methods and techniques.*

Waiting for the Phoenix

Perhaps the most hazardous course is one that requires management essentially to gut the old operation and replace it with a radically new one. This kind of attack is tantamount to dropping a "change bomb" on the workforce that disrupts, even destroys, their work. That, in fact, is the idea recommended in *Don't Automate, Obliterate*, the challenging title of Michael Hammer's introduction to reengineering.[7] Tom Peters is preaching "revolution, everything else is tactics," and even Deming argued that fundamental changes in existing practices were required to achieve Total Quality Management (TQM). "Improvements," he said, "cannot be grafted onto existing management structures and systems" but require wholesale uprooting of the old and replacement with the new. One should use "discontinuous thinking" to prevent the new order from being corrupted by the old, which, once destroyed, will give rise to a new one that will emerge like Phoenix from the ashes.

Managers like the idea of the Phoenix; it is the ashes that give them concern. The Phoenix has become the symbol of the emerging new organization that will solve all the problems of getting work from people. That business process reengineering (BPR) seems to have delivered on its promises inadequately is attributed to the lack of "management commitment" to radical change. Certainly, a business culture that eliminates a quarter of a million jobs a year cannot be considered squeamish about administering pain. Even so, the Robespierre-like qualities needed to satisfy the proponents for absolute reengineering may be asking a bit too much. Besides, revolutions have a bad way of devouring their leaders and a lot of others as well.

Reformers and revolutionaries do not like incremental change. They see only the beauty of their dream and the flaws of an unredeemable reality but may have no real sense of how to connect the two. Unfortunately, revolutions are never predictable, tend to be painful and costly, and are often hazardous

---

* While no one probably has a complete list, some other new approaches are quality-function deployment, breakthrough teams, high-performance teams, cascading teams, flat organization, benchmarking, reinvention, cultural change, root-cause analysis, continuous quality improvement, performance management, broadbanding, empowerment, concurrent engineering, skill-based pay, gain-sharing, pay for performance, de-jobbing, just-in-time training, team management, knowledge management, intrapreneuring, learning organization, reenergizing, environmental monitoring, and management by walking around. When a managers have learned all these, and the others that will have generated between this inventory and press time, they may not be better managers, but they can have one heck of a discussion.

to their authors. And, when the revolution is over and the dust has settled, things seem strangely similar to the way they were before. The need to improve workplace productivity and quality is no longer arguable but, with rare exceptions, organizations require improvement, not replacement. Consultants and gurus need something like the Hippocratic oath of medicine, the first precept being "Do no harm."*

Major organizational change is not only risky but also requires enormous amounts of time, energy, and initial productivity losses from disruption of work processes. It can, like chemotherapy, be debilitating until the "cure" takes. No responsible manager would put an organization at such risk and through such turmoil unless faced by some pressing and terrible exigency. What is required is an effort that guides and rationally connects reality with a vision of what can be better. What managers want is a program that brings about significant improvement but still allows the organization to continue its best work, that is, a Phoenix *without* the ashes.

Fallacy of the clean slate

Most of us would do things differently if we could start over again, but we simply cannot. Such fantasy is fine for personal daydreaming but it can be disastrous when applied as a management principle. Certainly, if a company were on the edge of massive failure, then immediate and radical action could be appropriate. But this is not the situation most companies face. What they do face is a need to reduce the number of defects in production or process to increase customer base, to improve safety, and so forth. Circumstances within and outside an organization change, whether through success, accumulated bad habits, technology, or the market. Virtually every organization, therefore, needs to take stock periodically of its condition and direction. A fundamental reality is that most organizations are where they are today because they are doing most things right. Another fundamental reality is that most organizations need to review continually how they do their work and, on occasion, change it. The more appropriate metaphor for organizational change, however, is not the sick patient who requires radical surgery, but the athlete who needs to become better conditioned for new challenges. The model is fitness, not terminal illness.

Descartes used the term *tabula rasa* to indicate that each new person comes into this world with a clean slate and could start anew in anyway desired. Freud's contribution to understanding was that people did not, in

---

* As one manager told me, "Telling me I need to find ways to improve is like telling Noah about the flood." This gave rise to the thought that the story of Noah is about God trying to start over again with the human race, but even that effort required something from the old. And, it must be remembered, Noah had the advantage of God as his consultant, while most managers must do with a lesser competence.

fact, come in with a clean slate because they were creatures with instinctual drives and urges. Similarly, unlike the dream world envisioned by radicals and academics, every business organization is essentially structured by its own history, technologies, people, systems, markets, and operating environment. Even new organizations are staffed by people who arrived preprogrammed by their training and experience. Indeed, that is why they are hired.

Every new enterprise begins with some established set of models, values, practices, and perspectives. Any given industry has a typical workforce drawn by the nature and culture of that kind of work, technology, market, etc. which must be incorporated and utilized in order to exist at all. Open up a new bank and it is indistinguishable from the others. The interactions of people in this milieu are not attributes of the organization; they *are* the organization. All of this cannot be reinvented. Every company will essentially rise or fall depending upon what it does with what it has. There can be quantum changes to be sure, but true and enduring *positive* change will always be incremental, protracted, and evolutionary.

Some companies have actually tried to implement recommendations such as abruptly eliminating all first-line supervision with predictably sad results. It would not seem sensible for managers to implement wholesale changes as an act of pure faith or without at least testing in some smaller part of the operation first. Even the idea of closely following demonstrated "best practices" can be misleading. Companies will try a new program and tout its seeming early success. By the time another company has begun to implement it, yesterday's "best practice" can become today's "failed program" replaced by yet another "flavor".

Sometimes a good practice at one place does poorly at another. Many companies have tried the DuPont safety program but often with disappointing results. DuPont's safety record is outstanding, but it is probably more the product of its culture and method of operations than the specific program itself. To truly begin anew is say-able but not really doable. Any realistic expectation of organizational change should be to craft an improved version of what one now has.

Confusion in the cornucopia

For managers, it is the best of times and it is the worst of times. It is the best of times, because there are many new and promising ideas on effective management that are much more sophisticated and capable than the old school of clunky, mechanical organizations. It is the worst of times, because the very cornucopia is issuing not a neat fabric of management strategies and tactics but a flood much like an explosion in a paint factory. People often disagree about what many of the terms they throw around actually mean.

Deming never really defined TQM, but many have tried since, making the term so embracing as to be as generic as aspirin, perhaps really more like pain killer. In one review of the use of the term TQM, the writer found TQM to be a:[8]

- Program, i.e., a way to deal with immediate problems to get quick results
- Approach to employee involvement, i.e., quality circles
- Way to process management, i.e., teamwork
- Toolbox, i.e., techniques to be used on appropriate occasions
- Marketing focus, i.e., treatment of vendors and customers
- Paradigm, i.e., corporate culture and Deming's 14 points
- Postmodern theory

In common parlance, TQM often means *any* improvement effort. Anything that means everything, in essence, means nothing.

This same problem is evidenced in many other areas. For example, teams, including the more specifically titled self-directed work teams, can vary from having a kindly supervisor who helps out his subordinates to groups of peers with true management powers. There are even high-performance teams, but hardly anyone really knows what that means. There is also the frequent problem of incompatibility of concepts where, for example, a worker may be empowered by her manager only to be pulled into the group will of a team. Some new strategies may have strong advocates, but they cannot bear much critical analysis. Studies suggest that some of the most cherished notions of participatory management such as "leadership style" and "involvement in decision making" have little actual effect.[9]

Discussions of problems encountered when trying to use various change strategies should be married to discussions of what these things really are. One does not know what has failed or succeeded. As the discussion regarding the various kinds of TQM (above) suggests, one may begin with one idea and end up somewhere else, either by changing one's mind in the process or because the approach itself has not been well understood to begin with. A company might be pursuing some version of TQM and reengineering that the authors of those strategies might not recognize or even agree with.

Snake oil and silver bullets

Management seems forced to choose between today's magic potion and what was yesterday's magic potion, now called snake oil by proponents of the *new* magic potion. Some people exhibit an almost religious fervor and devotion about some guru or other, speaking about their favored guru in the semi-hushed tones normally reserved for churches. Proponents of teams and empowerment are often Rousseau-like in their faith that the noble worker will, once freed from the corrupting confines of management control, blossom into self-managed, quality-committed, and work-dedicated employees.

Academe, normally a place for considered contemplation, now, in a unique role reversal, seems to be following the ideas of the trades as the workplace has become a fountainhead for new improvement ideas. The intellectual disputes that once took place in textbooks are now found in professional and trade books as each new proposed system tries to reach the top of a heap of discredited bodies of the others. Most management thought today seems to be the product of consultants rather than academics. That does not lessen the fury of the battle. Deming disdains any kind of exhortations, i.e., campaigns to motivate employees, while others advocate motivation through improved top-down communication. A book on the subject of performance management reviews all of the major quality approaches, finds them wanting, and then proposes an approach that is claimed to have astonishing power, while another book on leadership promises to show how to get extraordinary things done.[10]

As management keeps searching for a silver bullet to cure its organizational problems, and as new approaches continue to pop up on bookstore shelves, the whole arena is beginning to take on the flavor of the absurd. People, as one corporate manager stated, have had so much "reinvention, restructuring, reengineering, re-*this,* and re-*that* that no one pays attention to that stuff any more ... they just try to do their jobs." Ironically, he was referring to a company that advertises itself as a change consultant and headlines one advertisement for its services with the sarcastic, "Oh, great. Another paradigm shift."[11] The ad goes on to say that, unlike other consultants, this company really knows how to improve business processes.

Not a passing phase

It has gotten to the point where management improvement has become the stuff of novels and comedic mills. Humorist Garrison Keillor writes in *Time* magazine:[12]

> "The words holistic, leadership, process, quality, and commitment crop up everywhere — sentences like, 'The commitment to quality is a holistic value structure throughout the leadership process that is accessed dynamically through all functions of the organization from the bottom up.' Sentences that, the moment you hear them, they're gone like gas."

Hardly anyone has not seen and laughed at the bitter humor of Scott Adams' *Dilbert*, which is only the most popular of a new spate of workplace cartoons. Much of the *Dilbert* humor rests upon a chillingly realistic dialog of what could be called "quality-babble".[13] In one cartoon, the manager asked each of the "staff" to undertake a different quality initiative and asked them to suggest a name for the overall effort. The suggestion was "qaulicide".

Perhaps most telling is that management change efforts have become so ordinary and interwoven into our cultural fabric that they have become the stuff of literary settings. In his murder mystery novel, *Vertical Run*, Joseph Garber sets the stage and outlines a character in this manner:[14]

> "During his six-year tenure on the forty-fifth floor, Dave had been subjected to the ministrations of quite nearly a dozen motivation ju-ju men, managerial messiahs, and behavioral gurus. He had sat through interminable weekend seminars staged by temporarily popular business school professors, wallowed with his fellow executives in hot tubs at the Esalen Institute, and sweated with them in saunas at the Aspen Institute. He had jogged side by side with his wheezing and purple-faced boss at an *In Search of Excellence* 'skunkworks boot camp' and, a year later, had helped carry him down from the mountain upon which, during an Outward Bound 'team-building adventure', Bernie had sprained an ankle."

Mixed reviews

Whether quality programs are effective or not depends on who you read. A national study by the General Accounting Office found that quality management efforts can improve profitability, market share, and customer and employee satisfaction.[15] The 16 Malcolm Baldrige winners since 1988 have performed three times better than the Standard & Poor's 500-stock index, and almost 50 companies that made it to the final award rounds outperformed the index by 2 to 1.[16] One can identify many companies that have demonstrated the power of what might really be called modern management techniques, for, when we push aside the disparate labels for the various approaches, that is really what we are talking about.

On the other hand, there is strong evidence that proposed panaceas have often failed to deliver on their promises. Reports abound and conclusions vary in such publications as *Forbes*, *Harvard Business Review*, and *The Wall Street Journal*. A report in *Business Week* noted that 14 of the 43 companies praised in *In Search of Excellence* no longer met the "excellence" criteria. Some winners of the Deming Prize and Baldridge awards went immediately from accepting the awards to financial troubles. Some note that only one third of 500 manufacturing and services companies felt that their quality program had a significant impact, and only one fifth of the British firms thought they had achieved "tangible results". In other reports, quality efforts have yielded a perceived impact of less than 20 to 60%. One report of company surveys found TQM success rates between 1 and 8%, and a Harvard economics professor stated that he knew of "no empirical evidence that any of these things increase productivity."[17]

Trade journals are full of articles trying to explain the reasons, several of which have been cited in this chapter. Most of these say the same thing — inadequate management commitment, lack of adequate training, or wrong approach (that is how most articles or books suggesting the "correct" approach begin). One study of 17 articles and books analyzing TQM failure determined the 15 most cited causes, the top ones being, in order of frequency:[18]

- Improper planning
- Inability to change organizational culture
- Lack of continuous training and education
- Ineffective measurement techniques and lack of access to data and results
- Paying reduced attention to internal and external customers
- Inadequate use of empowerment and teamwork and lack of management commitment

The reality is that, slowly and subtly, American companies are changing in their operation. These efforts are bringing change, although not necessarily what was intended, and in many cases the price has been high in money and pain. The problem is not that things have not been improved, but rather they often seem to have ended, well, disappointingly. The improvements either have not reached as far as they should or things have simply been allowed to fall back the way they had been. Ask management about its quality improvement program and one may hear of considerable accomplishment. Ask the front-line workers or supervisors, and one is more likely to hear that "they're" always trying some new program or other that never makes much difference "down here".

As many managers have discovered, unfulfilled expectations are only the tip of the iceberg. There is considerable cost in radical change, and the consultants are a relative trifle. Existing practices, however flawed, were reliable, and people were skilled in making them work. Replacing these with unfamiliar methods and new skill requirements can result in confusion and organizational failures. With the uprooting and severing of the vast informal networks that got work done, efficiency suffers. One of the more harmful of these side effects is the general demoralization and disenchantment of staff. With each new program, confidence in management suffers and resistance to new changes increases. The team qualities the systems purport to produce are undermined.

Still, most quality programs can bring some degree of benefit if, for no other reason, they afford management an opportunity to take a fresh look at what it is doing. Work practices in the form of individual and organizational habits generally become hidden from view. Problems may get attention but the unseen host of activities that present the problem rarely does — and that, of course, is what the quality movement seeks to cure. The difficulty comes when techniques become tattooed on old work practices, which, though mutilated, do not become fundamentally changed. That is why Hammer urged management to obliterate these old practices.

Promises and pitfalls

There are numerous and varied approaches to management improvement, and many companies have tried most of them. Most any of these will bring benefit if properly utilized. By themselves, however, they generally lack a necessary overall framework within which they can be used as an overall management improvement strategy. Rather, they tend to be techniques or philosophies that, without an overall strategy to guide and measure their use, can be highly useful but do not provide excellent knowledge. Indeed, they can bring a number of sometimes unpleasant surprises in the countless ordinary daily decisions and actions that occur throughout the organization and which tell the tale of every operation. Many approaches, while rational in themselves, do not provide the right combination of concept and technique to achieve total organizational rationality.

In reviewing the various approaches (listed in Table 1), which are insightful and even wise, one cannot help but be struck by their paradoxes. For example, one of Deming's key points was to get fear out the work place. Nonetheless, fear is so universally pervasive, and management so reliant on it, that one wonders whether Deming was seriously advocating this or just wishing. Covey joins the ancients by arguing that principles and competence are necessary to earn trust. However, definitions of what constitutes management competence is one of the raging issues of the day. Hammer's reengineering was not designed to put fear into the workplace; actually, it was intended to take much of the fear out by rationalizing work processes. Still, his work has been used to terrorize thousands of people. ISO 9000 and Malcolm Baldridge are excellent standards, but many people try to cheat because their eye is on the award rather than the benefits of the standards.

Table 1 Seven Major Improvement Approaches and Their Potential Pitfalls

Approach	Example	Potential pitfall
Start all over again	Hammer and Champy	Large-scale disruption, confusion
Start with reducing variation	Total Quality Management (TQM)	Focus on conformity over change
Start with specific systems	Cycle-time management	Devaluing vital support systems
Start with specific problems	Breakthrough teams, SPC	Neglecting systems that drive behaviors
Start with behavioral modification	Aubrey Daniels	Neglecting technical processes
Start with leadership	Covey	Neglecting systems and processes
Start with empowerment	Human relations	Neglecting systems and processes
Start with standards	Malcolm Baldridge, ISO 9000	Becoming *pro forma*, not pursued in good faith

Teams have as many horror stories as success, perhaps more, and the process has been likened to bringing a tiger in your house to rid it of mice. Human relations programs make everyone feel better, but the benefit often does not stick much longer than the workshop itself.

Need for a strategic rudder

The disenchantment with BPR is not its logic, for that seems quite sound. Rather, it seems to require absolute organizational restructuring that never seems to be enough. The pitfall of many new ideas is that they are offered as organizational improvement strategies, not merely as one arrow in a manager's quiver. While these techniques are indeed likely to bring about system-wide changes, in themselves they do not serve to manage the full array of changes they instigate. Hence, they can become a new source of problems.

Any self-conscious, systematic and rigorous technique replacing a process low in these qualities is likely to bring about improvements in discipline, focusing, and communications. Quality circles — getting people together to talk about ways to improve things — still make a lot sense. Indeed, managers constantly use some version of them today with some success. The key variable in their success is the environment in which they labor. As the experience of many has proved quite clearly, a technique that is plopped down in the middle of an inappropriate environment is less likely to be successful than to stir up passions and expectations that can disrupt an organization. Perhaps that is why quick-fix efforts such as quality circles have not borne fruit. For example, a 1985 study of Fortune 500 companies that started quality circle programs found that only 17% of them lasted longer than 18 months.[19]

There has been failure in that these approaches, despite some claims, have not provided managers with a unifying, ongoing, universally applicable, and readily available tool to guide and measure these change efforts. This omission is often noted by critics and would-be gurus who then proceed to outline their change model which purports to remedy this oversight, much like the present writer.[20] Deming, Senge, and others wrote about systems thinking because any event in organizational processes will have an impact in other parts of the system or in other systems.

The value of process and systems thinking is that it helps managers connect a number of related activities and helps make sense of what may be, on the surface, disparate functions. It provides a more realistic context for managers to understand and act upon the situation immediately facing them. Every action should be toward the corporate value-adding effort. Value-add, however, requires both an overarching end goal and a strategy to achieve that goal. These goals and strategies are realized in the specific and situational challenges managers face. It is imperative, therefore, that managers have some fundamental understanding of the strategic implications of these local events.

To keep the situation at hand from being viewed too parochially, the desired outcome of that process must fit comfortably and rationally with the general organizational goals. Rationality exists to the degree that the activities of an organization are logically and reasonably pursuant to its purpose. Business process reengineering, or any other technique, is not scary or damaging if properly contained and controlled through an overarching management rationality. It only becomes destructive when it becomes a reason in itself and drives the organization into a truncated and misleading rationality which creates, overall, a condition of irrationality.

Search for rationality

When companies are undergoing Covey training, cycle-time reductions, reengineering, downsizing, and an ISO 9000 effort (and some companies are doing much more of this), their greatest need is for some general, strategic organizational management perspective. This is not only to optimize the value of these initiatives, but also simply to maintain the good order of the organization. Despite this pressing need for managers, many gurus continue to preach the virtues of discontinuity and even irrationality.[21] It may be the age of discontinuity or unreason, but true disconnect is not realistic, and irrationality has never been demonstrated to be a virtue.

What this means is that managers must have better understanding of what they are now doing in order to understand how to use the available change tools; otherwise, they will keep going from program to program, disrupting their operations, wearing their people out, and inculcating cynicism and pessimism toward change efforts in general. Organizations will labor through one program and then, as their operation is disrupted and productivity suffers, will go through a renewal, which is simply trying to get back to where they were before.

The logic of many change approaches can be beguiling, but logic is not rationality, and that is the reason the new approaches do not "make sense" to many of the managers and employees who are expected to make them happen. And, when one change program is followed by another, employee skepticism turns to cynicism as faith is lost in one's own management. The middle managers and employees, who for years created the organization's success, are now seen as being benighted obstructionists, with such facile and self-serving explanations as "people don't like change".

People like change. It is risk, particularly unknown risk or risk in which there is little promise of reward, that makes people cautious. Many of the organizational changes today make employees feel as though a giant bird (perhaps a Phoenix) has snatched them up and deposited them somewhere else (perhaps in the street). It is a good way to get employees moved around quickly, but it is an experience that they will remember, and perhaps resent, for a long time.

In an internal memorandum of a Fortune 500 company, the corporate human resources executive told division HR managers that their aim was to spur continuous improvement. They would not, therefore, be able to supply clear answers to such understandable questions as, "What is our target?" "How will we know when we reach it?" "What, exactly are my function and responsibility?" It is no wonder that employees drew back to avoid the scary embrace of such activities. The real test of a new approach is not its radicalism vs. incrementalism, but rather its goodness of fit. This creates rationality aligned with the basic purpose of the organization, the one to which everyone is supposedly committed. The basic job of management is, after all, to provide a rational, goal-achieving structure in a chaotic and largely uncaring world.

Search for easy answers

For every complex, difficult problem there is an answer that is simple, easy, and wrong. According to Peter Drucker, the promise of a quick and easy fix is one of "the most degenerative tendencies in the human race" and can be seductive. With such faith, managers jump from the bridge in the hope that there will be some water. Drucker argues:[22]

"Simple solutions to complex problems — that's the universally seductive formula. That's why books like *The One Minute Manager, In Search of Excellence,* and *Megatrends* have been so successful. ...Problems are solved easily, almost magically, in the world depicted in these books."

One of the reasons that top management requires change in others but brooks none in its own prerogatives and methods is that they lack a perspective of what they themselves are about. Unless people in an organization can see that top management has a strategic understanding to guide its own change, they will be reluctant to change what they are doing. When management continues in its old ways, whatever the current preachment, employees read the "real" message of management's actions rather than what is being said. They know that this latest flavor will pass, things will get back to where they were, and if they are left standing when the music stops they lose. In such a situation, people will see change activities only as extra work and will not make the commitment to stay with a program for the long pull required to establish true, deliberate, and lasting organizational improvement. In the meantime, smart employees are on their guard for programs that threaten to tip the boat over.

Strategic rationality

The need for managers to have an effective and readily available model transcends the immediate problem of what to do with change programs. All management is constantly involved in making adjustments to the organization and, therefore, is in need of a constant tool. Fortunately, such a tool is quite available and has been around for centuries. It is the very quality of mankind that has made us the supreme species but one which many gurus ardently urge managers to abandon — i.e., common sense. There are two uniquely human faculties in all social endeavors: (1) an ability to imagine a different state of things, often called the vision, and (2) an ability to undertake a rational effort to achieve that state. The first we call *leadership* and the latter *management,* topics discussed more thoroughly in Part IV.

If managers are to use a common sensible and rational approach successfully, they must first understand common sense itself and how it both serves and undermines their efforts. Secondly, they must understand the behavioral material with which they work in an organization. Only then will they be prepared to master the skills necessary to develop true managerial virtuosity and to avoid the siren call of "skill sets for effective, empowering coaching leadership" or the glittering but elusive "high performance organization". Fire is a wonderful, dangerous tool. And, like fire, change must be controlled, with every step contributing so that one gets improvement, not ashes, for the Phoenix is, after all, only a myth.

Invitation to argue

This book is an invitation for the reader to think along with me as I share some ideas that seem to address the pesky questions in the fields of both management and thinking about management, i.e., management theory. It is an effort to dig beneath the obvious answers and find true, but perhaps hidden, causes of why things so often do not work out as we had hoped. For example, it is almost a truism that quality improvement efforts often fall short because of a lack of top management support or middle management resistance. This does not help us much until we can find out *why* intelligent and well-intended managers seem to have problems launching or maintaining improvements that are, in themselves, compelling in their logic and need. Only then can management operate with the kind of sureness and confidence needed for success.

As we explore these issues, the picture develops more as an emerging mosaic than a linear highway. This is because the issues themselves are often both partial causes of what we do and partially a result, and these causes and results are both multiple and interactive. Life is not simple but, if we wrestle with it and are clever enough, sometimes we can gain a greater understanding of it. If you disagree with what I have offered, that means you have at least engaged my ideas and I have done my job. Some of the best thinking germinates from critical disagreements and a reflection upon "why" one thinks, beginning an exciting discovery of one's own new insights.

Endnotes

1. There is little news in this litany of today's challenges. In governmental and nonprofit operations, the problem takes the form of increased expectations and stingier budgets. A new wrinkle may be the increased activism and aggressiveness of labor unions, as reported in Greenwald, John, The battle to revive the unions, *Time*, October 30, 64–66, 1995. In this article, U.S. Secretary of Labor Robert Reich observes that he has not "seen as much raw anger as I have seen in the workplace today."
2. Nohria, Nitin, and James D. Berkley, Whatever happened to the take-charge manager?, *Harvard Business Review*, January/February, 128–137, 1994.
3. Northey, Patrick, and Nigel Southway, *Cycle Time Management: The Fast Track to Time-Based Productivity Improvement*, Productivity Press, Portland, OR, 1993.
4. See Bates, David W. et al., Incidence of adverse drug events and potential adverse drug events: implications for prevention, *Journal of the American Medical Association*, July 5, 29–34, 1995. Also see Crosby, Philip, *Quality is Free*, McGraw-Hill, New York, 1979.
5. Byrne, John A., The craze for consultants: companies are hiring more soothsayers — and giving them bigger roles, *Industry Week*, July 25, 60–66, 1994.

6. For examples of trying to deal with the plethora of approaches, see Labane, Polly, Management tools must be managed, *Industry Week,* September 5, 78–82, 1994; Bookhart, Samuel, Reengineering or benchmarking? It's time to blend the two, *Quality Management Forum,* American Society for Quality Control, October, 10–11, 1995; Kelada, Joseph N., *Integrating Reengineering with Total Quality,* ASQC Quality Press, Milwaukee, WI, 1996; Carr, David and Henry Johansson, *Best Practices in Reengineering: What Works and What Doesn't in the Reengineering Process,* McGraw-Hill, New York, 1995.

7. Hammer, Michael, Reengineering work: don't automate, obliterate, *Harvard Business Review,* July-August, 104–112, 1990. This radical approach is found in other new notions such as that of W. Edwards Deming, who argued that to rid one's organization of the "seven deadly sins" required completely changing the way one operates. Some of these are discussed in Grant, Robert et al., TQM's challenge to management theory and practice, *Sloan Management Review,* Winter 25–35, 1994.

8. An excellent review of the split personalities of TQM is found in Wichter, Barry, The changing scale of total quality management, *Quality Management Journal,* Summer, 9–29, 1995.

9. Pelz, Donald C., Influence: a key to effective leadership in the first line supervisor, *Personnel,* November, 209–217, 1952; Locke, Edwin, and David Schweiger, Participation in decision-making: one more look, *Research in Organizational Behavior,* January, 265–339, 1979.

10. For examples, see Daniels, Aubrey C., *Bringing Out the Best in People: How To Apply the Astonishing Power of Positive Reinforcement,* McGraw-Hill, New York, 1994; Kouzes, James M., and Barry Posner, *The Leadership Challenge: How To Get Extraordinary Things Done in Organizations,* Jossey-Bass, San Francisco, 1987.

11. This advertisement for IBM can be found in the May 13, 1996, edition of *Fortune.*

12. Keillor, Garrison, You say potato ..., *Time,* April 22, 100, 1996.

13. Published in *Quality Progress,* April, 25, 1996.

14. Garber, Joseph, *Vertical Run,* Bantam, New York, 1995, p. 43.

15. U.S. GAO/NSIAD-91-190, May 1991.

16. Noted in the March 10, 1997, edition of *Business Week* (p. 75).

17. For example, see Bleakley, Fred R., The best laid plans: many companies try management fads only to see them flop, *Wall Street Journal,* pp. A1 and 6, July 6, 1993; Kotter, John P., Leading change: why transformation efforts fail, *Harvard Business Review,* March-April, 59–67, 1995; Rust, R. T. et al., Return on quality (ROQ): making service quality financially accountable, *Journal of Marketing,* April, 58–70, 1995.

18. Masters, Robert J., Overcoming the barriers to TQM's success, *Quality Progress,* May, 53–55, 1996. Also see Beer, Michael, Why change programs don't produce change, *Harvard Business Review,* November/December, 158–166, 1990.

19. Cited in Peters, Thomas J., *Thriving on Chaos,* Knopf, New York, 1987, p. 282.

20. For examples see Davidson, Mike, *The Transformation of Management,* Butterworth Publishers, Stoneham, MA, 1996; Gouillart, Francis, and James Kelly, *Transforming the Organization,* McGraw-Hill, New York, 1995; Vollman, Thomas E., *The Transformation Imperative,* Harvard Business School Press, Boston, 1996 (who argues that BPR and other change approaches lack an overall element that would provide organizational integration).

21. See Drucker, Peter, *Age of Discontinutiy: Guidelines to Our Changing Society*, Heinemann, Oxford, 1969; Handy, C., *The Age of Unreason*, Century Business, London, 1989. Analysis of the problems and programs at Xerox and Ford can be found, respectively, in Hammer, Michael, Reengineering work: don't automate, obliterate, *Harvard Business Review*, July-August, 104–112, 1990; and Davenport, T., and J. Short, The new industrial engineering, *Sloan Management Review*, Summer, 11–27, 1990.

22. Timeless truths about performing at your best, in *Working Smart*, April, 1–2, 1986 (a publication of Learning International, Stamford, CT).

chapter two

Common sense and organizational excellence

Why common sense is both simply unavoidable and
as complex as human behavior itself

> *What lies behind us and what lies before us are tiny*
> *matters compared to what lies within us.*
> ～Ralph Waldo Emerson

If there is one bugaboo against which most management books seem united, it is the concept of common sense, which they see as a form of managerial boobery. One author quoted the Webster's dictionary definition of common sense as being "the unreflective opinions of ordinary men." Finding this definition, however, requires one to read past the more commonly accepted definitions, such "good judgment or prudence in estimating or managing affairs" and "something that is evident by the natural light of reason and hence common to all men."

Working managers see common sense as the element that keeps the plant operating, the customers served, and people working together. Common sense to most people means being level-headed, an ability to act properly and effectively in a given circumstance. It is a combination of proper values, good analysis, judgment, and practiced skill in dealing with the practicalities of everyday life. Ingenuity is but common sense in a creative mode.

To use common sense is simply to make what seems an appropriate situational judgment and to take suitable action. It seems absurd for people to argue that common sense is bad, although anyone's judgment can be poor on any given occasion. Common sense is simply us in action.

What is needed is not to replace common sense with blind faith in some proposed improvement program, but rather to use more good judgment and prudence in the selection and use of these proposed methods and techniques.

Management problems are hardly caused by common sense, but rather a lack of proper observation, knowledge, and understanding. No realistic or useful definition of common sense includes stupidity, smugness, sloth, ignorance, or indulgence, the faults that get most of us into trouble. Poor discipline in making decisions or dealing with colleagues stems from a failure of common sense, not its worthy application.

Management sense and management science

A common theme by writers today is that management common sense should be replaced by management science. There can be no doubt that a person's ability to make sound judgments is improved with good knowledge and logic systems. Unfortunately, management science, even when it is sound, is not always clear in its application. Secondly, management science differs from managerial common sense in two significant ways. One is its purpose and the other its scope. Science is intellect, intuition, integrity, and carefully guarded passion raised to a higher order of rigor and system in the exploration of what is, why it is, and how it works. It is common sense exquisitely focused on understanding and new knowledge, especially in the inconsistencies between what we believe and what we can observe.

In our appreciation of science, we must remember that it can be quite wrong. Indeed, every new discovery means that some previous understanding is now questionable. For example, nineteenth century scientists believed an element called *phlogiston* was the component in material that determined its combustibility. Wood had a high phlogiston content and, therefore, burned easily. Rocks, on the other hand, had little or no phlogiston and did not burn. This truth could be proved with a simple match. That such proof was a fallacy of circular thought did not detract from the practical value of this "knowledge". Even today, one could go to a supply store and ask for high phlogiston wood, just as one can now select high R-factor insulation.

At one time medical science held that people who became sick from being near swamps were suffering from the swamp vapors. Proof was that, in draining the swamp, the incidence of swamp fevers seemed to decline. That the mosquito population also declined was not deemed relevant. It has been estimated that it was not until the 1930s that medicine cured more people than it killed, competing poorly with home remedies.

Science has it easy

The ambitions of science are modest compared to what common sense is required to do. Science selects narrow parts of the world to study, while common sense must deal with the entire world of human experience. Science deals with relatively simple things like quarks, while common sense must deal with people who, when it suits them (and it generally suits them if they think someone is trying to predict their behavior), can decide to change. Science deals only with the description and explanation of what is. Common sense imagines what could be and seeks ways to create that new reality.

Science has strict rules and stringent critical review of each finding or concept, while common sense is sort of made up as one goes along. Science is universal, while common sense is situational, reaching universality only when done to the level of wisdom. Science selects the information it chooses to consider, while common sense is constantly bombarded with an array of messages. In science, there may be a range of informed opinions, but common sense opinions are like belly-buttons, i.e., everyone has one and most can be deemed valid or, at least, legitimate.

The paradox is that the very strengths of science and common sense are also their weaknesses. For science, there is a limited utility in dealing with the everyday affairs of people. For common sense, the limit is in precision because of its vast range from genius to foolishness, often in the same person and even in the same thought. Management is a constant choice among what we want, what we want to avoid, and how to get there. It can be done systematically, but it cannot be done scientifically.*

Science can predict how a *population* might typically behave under certain circumstances, but it cannot predict what any one *person* will do in a particular circumstance. That kind of call, however, is precisely what managers are required to make all the time as a normal part of their work. Science, for all its value, is incapable of doing what people must do using their best common sense. It is through our common sense that management becomes an art, and the quality of our common sense determines the quality of our art.

Contours of common sense

Common sense is the place where intellect, intuition, integrity, and passion come together in application. It is Stephen Covey's character and competence,[1] plus creativity and caring. These four faculties of common sense correspond, in a general way, to four key areas of the brain shown in Figure 1.

---

* The social and behavioral sciences, while trying to emulate those of the physical and biological realms, are simply not mature enough for their findings to be accepted at face value. The "human enterprise" sciences still frequently suffer from a condition where that which is significant has not been proved and that which has been proved is not significant. Finally, the human sciences also suffer from fragmentation in the disciplinary structure of universities. "Organizational behavior" and "organizational communications", two highly similar areas in concept and methodology based upon the common root of social psychology, are seen departmentally as different disciplines. The result is that many dimensions critical to organizational management never make it to the business school curriculum because of such other values as departmental accreditation requirements. Thus, management education itself often lacks a more realistic, holistic perspective on organizational systems and behavior.

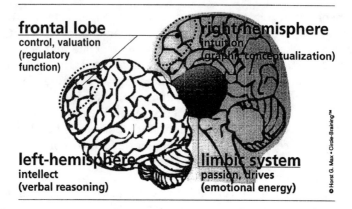

Figure 1   The human brain. (Reprinted with permission of Horst G. Max/Circle-Braining™, Lakeland, FL.)

Intellect refers to our powers to reason consciously, gather information, lay plans, and develop and utilize established methods and techniques. Intuition, which can be defined as knowledge that comes from no known process, gives meaning and portent to observations and reason, and allows us to see new possibilities that just "pop into your head". Valuation is the element of self-control that keeps us focused on certain standards and goals, while passion gives us mental energy and motivation. All normal behavior is the product of all these powers, usually in combination and with some elements typically predominating. How any individual tends to behave normally and under stress is what Myers-Briggs and other personality inventories attempt to determine.*

Management styles

The four faculties of valuing, analyzing, creating, and feeling combine to create the ordinary determinations that are a person's common sense. For

---

* Brain functioning is still in a rudimentary state and so we can claim locations of functions only generally. Moreover, while a part of the brain may be the most active or primary on any one occasion, all behavior seems to be essentially whole-brained. That is, all behaviors have elements of intellect, intuition, passion, and valuation but in quite different proportions. The four primary areas of common sense are similar to Karl Jung's four primary behavioral modes (thinking, intuiting, feeling, and sensing) which form the basis of many of today's personality inventories such as Myers-Briggs. Jung, and others neglect, however, the critical element of regulation and modulation in civilized behavior. Freud's superego and the parent of Transactional Analysis provide a regulatory element, but in a way that tends to caricature and depreciate our efforts at goal-oriented self control.

Table 1 Common Sense Faculties and Range of Balance

Faculty	Process	Inadequate	Balanced	Excessive
Intellect	Reasoning	Dull	Good analysis	Indecisive
	Calculating	Error prone	Problem-solving Planning	Overly concerned with process rather than results
Intuition	Envisioning	Lack of	Innovation	Unrealistic
	Creative problem-solving	imagination Easily stymied	Leadership	Impractical
Valuation	Self-control	Wishy-washy Jealous	Steadfast Good focus	Rigid Pigheaded
Passion	Motivation	Poorly motivated Lazy	Enthusiastic Energized	Fanatical Impulsive

example, the intellect determines that the loss of a client will cause financial harm to one's operation. Commitment to purpose, however, can still push one to continue to provide top service to the end of the contract, while intuition seeks opportunities for new business. These areas can also be a source of problems. For example, wrong valuation can cause resentment of one's customers because they disrupt the neatness of in-house procedures, emotions can cause resentment of customers, and intuition can dream of vengeful actions.

Excessive emotion can make a person a loose cannon, while too little may produce someone who doesn't care. Too much intellect can result in paralysis by analysis, while too little creates cowboys. An effective management manner is the same as a doctor's effective bedside manner, which is a combination of passion, intellect, and intuition evidenced by a caring competence. The key test of common sense is the balance and fit of these powers as applied in a given situation. Table 1 illustrates the range of balance for each element. Common sense is not all of a kind and varies depending upon the nature and quality of the intuition, intellect, integrity, and passion of the people involved and the circumstances at the time. Each of us, perhaps facing a common problem, views our situations differently.

Whole-minded approach

Most management advice tends to focus solely on the intellectual, but doing so misses a great deal of what determines how people actually behave. To truly understand management behavior requires an understanding of a how all four faculties are employed. While the study of logic and reason predates

Aristotle, and IQ tests have been with us for a long time, the role of emotions has usually been of interest only in the study of the socially dysfunctional; however, its role in common sense is now being explored seriously. The importance of this area as a part of common sense behavior has been reviewed by Daniel Goleman in *Emotional Intelligence*.[2]

Focus on valuation seems limited to studies in pathologies, ethics, and values or those of assertiveness training. Normal, healthy, self-regulatory, and purposeful behavior seems to get little attention. The work of Stephen Covey (principle-centered leadership) has been important in bringing more attention to the area of valuation.[3] That most people have a common sense appreciation for the validity of these four areas can be seen in the popularity of the works of Goleman and Covey.

Rationality is neither solely a function of one's intellect nor is intellect the sole measure. All of the faculties of common sense are involved. For example, the organizational purpose, which serves as the lodestone for organizational activity actions, must itself make sense to staff in a way that values their work and, consequently, them. Moreover, the purpose must engender commitment (passion, as in "passion for excellence"). Eileen Shapiro, in *Fad Surfing in the Boardroom*, discusses the limits of organizational improvement models by noting that "visions grow out of mindsets and passions, not mechanics and process."[4]

The discipline of various techniques can certainly be beneficial, but quality is more than a discipline; it is a passionate commitment to that discipline and the purpose it pursues that inculcates a willingness to exert effort even when one is tired, frustrated, or angry. When the purpose is unworthy, when the discipline is inappropriate, and when effort is not rewarded, this same commitment can be irrational. When management talks quality and pays off on volume (or worse, neither quality nor volume) or when management does not pursue action that makes sense to that purpose, people begin to seek a different rationality for their actions, with self-preservation being the most common.

The primary benefit from systematic approaches such as cycle-time management or Kepner-Tregoe is that their built-in integrity guides the intellect and, therefore, better enables a manager to operate more systematically and less emotionally. Many of these techniques are learned but never used, even though their potential value is clear. A decision that was well-derived intellectually may simply not sit well with others — they may just not like it and problems result, which is one reason managers often prefer not to use such techniques.

Sometimes, however, common sense tells a manager that the discipline is not worth the effort. Operating managers often see that, in the daily press of work, the results are simply not worth time-consuming, involved processes. For example, while many companies feel obliged to pursue ISO 9000 certification, it is not always with enthusiasm. The process is often seen as being laborious beyond any possible utility and a part of a European bureau-cratic examination mentality.[5] Peter Drucker laments the lack of practical, realistic, and cost-beneficial advice available to managers:[6]

> "Have you ever looked at a book on decision making?
> If you were to try to use a decision-making text to find
> a room in a hotel, you'd probably end up in the base-
> ment trying to trace the pipes to the room!"

Many, perhaps most, improvement efforts fail simply because they are seen, often quite accurately, as "just more work". That is why there seems to be such a resistance to change by employees whose common sense tells them, rightly or wrongly, that the best thing to do is what they have learned to do to succeed (or at least to stay out of trouble) in their organizations.

Situational common sense

To neglect pressing or localized problems with serious consequences in order to focus on long-term needs is no more common sense than calling a meeting to discuss how people will escape from a building that is at the moment ablaze. Everyone must deal with immediate situations because of circumstances beyond their control, a condition that can be improved but never eliminated, at least not in the real world. Certainly, preventing problems (rather than continuing to fight them) or involving the people in making decisions who are most knowledgeable and will be required to do the work would seem good common sense. When this approach is not supported by adequate resources or is penalized, however, it may not make good sense at all.

Rationality is situational in that, when someone feels wronged, a mali-cious act or malingering may seem quite appropriate behavior. When there is a great sense of urgency, making do makes more sense than it might when there is more time and resources. Prevention makes more sense than patch-ing only when the organization supports and rewards it and provides oppor-tunities to do so. A quality-oriented action may seem rational to one person but lunacy to another, depending on what they believe to be the controlling context.*

Measures of common sense

There is some validity to the criticism that common sense seems to be little more than that which is obvious in hindsight and, in that, is not very useful

---

* Psychologists refer to rational action in pursuit of inappropriate perceptions of reality as "irrational rationality". Phobias, such as a fear of spiders, can be viewed as fears of real dangers — such as Howard Hughes' fear of germs — that have gotten out of control

to managers who need to fashion rather than react to the future. This criticism, however, misses the point. Common sense is properly judged by its results. The first test of engineering, no matter how sophisticated or complex, is the common sense assessment, "Does it work?" It is also judged, however, by its *intent*, the purpose behind an action regardless of whether it failed or succeeded. If an intent is deemed noble enough, we will accept almost any action as acceptable, even laudatory, even those that seem foolishly doomed. Common sense is an assessment of appropriateness — in purpose, passion, creativity, and reasoning as much as anything.

As often as not, common sense operates on feel, as when one realizes that "it just seemed the right thing to do." But gut feelings and hunches stem not from the guts, but from the brain, and are the product of the subconscious weighing of purpose and values, likes and dislikes, and realities of the situation as we see them. We typically have a distinct liking or disliking about someone we have just met, called a first impression. Whether this impression turns out to be right or wrong depends on how prepared we are to make the initial judgment and, of course, how prepared we are to factor in new information.

Experience, instruction, and inference

Every normal person has the potential to develop his capacity for common sense to more sophisticated and powerful levels. Each of us starts off with certain basic learning, mostly about ourselves. For babies, experience is their sole source of information as they determine that the toes they are touching and seeing are their own. As people grow and develop language abilities, their primary source of information shifts increasingly to instruction, with experience being a sort of test of what one has heard from parents, teachers, and peers. This instruction, formal and informal, guides us by providing not only the group's knowledge base but its belief system, as well. It also shapes our understanding of what we should be passionate about and how that passion should be expressed. Thus, we acquire a common or shared sense of things.

When we think of the value of experience, we do not mean mere longevity but rather the learning that should come from doing. Nor do we mean mere hand skills but rather the expectation of greater understanding. As the mind becomes more mature from experience and instruction, the primary source of information and understanding becomes one's own mind through the process of inference. In the modern world, opportunities for actual experience in most of the events that affect our lives, even those of great significance, are quite few.

Maturity in many ways is the movement from dependency to self-directedness based on one's inferential powers.[7] It is this ability to think things out, to make sound intuitional judgments that is the payoff for the experience and instruction we have been afforded. How we behave is the outward manifestation of our inferences, our self-dialog. This, our personality, is our individual sound in the general cultural orchestra in which we perform.

Common sense and individual style

While everyone operates through intuition, intellect, valuation, and passion, the strength and intensity of these behavioral elements vary in each person. Even within a person, the relative strength of these faculties will vary on any given occasion. As every golfer knows, a person's basic skills do not change from day to day, game to game, or even stroke to stroke. Still, one shot goes straight and far and the next into the rough. The combination of emotional energy (passion) and our abilities to anticipate (intuition), to apply game strategies (intellect), and to maintain discipline (valuation) changes constantly.

It seems clear that people are born with certain predispositions and that these are altered through experience. Further, people with certain predispositions tend to move in the same direction and become engineers, lawyers, or artists. People prefer certain kinds of challenges and work styles and try to pursue them in their careers. The belief that all accountants are alike is, in some ways, largely true. Organizations seem to collect certain kinds of personalities, sometimes throughout, but generally in particular departments, levels, or geographic areas.

While there is much discussion about management style, style and substance are essentially the same thing in organizational management. The style of a manager is that person's typical way of operating, which is to say the way that person manages. Being open and responsive may be called a style, but it is part of the real communications environment. Quality programs in a hospital and a chemical plant will have quite different properties, even if they are trying to follow the same guru, because the organization's particular style or culture guides the inferences of all employees.

Organizational knowledge

It is the power of inference, based on our ideas about what things are and how they work and are kept viable through outside sources and experience, that constitutes modern common sense. Raw experience is rarely a great teacher. Certainly, one can learn quickly that fire burns, that Mr. Bigelow is an unpleasant fellow to be avoided, and that this company does not really care about its employees or customers. What a manager does and says often is assessed by a group that makes a sort of a collective inference. This group common sense guides each member's rational processing of the manager's action and strongly determines an individual's response to that action, which may be quality work or minimal compliance. That is why quality is determined more in the breakroom than in the boardroom.

Quality, to have any real meaning, must be more than an abstraction, it must be something that people do. In most situations, our work is shared with that of other people in a process stream, such as the programmer/ analyst, the person who does data entry, the data user, the respective managers, etc. They are not just bound together by a common string of information, but more strongly by knowledge about that information. Even though specific working knowledge is different, say, for the programmer and clerk, there is nonetheless a general knowledge of the organizational purpose and processes that binds their work together. Their models of interpretation, prediction, and understanding (what we call knowledge) are created inferentially, as each does his or her work, but they are affected in many ways by the work of others based on the shared understandings.

Management can do little about what goes on inside each person's mind, even though that is where the quality of the work is largely determined. Individual effort is the product of their common sense determinations about how fast or how well they should work, or perhaps even whether they should do it at all. Every day, every employee makes a stream of countless decisions about who should know about what, when, how much, and in what form information should be shared, and so on. Most everyone works because they must maintain a certain lifestyle, but *how* they work is a function of their own determinations. These, in turn, are the product of their individual common sense passion, analysis, intuition, and values. These individual determinations are influenced, but not determined, by their environment, especially management actions.

Quality as organizational excellence

A quality organization does not require the best engineers, managers, sales people, or equipment. Few companies have the best in any of these, much less in all of them. Rather, a quality organization is one that requires and enables these resources to reach their full potential, individually and collectively. A client told me that his problem was that he just had a "sorry bunch of supervisors." Having just trained these supervisors and been impressed with their dedication and willingness to learn, I advised the client to look around his plant. "Here," I suggested, "are the very people with which you will either succeed or fail." The difference would be in how he managed them. An organization rarely has all the best people, but it always can use them well if it has the will and the wit. In other words, quality is in the organization, not in specifications or technicalities.

An organization is a shared understanding or knowledge, the common sense of a particular set of people. Quality is a condition of excellent knowledge that drives the work of each person and that person's work with others. Quality is achieved when every person has both the knowledge and expectation of excellence and how that excellence is to be achieved. The working definitions of excellence may vary for the CEO and mailroom clerk, but they should be integrally related. Further, while Total Quality Management requires that all members of the organization pursue excellence, no one person can have total knowledge. It is the organization alone that can approach total knowledge, and it is the purpose of an organization to integrate the various kinds of knowledge into an effective, comprehensive, and rational whole.

If a person knows that quality is expected and is rewarded, then quality work is the likely outcome. Quality is not a hard sell, because the logic of quality makes sense to most people. They understand the wisdom of turning off the spigot rather than bailing faster. However, if working faster and dealing with emergencies are the real expectations — i.e., the expectations that determine one's job or career — then excellent knowledge becomes irrelevant. In such cases, a person's common sense will tell them to keep their improvement ideas to themselves and try to stay out of trouble. The flaw is not in the common sense of individual workers but in the poor knowledge of management.

As a level of knowledge, quality can be acquired through excellent learning. The job of management is to establish organizational systems that teach and reinforce excellent knowledge. Every organization is a learning organization, because it is full of people learning individually and collectively. Excellence, however, is always an extraordinary achievement. The quality organization does not merely learn but acquires and utilizes excellent knowledge. It is management's job to make it so. To do so, however, requires some understanding of different kinds of knowledge, and how these different understandings must fit together into an effective whole.

Endnotes

1. Covey, Stephen R., *The Seven Habits of Highly Effective People,* Simon & Schuster, New York, 1989.
2. Goleman, Daniel, *Emotional Intelligence,* Bantam Books, New York, 1995.
3. Covey, Stephen R., *Principle-Centered Leadership,* Summit Books, New York, 1990.
4. Shapiro, Eileen, *Fad Surfing in the Boardroom: Reclaiming the Courage to Manage in the Age of Instant Answers,* Addison-Wesley, Reading, MA, 1995, p. 13.
5. These survey results were reported in Weston, Jr., F. C., What do managers really think of the ISO 9000 registration process?, *Quality Progress,* October, 67–73, 1995.
6. Peter Drucker was interviewed in the April, 1986, issue of *Working Smart,* a newsletter of Learning International, Stamford, CT.
7. Knowles, Malcolm S., *The Adult Education Movement in the United States,* Holt, Reinhart & Winston, New York, 1962.

chapter three

The modern challenge of increasing complexity

Why things keep getting more confusing until we reach a new level of understanding

> *We shall not cease from exploration*
> *And at the end of our exploring*
> *Will be to arrive where we started*
> *And know the place for the first time.*
> ⌒T.S. Eliot

As things become bigger not only do they become larger, but they also become different. For one thing, growth brings an inherent complexity with it. For example, a business with few employees may require little overt communication. People work together in a familiar environment with frequent interaction and they often observe the same things. Over time, a high communications context develops and many things become just understood. As companies grow and people are added, work becomes more specialized and people interact less directly or frequently; communications are less understood and must be more specific and overt. When the organization becomes quite large, interactions become even more distanced, involving some medium or other, and they become more complex.

The challenge of complexity

Thirty years ago in the mountainous northwest comer of Georgia, women would gather to make chenille bedspreads, basically a sheet with patterns of tufted yarn. These spreads were inexpensive but pretty bed decorations used in times that were simpler, less affluent, and lacking the plethora of goods found in today's market. A truck driver who frequently passed through the area would buy some of the bedspreads and sell them to people farther north.

Business became so brisk that the trucker quit the road and started a small factory where women would find work space, machines, and cash income.

As the machines became more sophisticated, less sewing skill was required and the women mostly worked machines rather than handcrafting spreads. Someone figured that this same technology could also make tufted carpet, and the textile industry of Dalton, GA, was born. That part of the world had just moved from the simplicity of a cottage industry to the more complex state of a factory.

The effects of even this seemingly limited change were profound. The women no longer sewed for fun or pocket money but worked for wages away from home. Indeed, the women were no longer "sewers" at all, but machine operators, no longer unique craftsmen but standardized human factory parts. Quality control moved from very local personal pride and peer review to both immediate and distant bosses whose orders often seemed to make little sense, mostly because they were often based on factors other than the women's work.

And these changes wrought even more prodigious changes. The social fabric of sewing bees and parents in the home with children was in tatters. Women now needed cars to get to work and to learn how to drive them. Eventually, some mills were found to be unsafe and the government became concerned, or the workers were treated badly and unions formed. The entire society and economy of the area changed radically. The abundance of reasonably priced carpets meant that homes could have cheaper plywood or concrete floors covered with carpet rather than expensive wood, which had a major impact on the housing industry. This relatively small change in north Georgia generated great social, economic, and political changes. A seemingly local event can generate profound and widespread change which, in turn, comes back to change the situation of the original change.

Change not only breeds other changes, it breeds complexity. At one time, printing was a cottage industry. The same person wrote, set the type, and printed the newspaper, poster, or even book. Eventually the process became more complex as metal engraving and casting were introduced, followed by photography, screens, and color. Photographers became specialized, some with people in action, some with faces, and some with products. There were even subspecialties, such as photography of automobiles and food. The linotype hot metal typesetter was so marvelously ingenious that the inventor went insane shortly after creating it, although some say it must have been just before. By 1990, print production required a substantial array of technical specialties requiring high levels of skill and numerous pieces of expensive equipment.

By 1994, almost overnight, most of these techniques were obsolete and being replaced by computerized desktop publishing. Today the speed, power, and opportunities provided by new technology have rendered the publishing process almost unrecognizable. There is still a need for talent and skill,

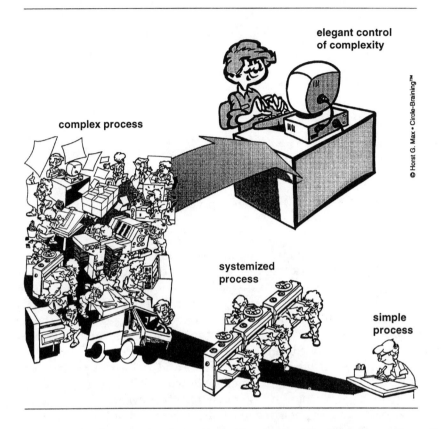

Figure 1 Levels of system (sophistication). (Reprinted with permission of Horst G. Max/Circle-Braining™, Lakeland, FL.)

but basic publishing skills have been put into computer programs and, hence, into computers and brought within the reach of many people. Desktop publishers can now strive to emulate the finest craftsmen and designers.

This complex process has been made more useful and controllable through the elegance of technology. But not only has this complexity become more manageable, it has also become faster and more economical, which has meant an increased demand and level of activity. Thus, a byproduct of greater complexity is greater intensity. The result is a world that continues to put greater stress on our abilities to manage it (see Figure 1).

Chaos and the difficulty of knowing

The concept that every change, no matter how small, changes everything else in some way is called "chaos theory", an idea that modern management

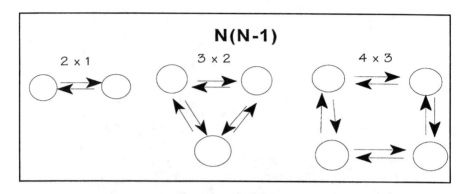

Figure 2   How increasing sizes increases complexity.

thinkers are trying to impress upon managers.[1] There are many areas in which people must work that display highly complex qualities where predictability is notably risky, such as weather, traffic at rush hour, the economy, disease, the market, and almost every aspect of human affairs. Managers have difficulty with the idea of chaos as an operating concept. The term suggests a condition of being out of control, and that which cannot be understood or controlled cannot be managed.

Perhaps a better term is "hypercomplexity", which recognizes a high and difficult condition of high complexity without seeming to give up on trying to manage it. Chaos has so many resultant events that one can only know or even observe but a fraction of them. Hypercomplexity, on the other hand, refers to those events that are important to you and which one must perceive, understand, and control to be successful at whatever enterprise in which one is engaged.

Anything can be either simple or complex, depending on the depth and sophistication of our understanding and interest; imagine the different perceptions when viewing a storm among a primitive native, a seasoned mariner, and a meteorologist. It can also be complex in different dimensions — for example, a sunset viewed by a primitive native, a honeymoon couple, and a landscape painter results in different experiences. Thus, complexity derives from our understanding of things and our needs, whether in regards to the weather, traffic, markets, manufacturing, or, for our interests here, organizational behavior.

As complexity compounds and common understandings diminish, management must find more sophisticated ways to assure a cohesive organizational knowledge. The complexity that stems from growth alone can be illustrated by the formula of $N(N-1)$ (see Figure 2). By viewing communications only in the simplest terms (channels, for example), one can see that adding another person multiplies the complexity.

Complexity and control

For an organization of 100 people, there would be 9900 potential chan-nels for interaction. There are, however, physical limits to how many of these channels can be used at one time. Also, limitations of technology such as memos and even e-mail tend to limit the practical experience of complex-ity. That is not good news for a manager who needs an organization that is in effective communication with itself. As an organization becomes larger, it becomes more complex in many ways that are less obvious but none-theless have significant effects on the messages that need to flow through these channels, such as special terminology, credibility of message source, disputations of purpose, competition over rewards, and so forth. More-over, complexity is compounded by the differing circumstances of all the parties which put them in different positions of time and ability to respond.

One has only to read the history of any major military battle to see how each unit was able to act, was prevented from acting, or even missed out on the battle altogether because of problems communicating the changing cir-cumstances each faced in their efforts to meet their assignments. The idea of an organization as an orchestra and a manager as a conductor has a compel-ling simplicity about it, but it "just ain't so". Managers who act in that expectation will find themselves constantly surprised by their operation, which is less likely to be a metronomic unity than a syncopation of surges and lags.

It is better to understand and anticipate the unpredictability of hyper-complexity and to set up the organization to deal with it, rather than to operate with the wrong expectations that come from inadequate conceptual knowledge. In such a situation, the prepared mind that chance favors is one that has a more excellent knowledge provided by modern understandings of behavior and organizational dynamics.

Search for elegance

While an organization might be hypercomplex, its management cannot be. Management must be sophisticated, but more complex controls only com-pound the problem of complexity. Control by humans must be operationally simple. Imagine the cockpit of a Boeing 747 with its hundreds of indicators, switches, buttons, and levers. The pilot does not try to manage everything in the airplane at once but rather relies on certain patterns of things to indicate the condition of the airplane and then applies, except in great emergency, gentle pressure or adjustment to coax the giant plane on its proper course. The pilot's seemingly simple and refined control of a highly complex opera-tion might be described as *elegant*. Organizations must be managed in the same manner.

Like pilots who must "get their scan working", managers must look for patterns of complexity and high probabilities and manage by controlling the things that fit with and control these patterns. Managers often suffer the illusion that simplistic actions are elegant ones, and then they wonder why things are not working out as expected. It has been said that, unless a person's knowledge is in order, the more of it he has, the greater his confusion. The key to elegance is in the ordering of knowledge so that people not only have a better understanding of what they are about, but can also continue to learn well and efficiently.

It is our concepts that order our knowledge, and it is the quality of our concepts that determines the quality of our knowledge. Excellent knowledge requires excellent concepts. In other words, how one understands the job of management will determine one's ability to create quality in the organization.

Elegance vs. simplism

Elegant differs from simplistic in that the latter, while usually quite plausible and seemingly graceful, tends to be effective only in solving the wrong problem and creating more problems. *Simplism* provides a false rationality by providing an improper context for assessment. An example is the plant manager of a major glass container manufacturer, who just two weeks before Christmas had to shut down the "hot end" of one of the bottle machines for repairs. The crew of about two dozen workers was furloughed until the machine could be put back on line the first week of January. When I asked the manager about the wisdom of this, he replied that he had saved the company $42,000 by that action.

While his answer was true within a narrow simplicity, his concept of savings failed to take into account the cost of injured morale, motivation, and loyalty that spread throughout the plant, embracing not only those who were furloughed, but also those who witnessed the action and realized they could just as easily have been sent home. If the full implications of such an action had been understood, common sense could have guided the plant manager toward a more rational line of thinking.

The difference between archaic simplification and modern elegance is an understanding of what one is doing. The better one's knowledge and mental equipment for dealing with complexity, the more one reaches toward management sophistication, which is common sense at its most refined. The ignorant oversimplify and confuse certainty, even passion, with truth. The sophisticated professional does not search for elegance in the form of simple, easy answers, but rather as solutions that fit the true nature of the events that are to be managed. However complex something is, there are still patterns that give it recognizable form. For example, we recognize a hurricane and a forest, and we succeed in our dealing with these things by our knowledge of their natural tendencies. Human behavior is similarly complex and, within the realm that our knowledge affords us, reasonably predictable.

We can comprehend but small portions of hypercomplexity, but that may be enough. We will continue to operate with the naturally recurring patterns found in all events no matter how complex, using the paradigms of our ideology to guide us. The more sophisticated our ideas of managing, the better able we are to understand and use complexity to our advantage. For example, each person's fingerprints are quite complex in that they apparently are different for every person who ever lived or will live. Still, there is a pattern to this infinite variation that we are able to understand as something we call a fingerprint. It is the infinite variation within a predictable, recognizable pattern that makes fingerprints valuable as a means of identification, rather than just being a feature of our fingers to help us hold things.

The complexity of the world, properly understood and managed with sophistication, can be a source of strength that ignorance misses entirely. The plant manager above made a rational decision to furlough employees according to a narrow and simplistic paradigm. Within that framework, it was quite logical and probably reflected the perspective of his company's home office. From a more sophisticated perspective, however, it was a terrible decision that was likely to defeat completely the economic purposes for the furloughs because of poor worker morale and, hence, productivity. The critical test of management ideology is its ability to provide a proper context for rational action which affords the right answers for the key questions about what one really wants and what one is most likely to get. Sophisticated management uses elegant management controls which take advantage of the natural patterns of complex things, such as the human need for self-esteem through accomplishment, to make them productive employees.

Elegant control

Leadership is the ability to control by eliciting the self-discipline necessary for performance. Control is the ability to obtain the desired and intended results, and quality is excellence in results through optimized work effort and processes. Organizational processes are dynamic work interactions which determine organizational quality by translating grand, strategic purpose to specific, situational purpose. It is these interactions that must be controlled. Elegant control is achieved by using the natural, ordering forces that are at work in the world, to work with them rather than against them. Control is Zen-like in that, to gain it, one must let go, because, in the end, people must control themselves through their common sense actions.

On the other hand, efforts to control by restriction and direct pressure tend to disrupt this natural order which, while giving the appearance of order and control, often achieves the opposite. Authority-based rule, through fear and denial of resources, is an effort to control by restriction and pressure.

The more one tends to exercise authoritarian control, the more one encounters the paradox of reduced contribution and capabilities by organizational staff. In an authority-based system, the ideology of quality does not stand a chance against the ideology of pure pragmatism — whatever works *now*, whatever will get me through *this* situation. When applied authority is the basis for action, the order of natural systems falls into a chaos of expediency.

Elegant control generates an organizational discipline to which all employees subscribe. Only in that way is productive order brought about from chaos. For example, a symphony orchestra has perhaps a hundred musicians playing a variety of instruments, each of which has a different sound, is played with a particular technique, and even has a different musical score. Still, when all play their instruments properly, particularly if they understand and are inspired by the music they are attempting, the result can be quite excellent for the conductor, the musicians, and the audience.

Endnotes

1. Two examples are Peters, Thomas J., *Thriving on Chaos*, Knopf, New York, 1987; Wheatley, Margaret, *Leadership and the New Science*, Berrett-Koehler Publishers, San Francisco, 1992.

chapter four

Excellent knowledge and organizational rationality

What is the nature of organizational knowledge and how does it relate to organizational action?

Chance favors the prepared mind.
◠Anonymous

When the gurus condemn common sense, they are not referring to practical, sound judgment, but rather the unreflective opinions of ordinary men, which may be one definition of common sense but common sense in its lowest form, the direct, immediate, and pragmatic form of understanding called *folk knowledge*. This primitive form of knowledge and its associated skills comes from extensive, intimate, and direct experience unleavened by conceptual understanding. It is the kind of knowledge typical of animals and of primitive societies.

A cultural anthropologist gives this example of an Amazonian Indian:[1]

> "Even under very difficult circumstances he will be able to find his way. When rowing or sailing he follows the river that he goes up and down. But upon closer examination we discover to our surprise that in spite of this facility there seems to be a strange lack in his apprehension of space. If you ask him to give you a general description, a delineation of the course of the river, he is not able to do so. If you ask him to draw a map of the river and its various turns he seems not even to understand your question. Here we grasp very distinctly the difference between the concrete and the abstract apprehension."

Primitive people and animals establish territory by practical experience according to what is required for an adequate supply of necessities, one's ability to range, the competition, and so forth. Conceptual knowledge, on the other hand, uses the idea of property, which allowed people to deal with all of these issues symbolically rather than through physical combat. With property, one can deal with matters through a system of laws and, hence, the transaction of business. These laws, in turn, have given rise to advanced civilizations. The principle reason that the Western nations were able to dominate and colonize less developed countries is that they could operate in any environment based upon general operating conceptual models or "abstract apprehensions".

Folk knowledge adapts to the environment; conceptual knowledge redefines that environment. These literal and figurative maps allow for exploration and exploitation, flexible military strategies and armaments, and establishment of social, political, and economic relationships. While the native savvy of the indigenous people made life difficult for the intruders, eventually the strength of greater mental tools overcame a strange and hostile environment.

Shade tree management

A modern, colloquial term for folk knowledge is *shade tree,* usually referring to mechanics who used to work "under a shady tree". These mechanics repaired engines with little or no formal training but learned through a lengthy period of trial and error, which probably involved some skinned knuckles. Shade tree mechanics began to disappear in the U.S. when engine designs became rapidly changing and complex. Now, even master technicians must continually study not only the engines, but also an array of increasingly sophisticated diagnostic tools. Organizations and the world in which they operate have become similarly complex. Unfortunately, while shade tree mechanics are fast disappearing, shade tree managers are very much still with us.

It is not that common sense gained from direct experience is bad. To hold that as somehow superior to common sense based upon the study of principles and their application, however, does not seem sound. Conversely, the understanding of concepts, no matter how grand, without the winnowing quality of experience is probably of little value. The idea that management requires little other than one's ability to work with people and, essentially, to wing it is often expressed by some managers. We all agree that some people make it on talent and others make it on heart, but in what enterprise other than organizational management have you heard intelligent people argue that learning about one's work and training for improvement does no good?

"It's just common sense" is usually a prelude or justification to some observation about a complicated affair about which the speaker knows very little and seems to take comfort in that condition. The self-styled "practical" manager, who denounces theories, usually begins with some insipid comment, such as "people work for money" or the thought-arresting "everybody knows...". These kinds of people cannot see their own logical disconnect. In a meeting of association managers, several boasted that they had never used a professional facilitator at any of their board retreats, then lamented that their board's planning retreats had been largely unproductive. Management of an organization is not just about winging it, but also about exercising good judgment based on a good conceptual understanding of what one is about. The manager who eschews conceptual sophistication reduces himself to a shade tree level and leaves the framing of the human operating system to others.

Lessons from experience

"Experience," it is often said with great solemnity, "is the best teacher." Perhaps, but experience, which is essentially learning through trial and error, can be quite expensive in a modern enterprise. When a person is operating a $10 million machine and making $50,000 worth of product a day, errors can cost way beyond their educational value. Worse, in terms of cost-benefit, the lesson is confined to those particular circumstances and has limited value. Folk or shade tree knowledge might be called local or particular knowledge, because it refers to knowledge gained from experience in a particular time, place, and set of circumstances.

Particular knowledge* is critical to good operation. For example, an engineer knows what an engine should do, but an operator or mechanic knows what a particular piece of equipment is likely to do under certain circumstances. He or she is able to give the equipment a particular tweaking to obtain optimal performance from it. These "knowledges" are not so much about different things but about different understandings of the same thing, although when unconnected they seem different. The function of an organization, of course, is to ensure that these different kinds of knowledge are connected to provide what we have called excellent knowledge.

Conceptual learning

Experience guided by a proper conceptual context can, however, provide a lesson, not only for that particular situation but for most similar situations. This larger context is the conceptual map that defines what a person is doing

---

* In an age of widespread standardization, however, various locales have much technical similarity to others. For example, all international airports are highly predictable in what they provide. Consequently, the experience of flying into one is often very useful knowledge for flying into another. For this reason, the term *particular* knowledge seems more accurate.

beyond immediate experience, the very thing missing in the folk knowledge described above. Particular knowledge is not common knowledge, although more than one person may have similar knowledge, but it is based upon each individual's unique experiences.

To learn particular knowledge is, essentially, to do it. Conceptual knowledge, on the other hand, can be shared with anyone who develops the mental equipment to understand its principles. It involves the *context* in which the technical skill is applied, such as the why, for whom, and how well. Particular knowledge eventually develops into more conceptual understanding, from animism to analysis, and with each development comes a new practicality and rationality. A technical field, a profession, or a work process represents conceptualized particular knowledge.

A technician operates essentially through particular knowledge in that the experience is direct, immediate, and limited to that particular set of activities. He learns established procedures and follows them by responding to the gauges, operating primarily through familiarity. He operates in a world that has been fashioned by a person who works at a higher level, one who has designed the equipment and processes based upon the scientific and technical concepts of one's profession.

When things do not work out as expected, the technician may fiddle and try one thing or another until things either are corrected or further efforts seem hopeless. The professional, on the other hand, takes it from there by reviewing the concepts of the process to see if they are validated by experience and, if not, adjusts the concept to be more effective as a means of understanding and prediction. Particular knowledge is confined to a specific set of conditions, but conceptual knowledge moves among categories of conditions. Particular knowledge is self-justified, i.e., it does what it does. Experience based on conceptual knowledge serves to validate, refute, or cause some adjustment in the model of reality within which one is working.

Organizational knowledge

While technical knowledge is essentially particular and professional knowledge is largely conceptual, there is another level of conceptual knowledge that lets the technician and the professional work together. When either one is concerned about being a good customer or supplier in a chain of activities, then each is operating under the concept of purposeful relationships. When one thinks in terms of vendor management and customer satisfaction, one is also looking at the quality of these relationships, which is the essence of quality organization.

But there is yet another level of conceptual knowledge in an organization, which is that of managing these working relationships. These relationships, on the whole, constitute the organization's work processes and systems, and it is to optimize these that is the proper goal of management.

Particular knowledge in an organization tells us, for example, that if we are having trouble with a person then he or she is not performing properly. The concept of performance management, however, provides a framework in which one can analyze a person's performance and determine the cause or combination of causes for the problem.

This kind of knowledge recognizes that an organization is not simply people who happen to find themselves together every day during office hours, but is made up of people who work together through a special relationship that is established by the organization and, indeed, *is* the organization. To truly understand anyone's performance is to understand that organizational relationship.

An organization exists in the minds of those who compose it and hold a special concept of self and others. It is a symbolic world composed of abstractions, such as *employee, job,* or *company.* "Supervisor" is an artifice, a negotiated understanding between people governed by the rules of that understanding. One's place in an organization is a self-conscious role that varies with where one is and with whom one is dealing. A person can change roles radically through professional education, promotion, or type of work. That all the parties share and accept that concept is what makes a modern organization work at all. When we speak of how these concepts are formed and guided, we speak of *leadership.* When we speak of how these concepts are utilized for the furtherance of organizational goals, we speak of *management.*

The practical implications of this are that efforts to reduce staffing needs by improving work processes make sense to employees, provided the employees are allowed to offer suggestions as to how this can best be done. As one can readily and widely observe, employee suggestions are rarely welcomed, and management efforts are often irrelevant or impractical in the workplace. To reduce head count arbitrarily in the expectation that the organization will become more efficient (a practice more common than one would suppose) is like shooting a gun in the air in the hopes of somehow getting a bird. Actually, it is more like shooting a gun in a crowd of people.

Essence of organizational being

Organizations do not do work; people do. Typically that work takes place in a social environment supposedly designed to guide, facilitate, support, measure, and reward their efforts. To the extent that the organization does these things it is in a condition of rationality. To the extent that it works against these things it is irrational.

One often hears organizational problems referred to as being a communications problem, which is correct but is like calling emphysema a breathing problem. The organization, a dynamic behavioral system, exists through interactions, and to what extent these communications are flawed or missing altogether determines the condition of the organization. Take, for example, the situation of a $400 million chemical processing plant (from a proprietary organizational assessment report):

> Interviews indicated a wide range of interdepartmental concerns such as engineers' not sharing information, work orders being submitted by operators who receive no word of their status, and the purchasing department changing the specifications on a procurement without telling anyone.
>
> Operations, maintenance, and other departments rarely meet to discuss critical common issues. New engineers are not oriented to lab procedures and order the wrong tests; the engineers in charge of information and control (I&C) mechanisms are rarely involved in reviewing capital project plans, nor are the I&C technicians involved in instrument and control plans. The chief process engineer sees little value in talking with operators, while operators see engineers and area managers making decisions based on outdated P&IDs (drawings) without ever asking the operators what the real conditions are. The (holding facility) shift supervisor gets three sets of conflicting daily orders from three area managers who do not always follow the same seemingly established procedures.
>
> There is no common information management system, no standardized memorandum or letter form, and many files and much resource information is incomplete or missing. Databases are fragmented and often incompatible. One department needs more clerical assistance but is not getting it because "there is not enough work to keep the person busy." Following a recent chemical spill, operators showed how they were being asked to do more than was physically possible under present work conditions. They were then told to slow down and be more careful; however, there has been no change in work load or manpower.
>
> Memoranda on critical policies and procedures are sent to plant control rooms but never seen because they are missed on already crowded bulletin boards. Operators come to the administration building to get their information. Work rule changes are initiated and made retroactive with no employee input, and a days-

off policy effective throughout the plant is announced without any explanation of why it was necessary. Many people, including department managers, feel that if they argue or object, they will be considered outspoken or not a team player and will suffer reprisals.

Organizational irrationality

The above describes not so much an organization as a bunch of people whose work is incidentally bound together only by the physical confines of the technical process. Most knowledge is parochial and concerned with survival. There seems to be little in the way of a comprehensive, rational management system of human operating activities. As an organization, it was highly flawed, and its productivity reflected it. In such an organization, there is little communication, and, with people largely left to decide for themselves what they should do, common sense drives everyone to do what is required to stay out of trouble — even if we know that's not what *should* be done. An operation out of touch with itself is deficient in cohesion and good order, two key elements of organization. In many ways, the ubiquitous "communication" problems and "organization" problems are the same thing.

Sometimes management loses sight of what it is after and undermines organizational rationality and communications. The general manager of an agricultural cooperative had mostly Mexican workers who were unable to speak English. He and his supervisors were forced to rely on two or three bilingual workers for communication. It was recommended that the supervisors begin to learn some Spanish, starting with 50 key words and then learning 50 more each month until they could communicate at least minimally. The process of learning would have been at least underway. Instead, the general manager took offense and said, "This is America and they should learn to speak English."

This may be a legitimate philosophical or political position, but it hardly solves the management problem of communicating with the workforce. There is a big difference between "hard-nosed" management and "hardheaded" management. In the case above, a hard-nosed manager would have kept his grand purpose in mind and had supervisors and managers learn some Spanish if they were going to supervise that workforce.

Organizational common sense

Here is an example of what organizational rationality looks like in real life. While interviewing employees of a large nursery, I asked each of them what their job was. The answers were typical descriptions of activities, such as "I answer the telephone" or "I'm a salesman." When I interviewed the young man who supervised loading the trees on trucks for delivery, he said his job was "to make sure that the trees get to the customer in good condition." I had finally found someone who actually knew what his job was. He could have said that "he makes sure the trucks get loaded." The receptionist could have described her job as "connecting customers with our services" and the salesperson could have worked to "help people solve their quality supply problems."

The function of an organization is to (1) translate its purpose into suitable terms for every employee, and (2) support their effort to fulfill that purpose. Most everyone knew what he or she was supposed to do, at least technically, but the loading supervisor knew *why* he was there. He had translated the organizational purpose into a suitable common sense understanding of his particular work. The organization surrounds each employee in an environment that defines common sense for that person. It is in the creation of that environment, that force field, that translation of purpose to specific application that constitutes the organizational manager's job. Unfortunately, many managers cannot themselves make the proper translation. The loading supervisor above had a much better understanding of his job than did his manager, who said that the supervisor "made sure the trucks were loaded."

Rationality exists to the degree that activities are aligned with purpose. The more these activities are aligned, the higher the degree of rationality. Clearly, a quality assured and optimally efficient operation is highly rational. When rationality is missing, people cannot make sense of what they are doing and usually try only to make the best of the situation to stay out of trouble. How many times has one heard the statement, "It's just a game; just do it." Such comments are generally attributed to employee attitude. Certainly, if one person says that on occasion it could just be that person's attitude or his blowing off a little steam. If one hears such as sentiment frequently, however, people have lost the connection between what they are doing and what they are trying to accomplish.

Another common remark is, "It is easier to ask forgiveness than permission." This reflects the idea that an organization's systems, which should serve to facilitate and support work, must be overcome to get work done. An organization in a low state of rationality is as unlikely to achieve quality as a thousand monkeys banging away at typewriters are to write a poem. People are forced to deal with the urgencies that plague them rather than align their efforts with the grand purpose of the operation. It is purposefulness, and the relationships pursuant to that purpose, that engenders a shared, rational common sense from their individual sense of things into a shared, purposeful social dynamic of human performance.

In the above example of the nursery, customer service had a practical meaning that reflected good common sense from both a situational and strategic point of view. The organization's goal and principles were manifest in everyday and ordinary work, a necessity if quality is to be something other than just another management program. This ability to infuse, maintain, and apply core principles is the difference between okay and excellent, between being only what you have to be to stay out of trouble and being all you *can* be.

Amoeba-like organization

Chance also favors the prepared organization. To managers, an organization often seems like a balloon full of water in that, no matter how hard one tugs, it just sits there like a blob. Managers would prefer a lance or an arrow that would bring necessary organizational power to bear on the concern at the time. Perhaps a better analogy is that used to describe Microsoft, a highly adaptive and effective company that thrives even though it has a number of imperfections in its products. Intel's Andy Grove says Microsoft's strength is that "when some situation turns up, [it acts] like antibodies, approaching the problem from all different levels of the company very, very fast."

Elsewhere, Microsoft has been characterized as being "amoeba-like", a quality of other effective organizations, such as Miami's Baptist Hospital, whose CEO noted, "If you're truly committed to good customer service, you've got to know exactly where you are and be ready to move the instant you detect a problem."[2] This illustrates, validates, and gives new meaning to Tom Peters' observation: "Self-generated quality control is more effective than inspector-generated quality control." It also gives clear operational definition to a bottom-line focused learning organization. When everyone knows why they are there and performance expectations are properly translated, organizations can be more alert and powerfully responsive to whatever their strategic situation.

The common sense of which each individual is capable becomes the common sense of an organizational member. Thus, individual common sense becomes an element of shared common sense throughout the organization. It is by this organizational common sense that individual efforts are judged by (1) their results, as measured against expectations, and (2) their operational rationality. If the translations of purpose to practice are fast and sure enough, an organization can rationally deal with the problems and opportunities it encounters. To the extent that purpose and practice are not rationally aligned, organizational focus and cohesiveness are impaired.

Translation and rationality suffer when management sends mixed messages, especially when there is a difference between what management says and what management does. For example, an insurance company tells its customer service people that their primary job is to ensure that customers who call in get complete customer satisfaction, but then warns them that they are spending too much time on each customer and no conversation should last longer than 7 minutes. Or, consider the medical clinic that tells its staff they are very important, but then says if they don't like something they can easily be replaced. Because there are inconsistencies in messages from management, particularly between word and deed, employees have no choice but to decide for themselves what management really means.

Managing knowledge

Most employee discussions quickly get to questions of planning and priorities, communications and cooperation, staffing and training, equipment and supplies, etc. That these are management issues does not mean that they should be sent off for determination by a group of remote managers. Almost any definition of management is okay, as long as it refers to a set of functions rather than a set of people.

Management, after all, is the guiding and adjusting of the organization, and virtually everyone is involved in that in some way. Those adjustments are made as people learn from their experiences, pursuing whatever is their purpose. *Managers* are those who lead and enable the process and ensure that processes are rationally aligned. Rational processes require excellent knowledge that is a good fit between purpose and effort. Perhaps that is what the president of the American Society for Quality Control (ASQC) meant by the statement, "Managing knowledge cuts to the heart of the quality issue."[3]

Sweden's giant Skandia and several American companies, such as Coca-Cola, Polaroid, and Young & Rubicam, have attempted to utilize their own knowledge more fully. The American companies have established chief knowledge officers to keep track of corporate information, but Skandia has gone further to establish the position of director of intellectual capital to manage "conversations within the group and to create intellectual capital from the dialogues."[4] The Skandia program takes a page from Peter Senge's *The Fifth Discipline,*[5] which proposes, somewhat recast here, that the organizational learning process occurs by discussions about the vision and thinking about work, or *rethinking,* as Peter Drucker would prefer to say.[6]

Learning may have intrinsic value, but beneficial organizational learning takes the form of translating how to best pursue company objectives. Translation, moreover, goes both ways. Experiential information from the frontline becomes translated into strategic intelligence. Strategic initiatives must, of course, be translated into frontline action. In this regard, an open, ongoing dialog among those charged with the work is not only generally beneficial but is also absolutely crucial to any quality operation. Moreover, this translation must be timely in order for an organization to make optimal decisions.

Almost every major problem management faces was, at one time, a much smaller problem that was observed, reported, and ignored by someone in the organization. These problems likely could have been resolved earlier at less cost and disruption and greater customer satisfaction. The information never got to the person who had the authority, expertise, or range of understanding to do something about it. Clearly, the person spotting the problem was not enabled or the problem would have been dealt with then and there. Reports of problems, when they are neither rewarded (given serious consideration) nor penalized (no action taken) will eventually stop coming, and the organization becomes both more numb and more dumb.

Andy Grove, CEO of Intel, argues that the successful management of change requires managers who "are smart enough to listen to their employees, who usually spot [changes] eons before boardroom execs see the impact on the bottom line."[7] A major manufacturer of food-processing equipment realized that its future success relied on continuous improvements to its machinery and that among the best sources of information for such improvements were its service technicians. When people were asked for their ideas, after a long cultural history of "we're not paying you to think" there was a resounding silence. The company eventually had to mount a promotional campaign offering stock and cash rewards to coax its own people to offer ideas on ways to improve products and manufacturing processes. This situation is not unusual given that less than 7% of employees contribute improvement ideas in a given year.[8]

The higher the level of management, the more it looks at the broad picture. So, the closer to the frontline employees are, the more they observe operational specifics that directly affect how the organization will be able to meet its intentions. Over time, employees develop common sense understandings of the nature, causes, and promising remedies for these specifics just as management does for the observations it makes at its level. In different parts of the organization, other people are gaining other knowledge that relates to the organization's accomplishing its purpose. Management must interweave these various perspectives such that (1) the broader view is well founded on the practicable, and (2) all applications are properly guided by organizational intentions. The organization is then not only prepared for action, but for continuous improvement as well.

Beyond amoeba

The idea of an organization being a collection of antibodies that form to attack problems has a major weakness. The most interesting thing about these lesser critters is their ability to adapt to suit the environment, but the most interesting thing about humans is our ability to create an environment that suits us. The advance of mankind has been from folk knowledge, which is primarily adaptive, to conceptual knowledge, which is primarily creative. Organizations must not just be "consciously preparing to move opportunistically" but should also be creating new opportunities when a new situation is conceptualized with new intentions.

A primary and continuing source of conflict within every organization is the conflict between the flywheel of ongoing activities (stability) and the pressures of change (disruption). George Bernard Shaw observed:

"The reasonable man adapts himself to the world; the
unreasonable one persists in trying to adapt the world
to himself. Therefore, all progress depends on the unreasonable man."

What Shaw failed to note is that, while the innovative person changes the
world, it is the adaptive person that consolidates that change and keeps it
going and, in an evolutionary way, growing. People do not just create and
change; they maintain that which at some point will be changed. While
change is inevitable and controlled change is necessary for quality improvement, effective maintenance of what presently exists during change is no less
so. Indeed, effective maintenance, the continued application of one's strengths,
is vital to continuous improvement.

Early management literature primarily addressed maintenance management. It emphasized ways to order and structure what one is doing such that
it was more rational, or at least based on the knowledge at the time. Modern
management literature emphasizes management of change at the near exclusion of maintenance management. That is one of the reasons that new approaches so often seem to fail or are rejected by those required to run the
operation. In a blind rush for the Phoenix, managers can end up with ashes.
What is required for truly effective and enduring quality improvement is a
management strategy that marries change to a well-maintained operation.
This marriage of old and new, like all marriages, requires good communications and understanding to provide a continuous translation of purpose to
situational action.

Parochial vs. management control

The rational translation of purpose to practice is the process of instituting
"management control" at every level and unit in the organization. For example, a work process system, assuming an existing operation, extends from
the monitoring and measuring of present operations, through design of
improvement efforts, both technical and organizational, and through operations, maintenance, and monitoring of the new system. A sure sign of poor
organizational rationality is a high degree of control by technical or parochial
interests rather than management, i.e., those responsible for the total organizational focus and accomplishment.

How technical and parochial control can seriously undermine the rationality of work processes is exemplified in a case involving the design,
construction, and installation of a new capital plant extension. The project
was controlled by engineers, with little involvement by those who were to
operate and maintain the new plant. As a result, there were numerous
operational and maintenance problems. When I asked the engineers about

the problems at this plant, they wondered why that issue was even relevant because the project had been completed 4 years ago. Yes, it was 4 years ago for the engineers, but it is today and tomorrow for the operators. What was seen as an engineering project was more properly a work process project, which should have been under management control, not engineering control.

In some organizations (and this is a condition found in many organizations), computer purchasing and maintenance are the responsibility of a single department. In an oil refinery, it was an engineer, because he "knew about computers", and in a city government, it was the finance director, who got the job by default because he wanted to computerize his operation and in doing so became the resident expert. Companies need the services of experts, but they do not want experts controlling their critical systems. Authority-reliant management tends to spawn little fiefdoms of technical expertise which then exercise parochial control over critical organizational systems as turf prerogatives.

Converting parochial into management control

The situation at the oil refinery provides a good example of converting technical and parochial control into management control by enabling the employees. The refinery had a variety of computer systems, acquired in an *ad hoc* fashion, over time, and by various parties. For example, operations had a system for running the refinery, maintenance had a system linked to purchasing that ordered and inventoried parts, administration had a system (although accounting had its own), the laboratory had one, and many others had different programs as well. There were problems with this arrangement, such as a lack of accurate inventory of who was using what programs and limited interfunctional capability. Many people who were supposed to be on a system were not because they did not know how, did not have the proper equipment, or were dedicated to another computer program. Engineers working on plant repairs, for example, were not on the maintenance-purchasing system of parts inventory, although they were supposed to be, and often had to do much of their work from whatever manuals could be borrowed from the repair technicians.

In the midst of this disarray, the worldwide corporation decided to install a standard office suite in all of its facilities. No one could get information on when this was to happen until the last minute when the engineer in charge of the refinery's computers announced that the programs would be installed in 2 weeks. Only then was the training department notified that it had to get everybody trained. By this time, however, responsibility for plant-wide information management had been given to an interdepartmental group of information system users, with the engineer assigned to support this team. Another manager, whose primary job was refinery performance measurement and information, was assigned as its coach and executive liaison.

The team first outlined a plan for the implementation of the office suite and introduced the idea of plant-wide e-mail. Next, it began to inventory the refinery's equipment and programs, determine training needs, identify expert users, and, in general, exercise management control over the information systems. Their first question was their purpose and the second was the purpose of the information systems, and thereby began the process of true control and rational translation. The team provided elegant management control of a complex, critical process that had floundered on the rocks of fiefdom.

Necessity of open dialog

The key to effective control is not simply to let go of the wheel, but to establish elegant systems to translate purpose into practice. The key to effective translation is effective interaction among the parties to the work. The reason for employee involvement is not "buy-in", which, although important, is a great oversimplification of employee behavior. Common sense can only be as good as the information with which it works. Therefore, people need to be free to get the information they require — from their particular perspectives — to do their jobs properly. And, since organizational work is a social effort, employees need to be able to get and share job-pertinent information so that everyone involved will know what to expect of each other.

Borrowed benchmarks and best practices are often rejected as not applicable because employees do not have an opportunity to assess these promising practices as they apply in their actual circumstances. As a result, they may comply with a direction to do something, but eventually implementation may require so much management push (assuming all management is for it) that everyone gets tired of it and it simply becomes a memory.

It is ridiculous to base a management strategy on supervisors' telling people what to do, except perhaps some expert coaching to assist someone new to a position (which is not what happens in most cases). For one thing, no one can tell people everything they need to do their jobs. Even if that were remotely possible, people will probably do their own version of it anyway. People rarely do as they are told, at least not exactly; otherwise, everyone would wear a seat belt and no one would smoke. What people do is to decide what they will do.

The application of purpose in a particular situation can only be understood and appreciated by everyone when the particulars of an action are understood, and this requires some sharing among the parties. Translation, like all learning, is greatly enhanced when it is interactive. Through the discussion process, the organization forms a sort of collective common sense with a clear and shared purpose, commitment, and information and with intuitive products that fit and support cooperation. The natural order of things is formed and the rational pursuit of goals is established. Certainly, not everything should be discussed, but in many organizations virtually nothing is really discussed. There must be some general understandings, and, overall, one could argue that an organization is only as good as its conversations make it.

The only viable management strategy, therefore, is to guide people in their work decisions. Just for starters, if supervisors would meet with their direct reports and establish clear and practical mutual understandings of the work to be done by each, probably 90% of the work problems would be settled. No one person can really control all the pertinent activities except through providing opportunities for discussions and negotiations to establish clear mutual expectations.

In most organizations, people are starved for information from management. The clear messages that are sent down are too few, too narrow, and often too irrelevant to real work situations to satisfy the needs of the organization. What is clear in the mind of top management may not be so clear to anyone else and, in terms of practical applications, not even clear to top management. In a study of corporate decision making, it was found that managers tend to establish strategy and organization change by a series of decisions that are more likely to be *ad hoc*, out of any explanatory context, and even contradictory. One General Motors executive reflected:[9]

> "When I was younger I always conceived of a room where all these (strategic) concepts were worked out for the whole company. Later I didn't find any such room. ...The strategy (of the company) may not even exist in the mind of one man. I certainly don't know where it is written down. It is simply transmitted in the series of decisions made."

Even when information is sent down, people may not have a clue as to what it means, so they make decisions as best they can with an eye for staying out of trouble. It may not be a condition of fear, but it can be high anxiety. It is no wonder that organizations that do not facilitate the work of employees (managers are employees, too) have difficulty establishing a high degree of rationality in their systems. People simply do not know what to do and are not allowed the opportunity to figure it out. Modern management thinking advocates unbinding organizations and making them open systems. This gives employees optimum access to work-related information and the opportunity to discuss this information to clarify their own work expectations, including its purposes.

Talk but no walk

Jack Welch of General Electric talks of "boundarylessness" where there is "an open, trusting, sharing of ideas. A willingness to listen, debate, and then take the best ideas and get on with it."[10] He is talking about managers, but he could just as well be talking about everyone. Without this kind of dialog, one has the situation of a state government agency where:[11]

> "Employees claim to get no feedback on their work unless they do something wrong. With the standards unclear and priorities constantly changing, one may not be quite sure whether he or she is doing the proper thing or not. Since there is likely to be considerable risk in trying to do something on one's own, employees and supervisors simply wait for someone to tell them what to do."

The truth remains that, for all the conversations about open communications and involvement, it is still not the norm. A 1995 survey of the nation's 1000 largest companies found that only 10% of their employees were significantly involved in management processes. Even those in work teams are given only information directly related to their jobs. In a sense, it is a matter of time, and the conflict of disagreement among employees is seen as a waste of both time and resources.[12] When one considers that the top companies are the ones most engaged in trying modern management techniques, the magnitude of the problem becomes more apparent.

It is true that employee meetings will turn into gripe sessions if (1) concerns have been allowed to accumulate and fester due to a lack of communications or management inaction, and (2) employees do not know how to turn their energies to a more constructive mode or they feel that their efforts will not make any difference, anyhow. However, the right kind of disagreements, even gripe sessions, can be beneficial and easily can be turned to productive discussions. It has been my experience, for example, that when employees complain about work rules it is less about the rules themselves than how they are applied — e.g., arbitrarily, unfairly, unevenly, or without due consideration of circumstance. Employees may complain about overtime, but their complaints tend to be about the *causes* of overtime — e.g., poor planning, arbitrary decisions that could be more accommodating, too few staff, or simply not knowing why. These are the kinds of things many managers are likely to dismiss as bellyaching (as in, "that's all they do"), but wise managers recognize this as valuable evidence of system problems.

Employee involvement requires time away from one's ordinary work which management tends to see as wasteful, even if it rationally serves to strengthen the operation and individual capabilities. In fact, time off the job is often not seen as "working" at all. It is not uncommon to hear that "we can't get our work done because of all these meetings," which is a warning sign that improvements are not considered a part of one's work. It is also somewhat ironic that high-priced managers can be gone for retreats lasting days while lesser priced frontline supervisors and employees can't be spared even for a couple of hours for training and coordination meetings.

Just how bad things can be was parodied in a *Dilbert* involving the "Grim Downsizer" looking for people who had time to go to training sessions and, therefore, could be spared. The bitter truth of this kind of situation was related by a client. He recalled how his former employer, in its run through management fads, began to send numerous employees into extensive training. When management saw that they were still operating as before even with these employees at training, they decided they were overstaffed and eliminated the positions. The bitter humor of *Dilbert*'s workplace-of-the-absurd is popular because its basic truths resonate so thoroughly throughout so many organizations.

Establishing organizational rationality

Hewlett-Packard (HP) provides an example of a company that has demonstrated how to translate its strategic purpose into specific action and to establish organizational rationality. According to CEO Lewis Platt, Hewlett-Packard sends designers, production-line workers, and others, as well as sales staff, to visit stores and talk with customers. They are charged with interpreting "what they hear in an imaginative way" and to apply themselves with "genuine care" for the customer's satisfaction. For HP, "quality is personal, for both customers and employees."

Richard Raimondi, General Manager of the HP LaserJet Systems Group, which enjoys 75% of the laser printer market, pursues both the emotional element and technical reliability by such principles as:

- A passion for customers
- Organizing around customers
- Understanding customers
- Responding imaginatively

These four HP principles align perfectly with the four faculties of common sense shown in Table 1. But HP has gone further than putting a statement on the wall; it has established effective organizational translation devices to put these principles into the hearts and minds of its employees.

The Hewlett-Packard model seems simple on its face, but, as they say, the devil is in the doing. How does one get to where one is now to a place like HP's? The easy rationalization, of course, is that HP's situation is different. It is true that HP started off being an enlightened company; however, its

Table 1   Operating Principles and Common Sense Faculties

Hewlett-Packard principle	Common sense faculty	Common sense translation
Understand the customers	Intellect	Sending employees from every functional area to stores to talk with customers and discussing interfunctionally how each area can serve the company's purpose by satisfying the customer best; use of direct data and analysis rather than assumptions
Respond imaginatively	Intuition	Supporting each area's efforts to arrange its work to achieve its purpose in new, innovative ways
Passion for customers	Passion	Constantly focusing on customer-expressed needs and responses to regulate rationality of work
Customer satisfaction	Valuation	Maintaining integrity by using customer responses to measure overall strategic accomplishment of purpose; quality is a personal relationship with the customer

situation today, although seemingly a natural development, was not an inevitable one. Companies can go astray, even do looney things. A number of studies have shown organizations that have done things that made perfect sense to management but were unwise to outside observers, although admittedly mostly in hindsight. These have been published in *Groupthink, The Abilene Paradox, The Neurotic Organization,* and *The Paranoid Corporation*.[13]

The Dilbert factor

Some of these books, such as *Groupthink* and *The Abilene Paradox*, illustrate how virtues such as loyalty and social cohesiveness can lead people astray. Sometimes people engage in behavior they know is crazy, such as the Border Patrol on the Mexican-American border who returned to Mexico most of the illegal entries and let them go, only to catch and return them again.[14] Activity without good purpose becomes an absurdity. It creates an environment, not where rationality is absent, but where anything can be rational. This creates a workplace of the absurd.

The humor of the Scott Adams' cartoon strip *Dilbert* is based on the logic of absurd work situations that nevertheless ring true. When people feel they are in a raft of rationality being tossed about by an irrational sea, they are quite reluctant to leave that boat for the promises of some new technique unless they are convinced that management is going to change the way it churns that sea. A situation where nonproductive activities seem rational is thus much harder to correct and is doubtlessly one of the major problems in any quality improvement effort.

When people don't like change, it may be for good reason, not just the lazy or benighted reluctance to which it is often ascribed. It is critical that any management strategy establish an overall condition of rationality so that people can move from defensive positions and pull together toward common goals. The strategy must also engender, facilitate, and render safe the necessary *disagreements* which must be resolved in a common sense way if there is to be any true community of purpose and action. It must also provide guidance to ensure that any subsequent agreements are properly focused and founded.

Hewlett-Packard has clearly established its purpose, but it also provides that this purpose is pursued by looking at different aspects of the situation such that some parochial or technical interest does not dominate its products and processes by default. The kind of productive disagreements and discussions that generate excellent thinking can only happen when the atmosphere is conducive, i.e., when the focus is on purposeful performance.

Our thinking is the strength of our species, but it is a strength that can get us into trouble as well as out of it. Before we can understand things outside ourselves, therefore, we must understand those things inside us that not only enable and guide our understanding, but that can also undermine and mislead that understanding as well.

Endnotes

1. LaRusso, Dominic, *The Shadows of Communication: Nonverbal Dimensions*, Kendall/Hunt, Dubuque, IA, 1977, p. 133.
2. See Schlender, Brent, A conversation with the lords of Wintel, *Fortune*, July 8, 42–58, 1996; Villano, David, Secrets of service, *Florida Trend*, September, 48–53, 1996.
3. Jones, Michael D. (pres. ASQC), advertising supplement, *Fortune*, September 9, 1996.
4. Training today: hail to the knowledge chief, *Training*, September, 12, 1996; Labarre, Polly, How Skandia generates its future faster, *Fast Company*, December-January, 58, 1997.
5. Senge, Peter, *The Fifth Discipline*, Doubleday, New York, 1990.
6. *Drucker on Rethinking the Organization*, a videotape by MTS Publishers, 1996.
7. Grove, Andy, *Only the Paranoid Survive*, Doubleday, New York, 1996.

8. Townsend, Patrick L., and Joan E. Gebhardt, Qualicrats and hypocrites: a troubling status report from the front, *Quality Progress*, January, 66, 1997.

9. Quinn, James B., *Strategies for Change: Logical Incrementalism*, Irwin, Homewood, IL, 1980, p.13. It is interesting to note that this study was done at a time when the full effect of the Japanese assault on the American market was just being realized. It was a time when General Motors was losing market share rapidly. The Japanese concept of *hoshin kanri* or "policy deployment" was not an arrow in the American management quiver.

10. Quoted in Tichy Noel M., and Stratford Sherman, *Control Your Destiny or Someone Else Will*, Doubleday, New York, 1993.

11. From a proprietary client report, changed slightly to mask the identity.

12. See Lawler, III, Edward E., Susan Albers Mohrman, and Gerald Ledford, Sr., *Creating High Performance Organizations: Practices and Results of Employee Involvement and Total Quality Management in Fortune 1,000 Companies*, Jossey-Bass, San Francisco, 1995.

13. Cohen, William A., and Nurit Cohen, *The Paranoid Corporation*, Amacom, New York, 1994; Janis, Irving, *Crucial Decisions: Leadership in Policymaking and Crisis Management*; de Vries, Ketz, and Danny Miller, *The Neurotic Organization*, Harper Collins, New York, 1991; Harvey, Jerry B., *The Abilene Paradox*, University Associates, San Diego, 1988.

14. Taylor, John, Border war, *Esquire*, October, 85–90, 1996.

Part II

Paradoxes and problems in management perspective

Chapter five: The paradox of language
How language itself can undermine improvement efforts
While we usually think of language as a tool for expressing our thoughts, it is actually the means by which our thinking is formed. Because of linguistic logic, we tend to draw lines in ways that cause us problems, such as threshold acceptability, management and labor, and success and failure. These arbitrary divisions are some of the most significant causes of quality problems for management today.

Chapter six: American management ideology
How our intellectual history causes us problems in management improvement
Our belief systems provide our understanding of our world. The difference between Japanese and American approaches is not just one of style, but of fundamental perception of the world. The rise of modern complexity, a function of our increased knowledge, requires more modern, sophisticated approaches to management.

Chapter seven: Authority and the paradox of control
Why authority-reliant organizations inevitably become wasteful and inefficient
Pressures on management today to control their organization are greater than ever. Traditional control by authority, however, only serves to undermine the very systems that actually control organizational behavior. The true controlling power of an organization is not through the threat of penalties, but through leadership and rational systems management.

Chapter eight: Decision making and work-place rationality
Why everyone is always a part of every decision no matter
what kind of management system one has
Managers see a decision as being a discrete action that puts into motion a set of given activities with predictable outcomes. Certainly, the outcomes should be predictable, but they will be less so if one has such a limited and simplistic understanding of what a decision is and how it works. A choice generates a dynamic interaction of behavioral shifts. These are the product of countless common sense decisions by the players as the game progresses.

chapter five

The paradox of language

How language itself can undermine our improvement efforts

> *The difference between the right word and nearly the right word is*
> *the difference between lightning and a lightning bug.*
> ᠬ⊷Mark Twain

Although they generally have some terms they prefer, most people take language for granted. They see it as sort of a "given" of life, an assortment of words to use as they wish. The role of language in our thought processes, however, is much more profound than that. For example, an essay in the American Society for Quality Control (ASQC) *Quality Management Forum* was concerned that problems in quality management often "lie within the ... terminology itself, the terminology used for teaching and implementing" quality activities.[1] There is no question that language itself causes considerable mischief in our affairs, and sometimes it can be profoundly harmful. The truth of this is evidenced in some of the fundamental problems in American quality management.

Language and thought

The contentious question as to whether the glass is half full or half empty is largely a linguistic one. It frames the question in such as way as to give us only those two choices and forces us to take a side. This is a condition in which language continually pushes us. We are constantly arguing over winning and losing, success and failure, labor and management, where matters are forced into two separate and opposite conditions. Many companies separate the concepts of safety and environment from production as if these were quite different things rather than aspects of the same process. Language is not only an expression of thought; it provides the building materials of our thinking. As such, it guides and restricts our language-based thought processes, i.e., our reasoning.

Table 1 Illogical vs. Logical

Illogical	Logical
All men have beards.	Only men have beards.
That person has a beard.	That person has a beard.
That person is a man.	That person is a man.

This tendency to separate the world into discrete things stems from the predicate verb "to be", a logic structure inherited from the Greeks along with their grammar. A person who is being idealistic, by exclusion, is not being realistic. One who seems to side with another's position cannot side with ours, because one must be either "for us" or "against us". It seems only logical, and by definition it is. Aristotelian or syllogistic reasoning is based upon such categorical exclusion in which one thing cannot be another (see Table 1).

Or, more to the point:

> All employees do is complain.
> That employee wants to talk.
> That employee wants to complain.

The dichotomous logic of our language has served us well in the sciences and is the basis for scientific hypotheses and mathematical equations, e.g., *x is a function of y*. Science works by holding other factors constant and manipulating the ones of interest to see what happens. In the real world, virtually nothing can be held constant and everything affects everything else all the time in different degrees. Those who recommend that managers suspend their common sense and try to operate only through the scientific method are asking managers to operate in a world of inadequate dimensions.

Undermining common sense

While the separation of things has advanced science,* it tends to undermine managerial common sense in many ways. Primarily, it forces us to make decisions we do not have to make and probably should not make. An example is the typical hiring process during which every candidate must be found unacceptable except one. If the selected one declines the offer, the

---

* Science itself is moving from Newtonian mechanistic thinking, where the world is comprised of separate things, to quantum or relativity thinking, where the world is made up of energy which becomes a dynamic form in relation to other forms. This move toward relativity and its impact on management thinking is explored in the next chapter.

employer, having rejected all other candidates, finds itself having to adver-
tise the position again, even though the best available candidates may have
already applied.

American reasoning is essentially linear and distinguishing, where one
element is logically separate but, perhaps, linked to the next. Japanese reasoning is more like building a mosaic, where pieces are added until a picture
emerges.* Americans think of a world of separate individuals who band
together into separate groups, while the Japanese see groups for which the
members are inseparable. It is not surprising to see American managers
struggling over the choice between Theory X (employees are basically lazy,
don't care, and don't want to work so managers must make them) and
Theory Y (people will work toward organizational goals when they see them
as aligned with their own).

In truth, there are people who range from the reluctant, even hostile, to
the enthusiastic. Managers know that there are those who will take all you
give them and give only what is necessary in return and others who need
little except for you to get out of their way. Most people, however, are
somewhere in between. On the whole, American managers have done much
better historically in creating Theory X conditions than those of Theory Y.
Being forced to choose between these two highly theoretical and unrealistic
extremes, the X approach seems both safer and easier. Many see Theory X as
necessary and Theory Y as pie-in-the-sky and have difficulty thinking in
terms of the much more realistic Theory Z at all.

It took a Japanese writer, William Ouchi, to overcome the X/Y dichotomy
and to suggest Theory Z, which recognizes both (1) the potential benefits and
limitations of employee involvement and non-financial work rewards and (2)
the needs of management for organizational control.[2] Ouchi based his thinking upon observations of Japanese firms that adapted successfully to the
American environment and of American firms who effectively employed
some Japanese techniques.

Acceptable is okay

The primary difference between Japanese and American views on quality
may be in language-driven logic. Quality to Americans is often a separate
aspect of production with special and separate organizational elements to
pursue it. For the Japanese, quality is an overall, integrated nature of effort,
and the idea of separating quality into different organizational responsibilities is almost inconceivable.

---

* As an illustration of just how important the relationship between our language and thought
is, as well as how different American management thinking is from the Japanese, American
reasoning takes place primarily in the left hemisphere of the brain, but for the Japanese it takes
place primarily in the right.

Kosaku Yoshida, a Deming disciple, notes a key distinction in American and Japanese views on quality.[3] The Japanese, he argues, have a realm of desirability, within which one moves from the not so desirable to the most desirable. Quality has a threshold but, within that, a growing level of desirability. For the Americans, the operating concept is threshold acceptability, sometimes expressed as conformance or compliance. Inside the realm of acceptability, everything is okay; outside of this realm, everything is unacceptable.

The critical difference in this thinking is that for Americans something within the circle of acceptability is good enough, while, for the Japanese, being within the circle of desirability is only the beginning of a journey toward excellence. Often the key reason for the poor acceptance of quality improvement efforts is that managers who feel they are within the realm of acceptability are not interested in the additional effort required to achieve excellence. Indeed, such "excessive" efforts are often viewed as a cost that is difficult to justify and as being a prime candidate for cutting, reengineering, or whatever.

"Okay" becomes "excellent"

Many managers doing acceptable work already feel they are doing excellent work, considering the circumstances. These circumstances, of course, are usually problems that have been generated by management's failure to establish a truly rational situation that provides quality assured and efficient operation. They have good reason to feel this way, as, given the poor state of performance management in most organizations, they have been rewarded mostly for doing acceptable work by superiors who feel the same way about excellence as do their direct reports. Most performance reviews really cannot tell the difference between "okay" and "superb". "Good enough is no longer good enough" is a catchy slogan, but for most managers good enough is actually quite good enough.

Examples of this abound but perhaps no where more exquisitely than in the process of ISO certification. This process is often a game between an auditor and a company in which the company tries to hide its inadequacies from the auditor. One Fortune 500 company even trains its employees on ways to defeat its own internal auditors. The ISO auditor, however, is merely trying to see if the company is doing what it said it would, such as ensuring that design output performance matches design input criteria, that rejected production items do not get back into the assembly process, and that customer complaints are acted upon. The company, however, is trying to cross into the threshold of certification, i.e., compliance, rather than trying to find ways to operate better. In this case, "okay" was not getting caught doing "not so okay" which apparently was the standard for acceptability. So much for quality.

When compliance is the goal (with "minimum" usually being the un-stated qualifier) — that is, when the highest expectation is mere acceptabil-ity — the level of typical and usual operation is generally *below* that mini-mum level. That is why organizations who try to comply with ISO 9000 or Malcomb Baldridge standards can find themselves in such as poor state of quality assurance and efficiency. Managers often seek the minimum accept-able level, generally a continuation of meeting past expectations for which the customer does not seem to be complaining too loudly or often. It is no wonder that managers, with rare exception, create an environment where employees work to comply rather than contribute. Managers often complain most about worker attitudes, but most employees actually follow their leaders.

The power of a compliance culture feeds on itself by instilling this thinking through the very processes that should be changing it. A good example can be found in an organization's approach to employee develop-ment. For American companies, a new employee with some related job skills or education is "good enough". They are, therefore, rarely given effective company and job orientations. Subsequent training is often a major manage-ment decision, and often the decision is no. For the Japanese, however, a new employee is only beginning the journey of guided and supported profes-sional development. It is not uncommon for an American manager to ask, "What if I train an employee and she leaves?" For the Japanese, the question is, "What if we don't train that employee and she stays?"

Us and them

The separating quality of our language gives us problems that we really need not have. Worse, because these problems are built into our common sense problem-solving apparatus, it makes them difficult to resolve or even iden-tify. That language is a critical ingredient in our thinking has been recognized for the past 50 years in cultural anthropology,[4] but it has not gotten much attention in management studies. Even studies of corporate culture do not really emphasize this critical aspect of organizational management, although it would be a fertile ground for study.

In 1957, Herbert Simon wrote of "bureaupathologies" in an organization, an example of which was goal inversion, where the customer becomes the supplier.[5] This situation is precisely one of the major concerns of the quality movement. Internal support activities, such as human resources, become demanders of accommodations from their internal customers, a perversion that corrupts the company's service to outside customers as well. When employees are shown an upside down organizational chart, they often put themselves at the bottom as one who works for many bosses. Human re-sources, purchasing, maintenance, and other service departments are often demanding and unresponsive, classic cases of goal inversion.* In external customer relations, this takes many forms, all irrational for the organization. Customer work or requests go into a black hole because of poor systems or wrong priorities; company representatives announce that something the customer wants is not company policy, or they expect the customer to know how to work the company system on their own. Sometimes customers are swamped with paperwork because the company has not seen fit to consolidate its information needs into a customer-friendly form, and sometimes it is just a "gotcha" virus caught from management through its treatment of employees. As bad as this is for a company, the treatment of internal customers stemming from organizational fragmentation can be even worse. Separate functions become separate goals and values and, hence, become forces of organizational irrationality.

Creating organizational classes

A great mischief stems from our dichotomy of management and labor. Perhaps no society is more conscious and respecting of rank than the Japanese, where managers drink their tea in a sequence based on organizational standing. Rather than separate individuals, however, rank serves to bind members of the group together. Senior and junior members exist in an integral relationship of mutual obligation and loyalty. In America, the Theory X relationships are often less a positive social bond than a forced, utilitarian, arms-length contract characterized by power and acquiescence.

For Americans, management and labor are two distinct and widely separated entities. The separation reflects a genesis from the feudal days, when there were knights and serfs, through to the development of anachronistic, present-day military castes of officers (who still have ceremonial swords) and the enlisted. With the growth of American commercial and governmental organizations beginning in the 1950s came the perspective of managers who had learned their craft as officers in World War II.

This is not to say that American workers suddenly had low status, for that had always been their lot. The rise of labor unions in the U.S., Europe, and even Japan, not to mention the rise of socialism and communism, was the product of worker treatment by industrialists. This, of course, is not news to anyone. The point is that the distinction between management and labor has strong roots and is quite institutionalized. That it is historical, however, does not make it rational, at least not in present times.**

---

* Read this paragraph to any employee and most operations managers, and watch the heads nod in agreement.

** The reliance of American managers on Theory X makes sense only if one assumes that managers are motivated more and differently than labor. A given person's level of virtue is to be found, we are asked to believe, by looking at their place on the organizational chart.

The arbitrary distinction between officer corps management and enlisted labor has justified a financial disparity that is a constant problem, especially in regard to organizational improvement. For example, American managers see employee salaries as "costs" and management bonuses as participation in the "profits" from cost control. This allows one to justify a reward system where labor costs should be minimized with a grudging raise, while management bonuses should be maximized for a job well done. During hard times, management perquisites and positions have been the last things to go.

Another historical twist, found in many performance management systems and conforming to the noble-serf model, is the treatment of employees as child-like people who must be punished for their transgressions and weaknesses. This fits well with the Theory X school of motivation. Similarly, employee newsletters are seen as "doing something for the employees" rather than as a critical communications activity for the organization as a whole. Initially, quality circles were viewed by many American managers as an employee incentive program, not as an opportunity to improve the operation.

Price of separation

For organizational change programs, the perceived separation of management from everyone else can be fatal. Many programs aimed at encouraging employee participation are launched by dictate from top management who nonetheless keeps its parental power unfettered. The CEO of a major regional bank, when introducing the new improvement program, never once said "we"; it was always "you" who were going to change. The higher one goes in an organization, the more one finds the conviction that a quality program is for those below who just can't seem to get it right. Such executive self-exemptions make the rest of the organization wary and are probably the primary cause of failure in most improvement efforts.

A good example of how management undermines what it says it wants by what it does is an international company that uses its plants to "warehouse" headquarters staff that it cannot presently justify but does not to want to let go. One of its plants was being pressured both to warehouse headquarters staff and to reduce its head count, even though its staffing level was already below industry standard. These warehoused employees comprised 3% of the plant's staff.

The "us vs. them" perspective is a fundamental and ongoing problem in almost every company in the U.S. That the Japanese, with their feudal traditions, would think in organic terms while American managers, with our democratic tradition, would think in terms of management nobility and employee serfs is truly a puzzlement. This is explored further in subsequent chapters, but certainly much of this problem stems from the forced dichotomies in our language. One must be management or labor; one cannot be both. We are still struggling with what to do with frontline supervisors who are typically expected to act like managers but are treated like hourly employees.

The perspective of difference and separation between management and labor can get quite hostile. Some companies see their own employees as an enemy to be fought and beaten. Most people are familiar with bitter labor disputes but these are just the tip of the iceberg. United Way agencies have found that some companies will not allow an employee campaign because managers are afraid that if the employee had meetings they might talk about unions or have a "bitch session".

In other words

A major paradox in the quality movement is that, while many writers denounce and bemoan the mechanistic thinking of American managers, they have provided terms that do exactly what they denounce. Take, for example, three of the key terms used today: *quality*, *productivity*, and *empowerment*. Quality, as a term, has confused as much, perhaps more, than it has guided. It is a term that forces us into "is or is not" choices and often pulls us off in the wrong direction. For example, some of the more successful products on the market are not particularly quality goods. Matsushita Electronics makes both Technics, a high-end stereo system, and Panasonic, a lower quality product. Panasonic costs less and sells far more. Do they both have quality? Yes, but not the same quality.

To talk about high quality and lesser quality only serves to undermine the idea of quality as a guide in organizational management. Trying to resolve the "What is quality?" question has wasted much time for both managers and academics. Compounding the problem, when words lose their distinguishing integrity, primarily through common usage, they become virtually meaningless. Worse, they contribute to a dichotomous logic that ends up painting one into a corner from which no useful action can be taken.

As discussed earlier, quality and reengineering have been absorbed into the management lexicon so readily and rapidly that their specific and accurate meanings could not catch up. At present, quality, reengineering and many other terms (such as teams) mean just about anything when one attempts in organizational improvement. Such problems that emanate from the terms themselves are probably a major reason working managers turn from the urgings of consultants and academics and instead focus on immediate pragmatics.

A more effective way to frame what management is after through its improvement is value, that is, the benefit or utility that has been gained and its cost. "Adding-value" is a common term for managers and, given its commonly accepted meaning, it would seem appropriate for dealing with quality issues. In a rational situation, such benefit would logically and, it is hoped, measurably contribute to accomplishing the organizations purpose and at a reasonable effort and costs. Value also allows the manager to make comparative assessments instead of being forced into win-lose choices. It is only when there is a reasonable and logical contribution that one can call it "value-add". Responsible managers make such choices everyday, or at least that is the kind of choices they *should* be making.

Unfortunately (and this is another ill the quality movement seeks to cure), many management decisions are made on the basis of cost (such as the international company that saved money by not buying the operating manuals when it installed Microsoft Office worldwide) or benefit (such as the auto companies that obtained wage reductions from employees and then gave large bonuses to management) alone. That one can separate cost and benefit at all is, itself, a linguistic trap. Cost decisions, without regard to the effects of that resource reduction, seem quite irresponsible. Similarly, benefit decisions, without regard to cost or contribution to company purposes, seems indulgent. Both qualify as a breach in organizational rationality.*

Value is a relational concept that provides a basis for a rational, logical decision based on what we want, how much we are prepared to pay for it, and what constitutes the proper balance of the two. Perhaps a more critical use for value in organizational management is its definition as a utility which provides a more realistic appreciation for support services and operational meaning to internal customers. Quality seems primarily to provide a basis for disagreement, rather than for a rational and productive working arrangement among the parties involved. Value is something employers and employees, manufacturing and marketing, buyers and vendors, and even bean counters can understand and appreciate. Value is a dynamic standard of guidance and measure, and it is difficult to imagine a management decision where it cannot be applied.

Enabling the organization

The idea of empowerment is quite compelling in that it seems to speak of freedom to do one's job. In practice, however, it is often frustrating and threatening. Freedom to act, without a commensurate adjustment in other areas, is an invitation to high risk for both the empowerer and the empoweree, whether an individual or team. The subordinate is unsure as to what can be done, and the supervisor knows that responsibility, no matter what assurances were given, remains with him or her. Empowerment misses the point entirely. The problem lies at its base in that empowerment sees power as a sort of discrete commodity that can be portioned and passed around. "To

---

* When you think about it, cost without regard to benefit makes no sense, at least from the point of view of organizational quality. From the perspective of portfolio management and executive compensation, benefit becomes differently defined.

give some of your power means you now have less of it" is a quaint and archaic concept at odds with the nature of human behavior.

A more common sense and rational concept is *enabling*, which refers to the conditions for which a person is not only authorized to undertake certain actions, but also has the resources and wherewithal to do so successfully. It assumes an understanding of the enterprise, its goals and the responsibilities involved. A person may be empowered but not enabled unless provided proper guidance, training, equipment, organizational support, etc. Enabling also includes the relationship between the employee and authority such that each party to the effort knows what they can do and when they need to bring in others. Enabling is a performance-oriented, organizationally integrating, and continuous-improvement perspective.

There is a more important reason, however, for thinking in terms of enabling rather than empowering. Empowering must mean the authorization to commit organizational resources if it is to mean anything. In this, empowering or authorizing would certainly seem a necessary part of any delegation of work. Enabling is making available whatever is sufficient to make a successful effort possible. As such, it is a more realistic way to assign work responsibilities, whether to a person, group, or facility.

Finally, enabling is an action word that implies relationships and duration. Enablement means that one is put into some sort of condition with the implication that the condition will somehow sustain itself without further attention. This invites neglect and, consequently, often unpleasant surprises. Managers who think in such terms often assign work and then see what happens. If they were required to address the question of sufficiency for the duration of the work process, they would have more excellent knowledge, and the odds of success on everyone's part would increase.

Winning performance

Productivity is like scoring in sports. It is what you are after, but not what you do to win. Consider the approach of John Wooden of UCLA, one of college basketball's greatest coaches. He kept winning, although he never focused on it. Rather, he saw his job as working with the only thing that anyone can control — performance. Even though "winning" and "productive" are great adjectives, "winning" and "productivity" are lousy nouns. Productivity is like the score at the end of the game; it is a measure of management effort but not of the effort that is performance. A "win" you can work toward; a "winning" performance describes how you have worked toward it. How you achieve that performance is what you actually manage. Productivity is a numerical measure of a qualitative effort and, as such, offers an opportunity for the bean counters to wreak havoc.

By focusing on the measures and not the requirements of the performance, cost reductions often get into the operational sinew. Or they become arbitrary, such as reducing the number of secretaries so that highly paid professionals and managers can stand in line at the copier. Reducing training, equipment upgrades, maintenance, etc. makes the numbers look better, at least in the short term. The object of both management and sports is not to make a score or even win a game, but to have a winning season every year. The primary objective of management, like coaching, is to provide the wherewithal on a protracted basis, for optimum performance from each employee and the organization as a whole. If an organization is rationally structured, its performance expectations and support systems are aligned with organizational purpose and it will achieve its potential productivity.

Between success and failure

Kenneth Boulding once observed that the U.S. was the only true Marxist country because it was the only one where the workers owned the means of production, the capital being provided through employee retirement plans.[6] While not generally viewed as a management guru, Marx provided another lesson for American managers when he observed that if you change something enough it becomes something else.[7] Enough changes in quantity eventually become a change in kind. A prosaic example is that a brown cow with a growing white spot eventually becomes a white cow with a shrinking brown spot.

Much of the perceived failure of quality initiatives doubtless stems from the quantity-quality enigma. First, one must realize that the enigma itself is language based. All changes in amount, to some degree, inherently constitute a change in kind. Highway safety and automotive performance change constantly with speed. The world is such, however, that we can deal with changing amounts as if they were not changes in kind. There are thresholds of action — such as when to computerize, get new trucks, or add an employee — that are addressed as quantities but are really qualitative decisions. This is generally the hard part of making a decision. It would be difficult to find a quality program that did not bring lasting and observable improvements to an operation. Likewise, it would be difficult to find a quality program that solved all of an organizations problems and, indeed, did not create new problems.

All change is incremental in the sense that, at some point, there must be an adjustment in the particular knowledge or its application where the work of the organization is done. On the other hand, all change is strategic to some degree in that the systems that support and enable technical applications must change if the application is to be effective. When does reinvention stop and adjustment start, or vice versa? In that one expects a mechanically tidy or complete perfection from a change effort, any such program will be a "failure".

Florida Power & Light won the Deming Award for quality improvement in 1989 and shortly thereafter laid off most of their quality improvement staff.

The Wallace Co. won the Baldridge Award in 1990 and 2 years later filed for Chapter 11. Although there was a substantial downside, it would be hard to imagine that the operation of both companies was not improved. On the other hand, Taco Bell is offered as an example of successful reengineering by centralizing its food preparation and enlarging its dining area, but one wonders what the downside was.

The truth is that every effort brings both benefits and costs. Further, an organization is not a thing. It is a dynamic condition and, therefore, is always on the verge of a different condition. BPR and TQM, by arguing for an all-or-nothing application based upon ambitious claims, can set themselves up for harsh judgment. Reengineering suggests, for example, a dichotomous choice of approaches where one can either (1) either fiddle with the present system, or (2) replace it with a completely new system. The reality is that there are many more choices than these, such as doing nothing, an option chosen by many managers and one that often works.

Endnotes

1. Kolbe, Andreas, Does FMEA terminology cause preventable errors in FMEA development?, *The Quality Management Forum*, Winter, 1–3, 1996.
2. See McGregor, Douglas, *The Human Side of Enterprise*, McGraw-Hill, New York, 1960; Ouchi, William, *Theory Z*, Addison-Wesley, Reading, MA, 1991.
3. Discussed in Thor, Carl G. (pres. ASQC), in *Total Quality Transformations*, Caroselli, Marlene, Ed., Human Resources Development Press, Amherst, MA, 1991, pp. 231-254.
4. See, for example, Whorf, Benjamin L., *Language, Thought and Reality: Selected Writings*, MIT Press, Cambridge, MA, 1956.
5. Simon, Herbert, *Administrative Behavior: A Study of Decision-Making Process in Administrative Organizations*, The Free Press, New York, 1957.
6. A curious and ironic twist on layoffs is that when a worker layoff causes stock prices to increase, the value of each employee's 401(k) plan increases; see Lieber, Ronald B., Who owns the 500?, *Fortune*, April 29, 264–266, 1966.
7. According to the Marxist dialectic, as there are changes in quantity, say increased industrialization, there is also a change in quality — that is, an agrarian-agricultural society becomes an urban-industrial one. These two kinds of societies may have some similarities but are fundamentally different in their social, cultural, economic, and political properties. One of the things that makes Marx out of date is that today there seems to be almost every kind of social, economic, and political mix one can imagine.

chapter six

American management ideology

*How our intellectual history causes us
problems in management improvement*

> *The problem with people ain't so much their ignorance;
> it's knowing so much that just ain't so.*
> ᐁJosh Billings

Looking up at the sky on any clear night, one can easily discern from among all the stars the cluster known as the Little Dipper. If one were to point out that constellation to a young person today, the response might well be, "What's a dipper?" A dipper, of course, is a long-handled cup that everyone used to get a drink from the water bucket. "The what?"

What was a "dipper" to Americans until not very long ago was the Little Bear to ancient Greeks. To others it was probably something else. In any case, it takes a lot of imagination to see the constellation as anything else except, of course, a dipper. The point being that people use the familiar to understand the unfamiliar. The ancient Greeks were familiar with animals and their pantheon of gods and tended to see them in things. If one could move a million or so miles to the right or left, the Little Dipper would become something else, perhaps a picture of Elvis or nothing at all. The reason is that the Little Dipper does not really exist in the sense of being an astronomical presentation of stars on a picture plane. Rather, it is the illusion of a picture created by a group of stars which actually are on quite different planes. It is only because of our position, both physical and mental, that the Little Dipper exists at all.

Ideological lens

Our view of the stars tells more about us than it does the heavens, because it reveals our beliefs about what things are, how they work, and what meaning they have for us. Our ideology is our system, actually more of a loose-knit package of abstract apprehensions. These constitute our conceptual knowledge, our "beliefs in" and "beliefs that" which, together with the artifactual results of these beliefs, are called culture.* Those elements of our mental framework that tell us what we need to be doing and how to do it are called, in modern jargon, paradigms. These concepts define for us the world and all of its parts, including our organization and the role of a manager in that organization. Only by understanding why we think as we do will we be able to understand why we should think differently. Only then can we consciously and deliberately move toward excellent management knowledge.

There are several aspects of ideology/culture that we should bear in mind:

1. Ideology/culture is a reality that we have contrived or learned from contrivances of others, such as this book. Social tendencies may exist in nature, but our organization is a shared set of manufactured beliefs among its members.
2. Because ideology is our creature, we can make it be pretty much any way we want — that is, we can shift our paradigms provided we are aware of what they are.
3. Ideology is not something that we carry around in our minds; it *is* our minds. Because of this, much of it is implicit and beyond our abilities to observe. Like a fish trying to understand water, we just assume that what we see is what is there, rather than being the product of our conceptual lens.

The distinction between managers and other employees is assumed. Bonuses and higher raise increments are often given to managers because they are managers, while the other employees are often given grudging and minimal raises. Why is that? Well, because.

This also gives us insight into another major reason organizational improvement efforts fail. Those that do not fit within the existing belief system (fortified and institutionalized as reward systems and a belief in the singular ability of a command hierarchy to achieve accountability) tend to get crushed under the overwhelming weight of the presently held reality. Although heads may nod dutifully regarding the virtues of new paradigms, once out

---

* If our "beliefs in", those things we find valuable, and our "beliefs that", those things we find credible, involve a divinity, it is a religion. If they are secular, they are an ideology. If they are metaphysical but outside our credibility, they are referred to as mythology.

of the workshop people are continually admonished to be realistic. That is why managers are able to mouth all the latest buzz words while still doing the same old thing. As William James noted, "A great many people think they are thinking when they are merely rearranging their prejudices."*

Adaptive thinking

The American culture is incredibly absorbing, even faddish, and this includes its intellectual artifacts. It seems less a rigid system of thought than an eclectic grab-bag of ideas that have been collected over the years. The ideas seem to be a loose fit and in constant flux. Americans who have been assigned overseas for several years often find themselves more in a culture shock upon their return than when they first went to another country. The flood of management improvement books is just one area of rapid development and adaptability that characterizes the U.S. and, increasingly, the rest of the world. This cornucopia of new management thought also reflects the vigor of American thought, enabled by its ideology and as rich and varied as its language. Indeed, the American language has grown twice as large as any other language primarily through innovative thought and technology.

American ideology is highly flexible, absorbent, and expansive, allowing corporations to range from predatory to altruistic to high-tech and still remain within acceptable bounds. Most display some combination of values such as high-minded wholesomeness and imagination (such as Disney), or marvelous invention (such as Microsoft), yet are tough as nails (such as both of these companies). The American ideology is not scientific, but it provides for scientific learning and knowledge and innovation. Unfortunately, it also provides us with a number of plausible, archaic, and heretofore productive beliefs about managing organizations that persist past their effective value.

The job of management, indeed for all of us, is to find rational meaning in a world of inherent contradictions, contentions, and confusion by being able to determine a proper purpose and promising actions to accomplish that purpose. The ideology of management is the foundation for managerial (and therefore employee) rationality and provides the basis for appropriate organizational common sense. Deming's "profound knowledge" and Senge's "systems thinking" are efforts to help managers find rationality in work process. But such efforts crash against the managerial ideology that sees employees as individuals rather than as members of process teams. People become cogs in the organizational machinery, replaceable and of only technical consequence. Communication becomes merely the technical distribution

---

* Another quote that may explain why consultants are sometimes unwelcome is by Donald R. P. Marquis: "If you make people think they're thinking, they'll love you. If you really make them think, they'll hate you."

of information, and the organization itself becomes only an assembly of parts rather than a dynamic and organic entity.

Modern management requires moving away from such simplistic and irrational concepts of reality. It requires grasping and incorporating this new thinking as a guide for strategic and technical action, making a fundamental shift in the way it thinks about how people behave and can be caused to behave in an organization.

Rational reframing

Our framing does not come anew, although we add to it throughout our lives. It is the product of our place in the diverse streams of history. These streams are nudged by new insights and definitions, such as the wheel, zero, corporation, nuclear weapon, ballpoint pen, and TQM. Sometimes these nudges seem radical in effect, as for the transistor, and sometimes they seem, as the French say, more of the same. On the whole, however, each new event is viewed in the only context we have, i.e., that which we have learned through our education and experience.

As long as these models explain and predict events adequately, life can be good. When the old models fail us in explanation and prediction, we get into trouble and search for new approaches. To the ancients, the heavens were close up and powerful, to be placated by priests and the sacrifice of people. We find the practice barbaric, but it was really quite practical, even humane, given the understanding of things at the time. If the heavens could be satisfied by a select few, especially from other tribes, many of one's own might be spared. Today, heaven is an economic dominion, priests are managers, employees' jobs are sacrificed, and hearts are only torn out symbolically. The purpose, however, is the same, i.e., to control events as best one can given one's understanding of those events.

Managers today are being told nothing less than that they need to change their basic way of seeing and understanding the world. They are being asked to leave their mechanistic world of modular, static, and discrete things and to move into a world that is organic, dynamic, and seamless. They are being asked to forget thinking about personalities, activities, and hardware and to focus on behavior, systems, and process. Effective action requires good thinking which, in turn, requires an appropriateness of what one is thinking about. What these concepts should be, of course, is what the fuss is all about.

Having said that, however, one must hasten to say that what constitutes the latest in management thinking changes rapidly. It was not that long ago that leadership and management style was all the rage. This has been superseded by rational decision making, systems thinking, and a host of modern concepts that continue to flow upon managers who, after all, must spend their time shoveling off their desks and trying to keep the boss happy.

While the plight and perplexity of the modern manager may be understandable, it still does not eliminate the basic truth: Managers need to have excellent models that explain and predict the modern world or suffer the consequences.

The right questions

The bottom line for managers is determined by having something to sell that somebody wants at a price they are willing to pay. Commercial operations that do not make money do not survive for long. Two strategies to make money are to increase revenues and to cut costs. Government agencies suffer budgetary problems largely because taxpayers are convinced that the agencies are not efficient and are reluctant to provide more money. Nonprofit agencies get into trouble when their supporters feel that administrative costs have gotten excessive. Quality improvement programs are attempted in the hopes that they will help the bottom line by either increasing revenue or cutting costs, or both.

The problem comes when inappropriate mental models prompt the wrong questions. When this happens, there are no good answers. Take for example a question that reflective managers have asked themselves: Are the employees here to help me do my job or am I here to help them do their jobs? That this is an issue is demonstrated in the companies which have presented their organization charts as upside down pyramids. Like the choice between Theory X and Theory Y, the question itself is specious and, consequently, there is no good answer. To say that the employees are there to help the manager is to set the stage for authoritarian management. To put the employees in charge can subvert the critical leadership role of management.

Whatever the answer, it will set the basic tone and direction for all actions regarding employees within that organization. It will determine the nature and amount of such things as rewards and perquisites, training budgets, and involvement. The choice has to do with who talks at meetings and who listens, with who is allowed to innovate and who isn't, and with who determines adequate performance and performance improvement needs.

A better question is that asked by Roger Milliken of the Milliken Company and Richard Teerlink of Harley-Davidson which, in effect, is, "How can we all work together to get where we all want to go?" This is the kind of question liberates all sectors of the workforce and joins them in a common effort. Milliken is one of the world's most successful textile companies, while the turnaround story of Harley-Davidson serves as a model for other companies. As the success of Milliken and many others illustrates, the change from archaic to modern management thinking is not impossible, but it can be difficult. To the thoughtful manager, change is much easier if one can identify what one must change from and change to. The powerful but unseen forces of our ideology must be brought before us so that we can choose those parts of our mental equipment that serve us best lest we be minions of our own ignorance.

The failure of the giant and seemingly indestructible Penn Central Railroad several decades ago, which sent shivers up corporate spines, was attributed to a wrong concept of what they were about. Penn Central Railroad was said to have suffered from thinking it was in the railroad business when it was really in the transportation business. Everyone thought that made sense, including a tile company that decided it was not in the tile business but the floor-covering business. It bought a carpet mill in Georgia only to discover that its core competency was not in floor covering but in tile. Within a few years, the carpet business was being dragged into bankruptcy. Only the death of its president and several million dollars in key executive insurance saved the company, which quickly divested itself of the carpet business.

Conceptually, the company was, in a general way, in the floor-covering business. It was also in the decorator business. Mostly, however, it was in the tile business and that is where it has profitably stayed. Penn Central was in the railroad business, as are many profitable railroads still, but it lost sight of what that business was in modern times. The question was what is the railroad business now, how can it manage its business and people better, how is its operating environment changing, and, generally, how must it change to continue to be successful? The fall of Penn Central was not a technological casualty like the buggy whip business. It was a failure by myopic management to pose the right kinds of questions that caused Penn Central's problems, as it is for most other organizations as well. The dinosaurs of Penn Central were not its trains but the management models of its leadership.

Low and high context cultures

Not very long ago Japanese management methods dominated this country's conversations about operational improvement. That such discourse centers today around American ideas and actions indicates the progress of American management in quality improvement and the ability of the American culture, including the management subculture, to absorb other ways of doing things that we like. American management has found a way to emulate the Japanese, not simulate them, which is the exactly how the Japanese have used the U.S. That two such diverse nations could both prove to be resilient, flexible, adaptive, and effective problem solvers is an example of equifinality, where the same result can be reached from two quite different paths.

While there may be some surface resemblances between the two models, as there are for the airports in Topeka and Tokyo, the underlying ideologies and their realities are quite different, as are their notions of common sense. In Japan, the idea of the modem corporation was absorbed readily into the organic feudal order and became essentially a new feudal order, both corporately and

nationally. Modern Japanese corporations reflect the feudal spirit or recipro-
cal loyalty, community focus, and high value on sacrifice for the group good.
In mechanistic, individualistic America, the corporation has been reflected in
organizational charts made up of modular boxes with connecting linkages
and showing a dispassionate disregard for employees. Interestingly, the
difference between the countries is also reflected by the fact that Deming, the
personification of the Japanese vs. American approaches, provided the Japanese only with statistical methods for quality control. The famous 14 points
were "strictly for the benefit of American industry."[1]

For all of his insight, Deming missed a critical and fundamental difference between the American and Japanese systems which caused some problems for those who attempt to implement his tenets in this country. For
example, Deming preached against performance appraisals, and some companies have either done away with them or attempted to fashion them to be
more developmental than critical. In Japan, organizations reflect the general
group-oriented culture in that they are close communities where much of the
communication is subtle and intimate. Performance expectations and feedback take place largely through a person's knowing what is expected without
being told. American organizations, on the other hand, reflect our general
culture in which workplaces, like everywhere in our society, are where
people gather to work, on an increasingly temporary and functional basis.
Work relationships tend to be more temporary, modular, and utilitarian.
While a great deal of performance regulation may occur through social
subtleties, much of it must be overt and explicit, even when effected through
peer pressure.

When a high degree of understanding is imbedded in the social environment, it is called high context. The U.S. is considered to be low context, as
communication is largely overt and explicit.[2] Sometimes this works to the
Japanese advantage, such as producing a higher commitment to team success
rather than individual recognition. Sometimes it works to the American
advantage, such as our being more comfortable with e-mail and other medi-
ated, impersonal communications. Americans are more diverse, more individualistic, more mobile, and more inclined to do things their way. If an
American company fails to have an explicit performance management system, it unlikely to have much performance management at all, at least not in
the sense of effective management control of the organization.* (See Table 1.)

Weakness through strength

Every strength, wrongly used, can become a weakness. For example, characteristics of American thought are effort optimism ("where there's a will

---

* "Management control" refers to management's ability to ensure desired organizational performance, not the restrictive condition most often associated with that term.

Table 1 Comparison of American and Japanese Cultural Contexts

Country	Basic concept of the universe	Primary work element	Cultural communication	Performance management
America	Separation of things; big things of many little things	Individual	Explicit	Explicit and clear messages required
Japan	Oneness of things	Groups as a whole	Subtle social messages	Little formal evaluation required

there's a way") and an action orientation ("don't just stand there; do something!"). While this attitude has energized and encouraged American management to be innovative and to take risks, it also leads to impatience and short-term thinking. Much of American management's short-term thinking has been attributed to greed, and that certainly can be a factor. Still, there seems to be a constant, abiding cultural pressure to take action and show quick results for any situation.

One of the biggest problems in trying to institute a quality program in any company is impatience, not only with the process as a whole (which can take years to reach fruition), but also for its components, such as clarification of goals and development of effective support systems. Impatience with the change process is the primary cause of failure of operational improvement programs according to one analysis.[3] This illustrates a critical point: Ideology, as the framework of common sense and rationality, can be a strength or weakness, depending upon how it is employed and the circumstances one faces.

Both the American and Japanese share the weakness of *hubris*, pride in our way of doing things, until some major change forces us into self-reevaluation. Japan and the U.S. have a history of challenging each other. In 1945, Japan was devastated by the atomic bombs and defeat of World War II. In 1953, Admiral Perry forced his way into Japan's comfortably closed society and rubbed its face in modern technology and industry. In both instances Japan, about the size of California with only 20% usable land and few natural resources, responded to equal or better its tormentors. Fifty years after the American fleet anchored in Tokyo Bay, that country surprised the world by defeating a powerful Russian naval force, and its economic comeback from the harsh devastation of World War II is well known.

Americans have responded well, too. The Sputnik of the Soviet Union prompted major improvements in this country's educational and scientific establishments. Few events in our history have had the impact of the Japanese intrusion in the American market. The automobile industry, which was dominated by the U.S., went from General Motors' having a consent decree not to sell more than 51% of the automobiles in the U.S. to finding itself in a position of having to struggle to keep one third of the U.S. market. Both the American economy and confidence were seriously shaken.

The story of the American and Japanese competition is still being told. It is, however, almost becoming a side issue, as both America and Japan find they must be at their top form, not just for each other but for the rest of the world, which is joining vigorously in the worldwide economic fray. A fray, one might add, created largely by the U.S. and Japan success.

The irony of success

The American management ideology has, until recent Japanese successes, produced results that were the envy of the world. The American response to the material needs of World War II was amazing. In just 2 years, Oak Ridge, TN, went from being a small railside village to a thriving city of 75,000 people with the capability of making an atomic weapon. After the war, the country was so awash with success that by 1955 it had revolutionized itself and become an employee society, an urban society, and a wealthy society. The U.S. enjoyed a period of historically unprecedented growth and prosperity, and its only real rival at the time, the Soviet Union, collapsed under the weight of trying to keep up. In the mid-1970s, as the U.S. was celebrating its bicentennial, the Japanese were preparing to give American management a punch that would send the economy and American *hubris* reeling.*

It soon became time to reassess what we were doing wrong and what the Japanese were doing right. Deming and Crosby have become familiar names, although as late as 1990 they were found in only a few management textbooks. America was finding, as Peter Drucker and John Kenneth Galbraith had predicted at the very height of American success, that "what looked like affluence and ease was really slow but steady weakening."[4] This same thought drives the authors of reengineering:[5]

> "The American record of industrial and technological accomplishment over the past century is proof enough that corporate management is not inept and that workers do work. The ironic truth is that American companies are performing so badly precisely because they used to perform so well."

---

* Penn Central is a good example of corporate *hubris* as are IBM, Apple, and many others. Xerox is an excellent example of both corporate disaster from *hubris* and corporate revival through new thinking.

The U.S. ironically, by its very success, had changed the world and created for itself a number of new challenges at a time when it wanted to rest on its laurels. Again, Karl Marx was right; the dominant force in an environment changes that environment in ways that undermine its dominance, even existence. The historical lesson for management is that successful effort, if unchanged, leads to failure, some modern examples being Holiday Inn and Howard Johnson. These companies invented the assurance of travelers finding clean, safe, and predictable places to stay or to eat, respectively. Their success helped increase road traffic and gave rise to a score of competitors that almost put Holiday Inn into bankruptcy and did put Howard Johnson out of the food business. The managers of Howard Johnson, which introduced many flavors of ice cream in the past, now must buy their treats from Baskin-Robbins. It is interesting that several of the examples of success in John Naisbet's *Megatrends* and of excellence in Peters' and Waterman's *In Search of Excellence* are now examples of problems rather than successes.

The impact of the U.S. on the world — and on its own social, political, and economic institutions, for that matter — is too far reaching and complex to summarize here. There is, however, one aspect that has had a major impact on the ability of American management to reach rationality and good judgment using its traditional ideology. People so commonly speak of knowledge industries, intellectual capital, doubling of knowledge every few years, and such gee-whiz facts as "90% of all scientists who ever lived are alive today" that the true import of the knowledge explosion tends to get lost.

As knowledge has grown exponentially in amount, it has also grown in depth and breadth and become more global in its sharing. This new intensity and sophistication has led to new understandings, which, in turn, have led to more sophisticated ways of managing. The simplistic notions of human events and their management, so powerful at mid-century, have become primitive and quaint. The most critical challenge to "common sense" is the change from a world of relative simplicity to one of high complexity. It is a change of situational quantity that constitutes a change in kind, requiring, as one commonly hears today, a new kind of manager. This does not mean a wholesale replacement of the old guard; rather, it means that the effective manager today is able to grasp the "new" ideologies that have been developed during the past decade and continues to pour forth.

Newton vs. Einstein

Henry David Thoreau wrote, "A person is wise with the wisdom of his time only, and ignorant with its ignorance." He could have also observed that people are quite capable of holding onto past ignorance even though new insights and understandings are available. A manager who operates by mechanistic concepts is more than out of fashion. Such a manager, like a dentist who uses a slow drill, is painfully behind the times. The mechanistic view of the world is woefully inadequate to deal effectively with complexities of today and the increased complexities of tomorrow.

The physical world conceived by Sir Isaac Newton consisted of discrete things that combined to make bigger things or were broken down to make smaller things. Each of these things existed in its own right and had clear and set qualities and ways of operating. In quantum thinking, things are merely forms of energy occasioned by a relationship to other energies. Thus, the world is dynamic and any static condition is an illusion.[6] A flock of birds or a cloud, therefore, is not a thing but an event. Likewise, a market, an organization, or worker attitudes, which, like the flock of birds, are in a constant state of formation and reformation.

To American managers, mechanistic thinking has the warm patina of a long and comfortable familiarity. Mechanistic thinking is simpler and easier to understand and it allows a manager to justify discrete and limited (if inadequate) actions. It is a siren's song of simplism in an increasingly complex and frustrating world. It is so deeply imbedded and structured into our very language and thought processes that even the proponents of new thinking often cast their ideas in mechanistic terms such as feedback. Most unfortunately, the study of human affairs differs from the study of the physical in that almost anything anyone says about behavior has a certain plausibility that will convince someone as to its validity.

From Aristotle ...

It would be difficult to detect any real American management operating theory in the sense of a clear, cohesive, and comprehensive system that neatly pulls together facts and guides and measures actions. Managers may operate with a sort of pocket theory, as suggested by Peters, but generally these are simply those mental tools that seem most applicable to the manager at the time. They rest upon and are extracted from a larger grab bag of general American core values, cultural norms, metaphysical beliefs, models (some like to call them paradigms), slogans and catchphrases, scientific theories (usually in the form of slogans), and numerous assumptions.

We use war metaphors to describe sports, sports metaphors to describe business, and business metaphors to describe war. Like the American ideology itself, American management ideology is a complex and shifting bundle of characteristic ideas that may surface as a small cluster of practical thoughts as managers shuffle their working concepts around to suit the needs of a situation. There are, nonetheless, clear and consistent patterns of management practice that reflect a certain cohesiveness and predictability of this ideology, and the ideological underpinnings can be traced from present-day practices to historical sources. While an exhaustive tracing of American management ideology is beyond us here and the genealogy of ideas is always tricky business, it would be useful to illustrate some the basic tenets, how they fit together, and how they work in practice.

The separatist ideology in American management thought becomes clear with a review of its intellectual history. Aristotle gave us the language-based logic that rests upon the differences among things, a concept that St. Augustine used to separate the individual (soul) with free will from whatever particular society (organization) in which that person may reside. Thomas Aquinas developed this thought into a hierarchy of laws and tied economic and social laws to those of divine powers. This became a pillar in Sir William Blackstone's *Commentaries on the Laws of England,* which was the basis for much of the education of Jefferson, Madison, and many of the Founding Fathers. Other contemporaries of Blackstone are also central to American ideology. John Locke articulated the notion that all men are born free and equal and joined together in society for their utilitarian purposes. Sir Isaac Newton argued that the world was like a great machine and operated on mechanical principles. About this same time, Adam Smith and John Stuart Mill used the Newtonian model to explain the economic and social worlds. (See Figure 1.)

These were the thinkers whose ideas flourished in the receptive and open land of the new America but fared poorly under old world institutions. As the industrial revolution began to gather force, the Protestant ethic (one prospers from hard work and suffers from bad habits) was married to the concepts of natural evolution to form secular social Darwinism, which, in turn, gave the idea a mean twist by justifying material success for some and poverty for others as being scientifically natural and ideologically just, rather than being the product of something being out of whack.

... to the Peter Principle

Max Weber is given credit for best articulating the model of a mechanistically rational organization with a clear division of labor and specialization.[7] This approach was carried further by Frederick Taylor in his work with Henry Ford which led to the increased specialization and minimization of worker tasks and, consequently, a depreciation of worker skills. The organization as mechanism, in turn, led to a depreciation of the workers themselves. As Tom Peters summarized:[8]

> "The central idea behind narrow job classifications is the conception of labor as a mechanical tool; cost minimization (low wages) and the widespread application of labor-replacing automation are natural concomitants. So is the fact that old American firms and, more frighteningly, new ones thoughtlessly ship work offshore to find cheaper labor."

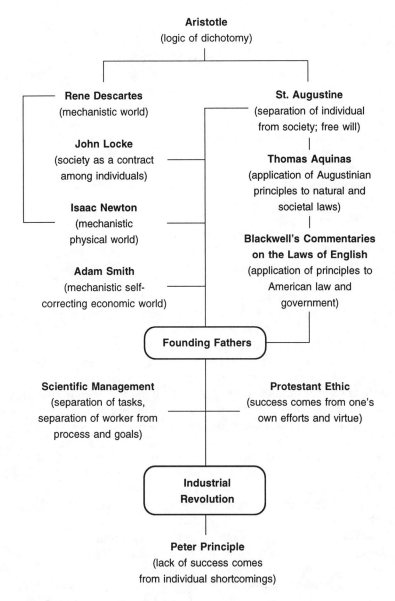

Figure 1 Partial geneology of American management ideology.

The paradox of American society, which places high values on the individual, and a management ideology that depreciates employees is illustrative of the mind's ability to nestle seemingly conflicting ideas. Still, the business of business is business, not social work. Peters' concerns were received with something like, "Yeah, and it's too bad but, hey, that's business."

The problem with mechanistic thinking is that it leads to wasteful and counterproductive actions that are not good business. The wasting of social capital is rational only in an ideological context that is blind to its real value.

The ideological composite of individual responsibility, freedom from social responsibility, and minimization of worker value requires only a clever turn of phrase to mold it into an element of applied management thinking. Such a phrase is the "Peter Principle". Given this rule of operation, people are promoted to their level of incompetence, from which they are either demoted (rarely) or terminated (often). The organization, or its management, bears no responsibility for the development of these people, their selection for the positions, establishing the expectations and requisite abilities for these positions, or for adequate support to optimize success after the appointments.

Those who do not work out are usually let go; it is sink or swim. As a result, a person who had demonstrated ability and promise, who had contributed to the organization and who had been judged worthy of greater responsibility, is lost to the organization altogether, along with his or her talent, skills, knowledge of the operation, and social contacts. The cost of wasting such social capital is difficult to calculate, but it must be tens of millions of dollars annually. Indeed, only a very rich society could waste its resources in that manner and survive.

Whether cause or effect, a characteristic of poorly developed countries, including in many ways the former Soviet Union, is the wasting of the genius and energies of its people. It would be difficult to find a more wrong-minded or mean-spirited idea than the Peter Principle. If the waste involved material or equipment, the irrationality of such an action would be readily perceived and much less forgivable. Had management been so irresponsible with a piece of equipment with a fraction of the value there would be serious repercussions. Because it is "only" wasting money in the form of human talent and experience, it is considered regrettable but all right. Because Joe just didn't work out, Joe bears the onus of responsibility, and there is no blame for the management that promoted him and presumably guided and assessed his work.

The problem is not that it is unfair to Joe, because he took his chances. The problem is not carrying dead wood, because Joe, if his management had any sense at all, was not dead wood before his promotion and did not become so afterwards, any more than the team coming in second in the World Series is a loser. Rather, the problem is that such a system creates, and wastes, a lot of Joes. The smirky Peter Principle, in that it justifies the waste of organizational resources, fails the test of rationality, which is an assessment of the appropriateness of one's activities to one's purpose.

Management decisions are essentially bets on the future, predictions based upon one's notions about how the world seems to work. The real power of a good ideology is that it helps us get a fix on what we need to be doing and what to look out for. Management is much like chess in that one rarely makes a move that is not without some good logic. These actions, of apparently obvious value, are later found, in a more excellent context, to have been foolish and to have jeopardized their queen. That is one of the fundamental problems of authority-reliant management, a topic to which we now turn.

Endnotes

1. This observation was made by Junji Noguchi, who worked closely with Deming for many years with the Union of Japanese Scientists and Engineers; see Noguchi, Junji, The legacy of W. Edwards Deming, *Quality Progress*, December, 35–37, 1995.
2. Those interested in gaining a better understanding of high-context vs. low-context cultures might be interested in reading Ishii, Satoshi, Thought patterns as modes of rhetoric: the United States and Japan, *Communication*, December, 81–86, 1982; Hall, Edward T., *Beyond Culture*, Doubleday, Garden City, NY, 1976. These works also suggest how simple-minded some approaches to integrating different "corporate cultures" have been during corporate mergers and acquisitions.
3. Kotter, John, Leading change: why transformation efforts fail, *Harvard Business Review*, March-April, 59–67, 1995.
4. See Drucker, Peter, *The Age of Discontinuity: Guidelines to Our Changing Society*, Harper & Row, New York, 1968.
5. Hammer, Michael, and James Champy, *Reengineering the Corporation*, Harper Business, New York, 1993, p. 10.
6. For an excellent comparison of Newtonian and quantum thinking and its impact on management, see Wheatley, Margaret, *Leadership and the New Science*, Berrett-Koehler Publishers, San Francisco, 1992.
7. Max Weber is credited with coining the term "Protestant ethic" which describes an individual's responsibility for his circumstances rather than environmental factors, including the organization in which the person works; see Weber, Max, *The Theory of Social and Economic Organizations*, Oxford University Press, New York, 1947 (edited and translated by A. M. Henderson and Talcott Parsons).
8. Peters, Thomas J., *Thriving on Chaos*, Knopf, New York, 1987, p. 21.

chapter seven

Authority and control

Why authority-reliant organizations inevitably become wasteful and inefficient

> *All silencing of discussion is an assumption of infallibility.*
> ∽John Stuart Mill

One of the funniest bits of the old comedy team of Bud Abbot and Lou Costello took place in Spain, where Costello was trying to ask a local person for directions to the bullfight arena. He was asking in English, which the Spaniard did not understand. After a few minutes of this, Bud Abbot, the supposed "smart" one said, "Let me try." Pushing Lou Costello aside, he put his fists on his hips, leaned forward, looked at the person sternly, and began to shout in English. The results, of course, were no different, except that the Spaniard was now more confused and perplexed. In many organizations, even though everyone supposedly speaks the same language, shouting often takes the place of effective translation and learning, and the results are not so funny.

Search for truth

If the world were simple, it would be easier for one person to have all the answers or even to know the questions. The real world, however, is invariably uncertain, untidy, and unclear. Generally when we fail it is in our inability to put events into some sort of understandable and predictable order. Our world is a place where the American health system can be both a triumphant success (medical breakthroughs) and a failure (affordable care to all). One cannot help but wonder why the managerial enterprise, pursued with such good intentions and effort, so often turns out so differently than expected. The answer is that we have not been given a straight deck with which to deal. The cards themselves are a problem.

Good common sense today requires many eyes and ears and an effective sharing of information if anything approaching the truth is to be known. Like beauty, common sense is in the eye of the beholder. One person's good coordination is another's red tape; one's diplomacy and tact are another's timidity or deceit. One person is too idealistic, while another lacks vision. One person's thorough analysis is another's paralysis, and one's forceful leadership is another's pushy overbearance. Should the advertising budget be determined as a percentage of sales? Should we contract out or do it in-house? Is 10% ROI profitable or an effective liquidation of assets? Should we fire him or not, and if so what should the terms be?

The real world is a place where one can do everything right and still, as the story unfolds, appear to have acted wrongly. To the dismay of managers, it is a haven for second-guessers. Certainly one of the most innovative, forward-looking, and meticulously managed companies today is Walt Disney. The design for the Contemporary Hotel at Florida's Disney World included modular rooms that could be removed, renovated, and replaced without losing rent revenues. Disney's considerable talent went into the design and construction of this innovative architectural showpiece.

Unfortunately, the ground under the hotel shifted, causing the framework to shift as well, and the rooms were no longer movable. A great deal of planning and cost were wasted. Disney could have played it safer and stayed with convention, but then it is Disney's nature, genius, and, indeed, business to do the creative and unconventional. The very nature of creative effort is risky. When one has done the best to optimize the chances of success and calculated the loss-gain ratio, that is how things should be done. It is common sense at its best.

Pressure to prevent

The cost of error today puts managers under even greater pressure to control their operations. Paine Webber settled with its customers for sales misrepresentation for $332.5 million and Sears Roebuck & Co. settled for $60 million for misrepresentation in its auto repair operations. The Standard Charter Bank has been banned from trading in Hong Kong, Food Lion Super Markets was investigated for improper meat handling, and Tropicana, the largest producer of orange juice in the U.S., was fined for dumping waste material into a bay for a third time. Because many of these activities can involve criminal charges, few in top management would knowingly allow them in their operations. In these cases there was an apparent perversion of the company's purposes at the operating levels.

In a more chilling case, a Union Carbide plant in India accidentally released methyl isocyanate into the air, resulting in thousands of deaths. Just months later, a plant in West Virginia almost released the same lethal material. These events, and the many accidents and releases of material from other plants in the oil and chemical industries, led to a government-required wholesale redesign of chemical process management. Still, it is not unusual for a company to be in the news because of management control failures. Less newsworthy, but perhaps more telling, are the problems with customers such as product recalls or just plain bad feelings in the market.

Pressure to produce

For several years, my consulting work involved following a plant manager who was a trouble-shooter for a major bottle-making company. In each case, the pathology was virtually the same. The previous manager had been quite authoritarian and, for awhile, had done quite well with the plant. Over time, however, plant productivity began to flag. Equipment began to have problems, and the decline of employee morale was indicated by the rise of union activities. Safety also suffered. In every case, the impact had been the same. Organizational systems had collapsed or were irrelevant, such as the union journeyman program, and the equipment had been neglected, usually through poor maintenance and improper operation. The focus for everyone had been on making the boss happy, not on the needs of the plant.

In fairness to the previous plant manager, squeezing the good out of the plant was not his idea alone. The home office loved the numbers and rewarded his approach to management. That the plant was now a mess was considered either a cost of doing business or something that my client trouble-shooter could fix. Sometimes he could, but sometimes the combination of poor morale and poorly maintained equipment could not be overcome, and what had been a state-of-the-art plant now operated at a much reduced rate of productivity. When plants like this are closed, the stated reason is rarely poor management, but rather high labor costs or a market downturn. One of the most important privileges of authority is being able to assign the blame.

Blind faith in "bossism"

The virtually blind and complete faith by management in nearly unqualified management authority is a major cause of problems in organizations today. It is not that authority is bad, any more than weather is bad, for both are natural conditions.* Rather, it is the manner in which managers use that authority that causes problems. To take the position that authority always acts in the best interest of the organization is an act of such faith as to be worthy of sainthood. Still, that is the position many, if not most, organizations take. One hears, "It's Joe's shop, so he should be able to run it however he thinks best." Only when the company is sued, turnover gets too high, or

---

* There seems to be both a natural psychological tendency for deference among individuals as well as a culturally determined one based on such things as position, reputation, wealth, etc.

there is some other major problem do we question Joe. It is a classic model of detect-and-correct management at its worst. Because good enough is okay, it is actually hard for a manager to get into trouble other than for political reasons.

Years ago, Lord Acton observed that "power corrupts and absolute power corrupts absolutely," a lesson applicable to American management. Unchecked authority is often typified by laziness and indulgence, with whimsical and arbitrary decisions being made that cost companies thousands, perhaps millions, of dollars. For example, the problem with performance management in most companies is that top management simply refuses to do it properly, and who is going to make them? Unchecked authority often leads to "rawhidin'", with the manager as drover or bully rampaging through the organization and cracking the whip. The organizational chart, typically a reflection of authority and privilege in an organization, allows managers to rampage from their block on down.

In one organization, the CEO did exactly that with the result that managers were constantly rushing from one concern of the boss to another. After awhile, the boss did not even have to say anything, as the managers would rush around in anticipation that the boss might say something. There were no real priorities, in the sense of organizational or corporate goals, but only an urgency to avoid trouble from the boss. It is no wonder that such power is addictive. The primary obstacle in any improvement effort is not the workforce, but management, who typically wants changes below them, above them, but not for them.

The bad habits of "bossism"

Because unchecked authorities are not required to manage well, such as providing clear expectations for the organization, they tend toward the sheep-dog type of management, which operates primarily by nipping at people who get out of line. Rather than tell people what they expect, other than in particular circumstances, they tend to tell them what they do not like about what they have done. Instead of focusing on their work to optimize performance, people spend their time trying to guess what the boss might want. The boss, lacking effective constraints, has little incentive to plan the work of others and makes increasingly arbitrary and wrenching decisions.

While this may strike one as a ridiculous way to operate, it is nonetheless a condition in many organizations. It is very hard to establish a rational program under those conditions, because authority changes the premise of rationality from organizational performance to authority pleasing. This kind of abusive authority is based on fear. Rationality becomes perverted to the common sense pursuit of staying out of trouble, avoiding risk, and sacrificing corporate goals for survival.

Often, actions are mere formalities meant to satisfy a need for compliance but lack the spirit and content of real action. A good example is a safety orientation for a chemical plant that processed dangerous materials. The requirement was that no one could enter the plant without going through a safety orientation, which earned a sticker for the person's hard hat. The safety orientation involved a review of the plant layout, a discussion of the plant's dangers, instructions for putting on a respirator, telling people the emergency telephone number, and instructions that, if the alarm whistle blew, to run in a direction that is generally upwind. Even if a person had remembered the emergency number, there were no telephones generally available nor maps to tell people where they were in the plant. The windsock was not visible from most areas of the plant. When these things were pointed out to the plant manager, the response was that it satisfied government requirements, and "besides, that's Joe's area and he is very sensitive about these things." So much for rationality.

The saving feature is, of course, that most managers are not tyrants, although the "authority trap" catches everyone at one time or another. Most organizations operate with a generally accepted purpose for most organizations, although it may be assumed and unarticulated. There is a productive logic in most jobs and technologies, people have an inherent need to do something constructive for their own satisfaction, and, finally, there is a fundamental inertia to every organization of any duration. Because of these forces, an organization may continue to produce despite various irrationalities.

Need for modern controls

Managers who rely heavily on authority tend to be suspicious, which, in combination with insecurity, lack of understanding, and inadequate sense of restraint, drives them to attempt to control what they see rather than what causes what they see. In earlier, simpler times it was not difficult for a manager to be involved in many of the details of an operation. If the manager were an entrepreneur, much of the value-adding knowledge of the operation resided with him or her. Much of the work was menial and semi-skilled. Indeed, part of the genius of the production line was that it minimized the skills required of any one worker. Today, one talks of knowledge workers, although the full meaning of that reality might not be fully understood.

A knowledge worker is not just a fancy version of a clerk who transcribes audiotapes to a word processor. Knowledge worker refers not just to dealing with information, but also the total condition of the working environment. The plantation system was possible because little in the way of complex or speedy information or learning was required to do the job. In modern organizations, sales and marketing, research and development, and production must coordinate and cooperate closely. This involves working with information and integrating their work into a broader conceptual environment. The levels of understanding for these diverse activities to act in mutually supportive harmony are high and likely to increase in both amount and sophistication. The problem in organizations today has become as much information overload as the need for more.

The tendency of authority-reliant managers is to thwart the free dialog necessary for effective translation and learning. To have information go through restrictive and rigid channels and to push up and down through layers of control is simply too clanky, clunky, and simple-minded a management control system for today's operating needs. The time required for decisions, the real limits on information flow and knowledge, or simply the abilities of any one person to attend so many matters render traditional management structures ineffective. Decisions come too late, are based on too little or the wrong kinds of information, and are often woefully inadequate or even counter-productive.*

Unfortunately, people under pressure tend to revert to the methods with which they are the most familiar and comfortable and not some new technique they are still trying to learn. A golfer trying to learn a new stance is likely to knock a lot of balls into the rough before incorporating the change into his or her natural swing after much practice. A manager trying to incorporate a new technique into his or her "game" rarely has the luxury of practice. More likely, they are under constant pressure to perform and are reluctant to try the new technique unless that pressure is even greater.

Paradox of overcontrol

People under pressure can lose system control by trying too hard to control the outcomes of some emergency or other. Because poor systems create the most urgencies, the process feeds on itself until one is caught in what George Odiorne called the "activity trap".[1] Focus on the particulars can undermine the bigger effort. Management wonders why its exhortations for others to take a bold stroke falls on deaf ears, all the while lecturing them about the cost of office supplies.

Piddling interest by management begins a cascade of that same mindset throughout the organization. The control focus gets smaller and more localized, and the general systems that generate the problems for managers receive less and less attention as solving problems is displaced by patching symptoms. One example is the president of a large-sized Goodwill operation expressing a common managerial lament. He could get things done if he personally got involved, but otherwise they just did not happen.

---

* This is not news, of course, because that is why there is so much interest today in new techniques which promise better control of work. Still, there is an almost irresistible need felt by many managers to try to control the particulars rather than the systems.

What he did not realize was that anything he wanted got done because he brought the full resources of the organization to achieve that one thing. Everything else in the organization was set aside, minimized, or seriously disrupted. People found the work highly unpredictable, becoming self-defensive and seeking refuge in following the rules.

Worse, since the work in which they were investing themselves could be so arbitrarily trivialized, they came to view it as not important. It took this executive a while to realize that the *he* was the problem because, when the organization was kept in such turmoil, its ability to function was being continually undermined. What he had attributed to a lack of ability and motivation in others was in reality his handiwork because he denied them necessary opportunities, resources, and, in the words of Deming, "constancy of purpose".

Thus, one finds the irony of overcontrol — the more one tries to control the parts without reference to their whole system context, the less one is able to control the sum of the parts, i.e., the whole. The ironic result is a lessened ability to control the parts by anyone and much frustration by everyone. Bureaucracies are created in the effort to control by reducing options such that only the "right" response will happen. But people are boundlessly creative, and circumstances change such that the "right" response varies with time and circumstances. When approached with a negative, restrictive perspective, policies and procedures beget more policies and procedures, begetting bureaucracy.

The effort to control particulars brings about the problems that result from the paradox of overcontrol, which is the antithesis of leadership. This may not be evident because, in the short term and in selected areas, the organization may perform quite well. Such immediate action can *seem* to bring about a rationality that the organization needs, but actually it is highly disruptive to the efforts of everyone in the process, creating greater irrationality, causing them to have problems in their areas, and validating the boss' contention that no one else seems to be able to get things done. So, everyone else just hunkers down, desperately trying to keep their own operation going and waiting to see where the boss will strike next.

As the rational systems collapse and people wait for orders, authority becomes increasingly necessary to do the ordinary work of the organization, taking a greater toll on both management time and employee morale. That is one reason managers in poorly managed organizations are "too busy" for improvement efforts. Good analysis is neglected as the boss becomes increasingly confident in his own insight, brilliance, and singular efficacy, and decisions can become increasingly arbitrary, even whimsical, and remote from the real work of the employees.

Because authority-based management requires little other than making the boss happy, it does not deal well with general organizational performance. Worse, it affords opportunities for people who are inclined to utilize the weaknesses in an authoritarian system to build fiefdoms from which they defend their prerogatives at the expense of the overall operational good. Understand that these people do not see themselves as feudal lords, but rather as rational islands of competence in that same irrational sea. There are numerous examples, but a good test for any organization is to ask who is in charge of what. If it is someone who dispenses favors or decides on the basis of technical expertise rather than user needs, you have a fiefdom.

The Soviet model

There is ample evidence of the paradox of overcontrol but perhaps the most dramatic is the collapse of the Soviet Union. Here is a system that knew control, but it was a control over its parts. It was a mechanical control that was rigid and closed, capable of preventing most anything it did not want. It could make selected things happen, such as Sputnik, by investing enormous amounts of resources that had been pulled from other areas. The price of this, however, was the loss of general adaptability and creativity resourcefulness. Everything that did not get the authoritarian attention was out of control. In short order, the very mechanisms of control, such as the secret police, became another control problem.

Power in the mechanistic Soviet system was seen as a finite quantity that was diminished when shared. The Soviet system demotivated people away from its grander purpose and, indeed, subverted it, pushing everyone into a defensive, self-serving rationality. The Soviet Union was undermined by its own passive-aggressive population, which, upon being denied the opportunity for validation, turned to vodka and cynicism.

One of the reasons that the U.S. and Japan have been able to thrive while the Soviet system failed is that the Soviet system was based upon a mechanistic model which expected a world of technical system attributes, such as an ideal state of operation. The fallacy of trying to force human systems into a mechanical mold was a strategic error that led to its consequent failure. The U.S. and Japan, although quite different from each other, are both flexible, adaptable, and highly effective problem-solving systems. Communism was a vision of a static human condition as an ideal state, which is like falling in love with a photograph. Democracies, however, are rules of process which can lead anywhere as long as one follows the rules, at least until everyone agrees to change them.

When analyzing companies in trouble, one finds many similarities to the flaws of the Soviet system. Where one finds a high degree of power that is seen as a finite quantity, efforts to control parts rather than systems, distrust, manipulation, and even contempt for those not in power, and so on, one sees an organization out of control. Attempting to set up controls for all of the parts of an organization will eventually tie that organization into a bureaucratic knot, frustrating efforts to make it productive. Such hide-bound, activity-focused true control of complex operations comes, as Zen might suggest, not from gripping tighter but from letting go, from leading through compelling purpose and rationality.

Rule-basing and bureaucracy

An insidious form of authority-based strategy is rule by rules. Its chief product is bureaucracy, reaching its most exquisite form in government. Rules are certainly necessary in any organized effort, and the problem is rarely the rules *per se* but how they are used. Rather than deal with situations through good management, managers may attempt to circumscribe behaviors with restrictive policies and procedures. Since people seem infinitely inventive when it comes to getting around rules, and because situations are always a little different, there is a constant need for more particularized rules.

Soon, no one can do anything without breaking a rule. Rules may not be changed for years, may become irrelevant (if they ever were really relevant), and are ignored or conveniently interpreted to meet immediate needs. Pretty soon no one has faith in the rules, which seem to have been written by someone in another place and time, and system credibility breaks down.

Students recently being suspended from school for having aspirin is an example of rules driving out common sense. One study of hospital-caused injuries and deaths of patients found one factor to be that system rules are ineffective, cumbersome, and sometimes used punitively.[2] It is as if a coach focuses entirely on the bounds and penalties, neglecting the playing of the game and optimizing the players abilities. One of the chief reservations American managers have about ISO 9000 is that is seems to be a pro-ceeduralizing process for rule-based management at the sacrifice of flexibility and innovation.

A defining quality of the pejorative bureaucracy, however, is that it does not allow for flexibility. Worse, as the rules proliferate, they begin to make it impossible to follow them all or to conform to one without being in conflict with another. Authority uses rules in the attempt to control others, and often they are arbitrary or simply indulgences. The rules lose all rationality, are given lip service, and become irrelevant to all but a few self-serving "coffee-pot lawyers" who use the rules for their own special purposes. Management's hands become tied up in particulars; the system wanders as its vision dissipates. The system becomes more irrational, and its ability to accomplish its grand purpose becomes less efficient and quality assured.

Authority-based management fails to optimize an operation (although it may produce some impressive short-term results), because it disconnects employees from the organizational purpose. Instead of serving as a translator of purpose to common sense practicality, the authority merely tells people what to do. Because employees often do not know what the purpose of management is, they often see its actions as arbitrary and usually change what they have been doing only to the extent necessary to stay out of trouble. People are not automatons, and they respond to how people treat them in a way that is in their own best interest. Because of various departmental satraps and because people are being told rather than asked, authority reliance tends to curtail the flow of communication critical to effective translation of purpose to practicality.

Disagreement is not a test of common sense; it is a *search* for it. The test of common sense is rationality, but, if these conversations are carried out conspiratorially to avoid detection by management, there is the danger of a "win-win" situation among departments at the expense of overall organizational goals. An example of this is a company where the operations and human resources, unable to keep up with the turnover in operations, agreed to lease employees so that they could step away from the problem. However, all employees, whether leased or not, will need to ask questions that clarify their assignment and its intent, to report anticipated difficulties, to resolve how they will work with others, to note necessary resources and training, and to surface and resolve relevant disagreements if they are to self-manage their work properly in terms of corporate goals and values.

For example, a city manager decreed that all breaks, no matter what the work situation, be promptly at 10:00 a.m. and 2:00 p.m. so that he would know when people were on a break and when they were goofing off. Supervisors then had to schedule all work around breaks rather than the breaks around the work. It is a system out of control that exacts a high cost in underutilized energy, talent, and creativity. In a competitive world based on the optimal utilization of human capital, this can hurt you.[3]

Leadership and control

The three elements in any enterprise are purpose, system, and effort. Leadership utilizes systems to elicit employee collective self-discipline to form an organized pursuit of organizational purpose. Authority focuses on effort at the expense of purpose and systems. Authority is, therefore, very personal and gives rise to hard feelings such that management is often at war with its own workforce and even within its own ranks. Because managing the bees rather than the hive never achieves the overall effect that is ostensibly the purpose for everyone's being there, authoritarians are often frustrated and feel unappreciated. This may account for their occasional, sometimes frequent, reassuring and gratuitous displays of authority.

In rational circumstances, control is the ability to ensure outcomes and power is the ability to drive the behavior of others in a goal-achieving way. Negative control can prevent some behaviors, but it tends to generate other undesirable behaviors, such as cooking the numbers or providing hollow safety orientation to comply. Efforts to achieve the desired behaviors by eliminating all others by rules and orders, a strategy more common than one might think, is realistic only for managers of a gulag. For managers in such an environment, work can be truly Sisyphean.

Control is a state of mind, and control of particulars (especially self-indulgent control) leads to the paradox of overcontrol rather than the optimized pursuit of corporate goals. The primary job of a manager is not to control every particularity but to cause the right things to happen, which occurs when everyone is self-managing with a properly oriented common sense. One of the most powerful tools of managers, although one that gives many managers great discomfort if not a little fear, is teams.

Most people tend to see teams as empowering employees when, in fact, it is the manager who has a new powerful means available if he or she can become skilled in its use. Because of management fear or inability, mostly through a lack of true understanding, teams are often too circumscribed or manipulated to be successful. If the teams are too bounded or in a hostile environment — that is, unless the entire operation is team-like — the benefit of team translation will also be bounded, even suffocated.

The primary benefit of teams or a team-like operation is not buy-in but rather an effective translation among those involved. They are the locus of the communications when the translation issues (who, what, when, how, why, etc.) can be determined fully, accurately, and in real time. When the team is functioning well, staff leaves the meetings with a clear sense of what they need to do. Teams also make it difficult to hide performance problems and such ills as supervisory favoritism.

A group of coaches in a team-managed plant were lamenting their lack of authority and were pressing for more authority to get the teams to do what they were supposed to. "Authority" in this case was the power to punish if people did not do what the coach ordered. Many of these coaches were poorly trained and their responsibilities were unclear, so they were understandably anxious about how to deal with their teams. The only model most of them had was that of authority-reliant supervision. Had they been properly prepared, they would have understood that the true value of authority is as a platform for leadership, to elicit the desired behaviors (performance) from staff. Authority reliance, however, is a hard habit to break.

The rational control of an organization does not require that management surrender authority, but rather that it use that authority in a way that establishes more effective organizational rationality, moving from command to leadership. In addressing this issue, one of the first things we explored was ways in which the coaches in the previous example could inspire the proper performance without authority. A great deal can be done by simply clarifying expectations, building pride, solving problems as a group, and providing appropriate incentives and rewards. One must wonder, though, whether someone who cannot think of anything to do without threat of authority should be a coach.

Authority is a necessary, even natural, quality in the workplace. Its improper use, however, is probably the single more important reason quality efforts fail. To truly drive an organization with true authority requires fear in the workplace and, paradoxically, creates turtles not rabbits. Adding to the harm, authority fails to develop the systems that make organizations capable of effective response during all those times when response is needed but management is focused elsewhere. Authority tends to neglect not only systems, but also the skills and knowledge of its workforce. It prevents critical organizational communications, sows mistrust and friction, and exempts itself from any change so nothing really changes.

Endnotes

1. See Odiorne, George, *The Human Side of Management*, Lexington Books, Lexington, MA, 1987.
2. Bates, David, et al., Incidence of adverse drug events and potential adverse drug events, *JAMA*, July 5, 29–38, 1995.
3. For one of the clearest and most incisive essays on the subject of human capital, see Stewart, Thomas, Brain power: who owns it ... how they profit from it, *Fortune*, March 17, 104–110, 1997.

chapter eight

Decision making and work-process rationality

Why everyone is always a part of every decision
no matter what kind of management system one has

> *"Nice tie, where did you get it?"*
> *"Why, it was right there in my closet."*
>   ∽Old joke

One the way home one evening, I stopped by a grocery store to pick up a few things, including a half gallon of milk. I get milk in half gallons because a quart does not last long enough and a gallon will spoil before I can drink it. I also get 1% milk, because it is low in fat but has non-fat milk solids added so it taste good, unlike skim milk which looks and tastes like cloudy water. At the store, I noticed that the expiration date on half gallons of 1% was only a couple of days away, and I would not have used the milk by then. This particular store brand seems to have a short shelf-life but the store is conveniently on the way. The store with more long-lasting milk is not. Had the kids been in town there would be no problem because the milk would not have lasted that long or I could go ahead and get a gallon. I could get a quart, but then I would have to get milk again soon. Geez, decisions are tough — and that's just for a little milk.

Actually, one often sees executives commit millions of dollars with quick decisions then agonize over some seemingly small matter, such as office arrangements. One of Parkinson's more famous laws is that time spent on deciding a matter is in inverse proportion to the amount of money involved.[1] The milk decision has many similarities with the countless other decisions we make daily, some big and some quite piddling. Which copier should we get? Should we build or buy? What should we do about Joe? Should we expand into Ohio? If so, should we make some changes in our product line? Should we let Russia into NATO? Which tie should I wear?

The decision stream

Each of these decisions has a number of things in common. For one, they do not start afresh. They are part of a stream of activities that is the product of countless previous decisions, such as making the purchases or keeping the gifts that comprise one's tie inventory. Even then, there have been a number of earlier determinations going back to a fundamental concept of self which have determined occupational and social expectations and, consequently, the styles of ties that are even considered. One selects from those things that have been historically established as one's range of options. In spite of a tendency to regard decisions as being right or wrong, most decisions concern preferences, not criticalities. They can be judged only as wise or foolish or, in terms discussed here, more rational or less rational.

Managers face a constant stream of such questions as how much capital expenditures or employee raises to allocate, whether to promote Joe or Sally, how much inventory one should carry, or whether to build or rent. There are always some pros and cons or no decision would be needed. A decision is merely a notion until some one acts to realize it; the actual decision is probably less important than what happens next. Because there are always limits as to what one can know about a given question, and even greater limits about what one can predict about the consequences, people can only make the best decision possible at the time. The trouble starts when a manager loses sight of that fundamental reality and feels that a decision, once made, is complete.

A decision is an adjustment in the stream of activities, preferably a minor one that does not disrupt and confuse. Every adjustment moves the activities to new circumstances such that new obstacles and opportunities present themselves. It is natural and unavoidable that people will construe what the decision, which is really only information, will mean for them. They will then act accordingly. If the people who are expected to realize the decision are involved in that decision, they will understand what they are doing and why. As situations come up, they can either handle them or get the decisions reformulated for a more pragmatic and rational translation into action.

When issued a command, on the other hand, people are less likely to understand enough to make adjustments and, worse, are probably not going to even get a reconsideration of the decision. Indeed, under such circumstances, employees are probably reluctant to even deliver bad news, much less offer suggestions. Every decision, however, should have the suffix, "Let's try it this way, be alert for ways to make necessary adjustments, and keep each other informed."

Decisions as translation

A decision is really the entire process of identifying, considering, determining, and taking courses of action. A decision is the point at which what happened becomes what happens. The problem with most decisions is rarely the choice itself but in failures of analysis and implementation. The analysis — asking the right questions and getting appropriate information — is where the Japanese reputedly invest most of their time; as a result, implementation is easier and more quality assured. Americans, on the other hand, have an urge to action and tend to give the formulation of the question less time, preferring instead to spend most of their time trying to make the decision work. The difference between being proactive and relying on detect-and-correct is largely cultural and ideological, between "then will be what we do now" and "that's then, this is now."

Managers may be unsure about what to do at times, but they rarely make decisions they think are bad. What managers often do that gets them into trouble, however, is make the mistake of novice chess players. They look at a decision facing them at any given time as a discrete act, forgetting that it is but a passing action in an ongoing stream of events. It is a trick of our language that allows, even pushes, us to turn an abstraction such as "decision" into something that seems concrete and discrete. Isolated decisions also create irrationality by missing the connection between the purposes of the decisions and those of the organization as a whole.

Actions that follow a decision stem from the way people now think about their work, i.e., how they translate ideas into actions. Every choice directs a number of subsequent actions that are themselves decisions that translate the purpose of the higher decision into situationally applicable purpose. While follow-through is generally seen as a finite sequence of consequent events, it is really infinite in both its duration and tangential ramifications, as it becomes the input of future decisions. That is the chaos effect in action.

Inevitability of multiple outcomes

Suppose one is given a bowl of water and the task of causing a ripple to go from the middle to a mark on the bowl's side. One simply puts a finger in the middle of the bowl to generate a ripple that will travel to the mark. But that action does more than intended because the ripple travels all around the edge of the bowl. It is the nature of things that any action does not create a single reaction but many reactions. Sometimes the ramifications are serendipitous, such as for Ray Kroc when he got the McDonald brothers to let him franchise their hamburger business so he could sell them more milkshake makers.

Invariably, however, there seem to be adverse unintended consequences for any action.

It is our nature that we generally see only those reactions of interest to us at the time. The game of chess is particularly instructive for decision makers to understand this principle. In chess, all who can play the game have the same basic knowledge as a grand master in that they know all the moves available for each piece. Games of chess, however, are not so much won as lost when a person, seeing a seemingly advantageous opportunity, acts. It is then that the other implications become evident, and a player finds himself in jeopardy. The master player, on the other hand, is the one who can better assess these potentially untoward implications. Chess, of course, is infinitely less complicated than organizational management.

Given the complexity and creativity of decisions, one can better understand the need for managers to think in terms of probabilities rather than absolutes. If this is true in the hard sciences, one can only imagine how unsure any prediction in the social arena is. Given this condition for managers, the only realistic strategy for them to maximize organizational rationality is to strive to get the best odds possible. Identifying the causal factors and optimizing the likelihood of a preferred outcome is not only a good working definition of quality management but also of scientific management.

Lack of excellent knowledge

One of the standards of judgment is intentionality, i.e., does the decision do what it sought to do? This is particularly true when the focus of the decision is on the technical process without due regard to the organizational effects. If the particular purpose and the grand purpose are aligned, intentionality is a good standard. When a decision only needs to satisfy itself, however, self-justification that only references itself can very easily allow an operation to get off track. This rarely brings quality because only rarely is it excellent knowledge, which must be verifiable at strategic and particular levels in an organization.

This discrete view of decisions fools us into making decisions that are not so much wrong as they are inadequate, in that they fail to consider the factors that influence the decisional situation and the decision's implementation. It is this inadequacy that causes so much trouble for an organization, because it fails to address the factors that determine the odds of success. Such decisions often contain a plausible, closed loop of logic, but they can lose their rationality as one moves to the larger organizational context that generates, implements, and sometimes makes by default the vast array of actual work process decisions. Sometimes managers are so focused on their decisions and what they are trying to accomplish that they are blind to the implications of what they do and what they ignore. It is the worst sort of gamble.

The example of a fruit shipper is instructive. Quality was so important that packing was done entirely by hand, rather than by dumping and topping, so that each grapefruit would be hand tested. The entire operation of growing and purchasing fruit, packing and shipping, and even establishing market position and sales rested on the efforts of these manual packers. One day while observing them working, it was clear that a number of simple steps could reduce the burden of their work and increase their work rate. Because the packers were on piece work, everyone would have made more money. When I mentioned this to the general manager, he responded that there were more important things to do at the time, thus the keystone activity in the entire operation was not a priority.

The fruit shipper shows what can happen when top management makes decisions without regard to the circumstances of the workplace. This particular fruit shipper, indeed, had several containers of fruit returned from Japan because the general manager discounted the concerns of the packers that the fruit was too ripe. The ability to detect and prevent this condition was precisely the reason that packers for this company had to pack every piece of fruit by hand.

Other examples abound where company quality and productivity failed because of poor knowledge, many of which are documented. Thomas Pyzdek, an expert in statistical process control, tells the story of a team effort that reduced the solder defect rate by 90% and increased productivity in that area fivefold. When a presentation of their work was made to the executive staff, one manager remarked that solder defects had never been a problem and "we haven't had a single line stop due to solder defects." While that was an accurate statement, it failed to note that 40% of its soldering costs were for inspection and repair. The problem had been "solved" by considerable investment of resources. As Pyzdek notes, the company had papered over the pain signals with money.[2]

Decision as creative process

The reasons that some decisions never bring exactly the anticipated outcomes are many and varied, ranging from poor research and poor focus to poor reasoning. Hypercomplexity is a considerable element, given the limits of our ability to know. There is, however, a more fundamental reason the efforts of even the best of managers will always have unintended consequences: Our view of the future is obscured because we have not created it yet.

Thomas Edison said his inventions were not from his head but existed "out there". He just captured them, and if he hadn't gotten them, then someone else would. Pythagoras, Keith Richards (Rolling Stones), and Bill Monroe (bluegrass legend) all said that they did not create the music they wrote. It just sort of came into their heads from "out there". In the creative process, things always seem to just pop into your head, and logic tells us that they must come from somewhere.

Like music, art, or even engineering, decisions are essentially intuitive — that is, they just sort of pop into our heads. Real decisions are rarely the choice between the obviously good and the equally obvious bad. They are a struggle with the "goods" and "bads" of various options or even the creation of these options. One may research, analyze, and calculate, but, at some point, one has to make an intuitive reach. Actually, the answer to the question of what to do does seem to just come to you, but it is a little more complicated than that.

The air is not full of ideas and tunes that, like radio waves, are captured by alert mental antennae. The way chance favors a prepared mind is by presenting potentials to the prepared observer. The potential is "out there" waiting to be realized in some special fashion by someone with the creativity to contrive it. Decision makers are presented with prospects and possibilities depending on their wit and knowledge. The nature of that knowledge and a person's abilities to use it are what determine quality. Since each person invariably has somewhat different knowledge and levels of ability, each decision will tend to be different even though the circumstances seem to be the same.

One often hears that no one is indispensable, which is true in a sense but misleading. It is true in that, even in the absence of a particular employee, a company very likely would pursue the same course, similarly blessed with both success and challenges. It is not true in the sense that different people make different decisions, relate to others in different ways, and cause outcomes that, while perhaps similar, are still different.

A strategic decision is actualized throughout the organization, as each person and group translates the conceptual picture they are presented into particular applications that make sense to them. When the challenge is put to them they make determinations that create an appropriate reality based on the potentials as they see them. This is what is truly meant by chance favoring a prepared mind. Taking advantage of chance's opportunities and positioning for these opportunities are otherwise known as decisions. Every decision, even the mundane choice of what tie to wear, is a choice of potentials that can be realized. Clothes are chosen for what we think they will potentially do for us. Every decision, then, is not merely a selection from an array of givens but a creative act that sets new forces into motion, a movement toward some vision of new possibilities.

Creating realities

The real world is a shifting, elusive reality where managers must find rational courses of action. There are always limits on information and conceptual understanding[3] and differences in priorities, cost, and impact for each person affected. There are, therefore, generally some necessary compromises and accommodations. Rationality, although it may involve objective measures, has no objective measure; it can only be judged by some sense of the thing. Costs and benefits can be measured, or at least their indicators can, but their suitability or reasonableness must satisfy qualitative, judgmental factors.

Decisions, therefore, cannot be purely intellectual because the faculties that make them and the standards that assess them are not themselves wholly intellectual. For example, our intellect can tell us if the numbers seem to support some course of action or other. The logic of the decision itself, however, is about values and is not susceptible to objective measure. Our intuition can look at other alternatives and weigh their possible consequences, but these are idealized until translated into specific action. Our passion can tell us if it is worth the effort, and our sense of purpose can tell us if it is what we are after — all non-measurable preferences.

Most of the time, our common sense faculties point us to a position from which we then use our intellect to find supportive facts and reasoning. If these four faculties are not in consonance, we are torn between alternatives and have to make internal compromises and rationalizations. In an organization seeking a common sense among its diverse elements, there can be much dissonance. Individual decisions are a search for harmony among that person's values, feelings, and judgment applied to a question or even the formulation of the question. Because a group decision is the factorial of these faculties and the number of participants, achieving effective communications, much less consensus, may require a great deal of dialog.

A good decision, i.e., one that provides a good translation of purpose to action, does not provide the participants with an objective truth, if such were available. Rather, a decision is an invitation to create a new shared reality. That new reality will still be subjective — it will exist only in the mind of each person who perceives it. Organizationally, it will be a new collective subjectivity that now constitutes the order of things in the minds of the participants. This new condition can only be as good as the understanding of it and only as effective as the people who are prepared to execute the proper actions. This understanding generally requires some dialog for all of the parties to understand whatever must be done, what will be needed, what the desired outcome is, and what are the likely consequences. This is the dialog that translates purpose to situational practice for the participants. Because the new reality is actually formed by the dialog, participation in decision making is critical. This is not only for due consideration of pertinent factors, but also for its proper implementation. It is not a matter of buying in, but one of true common sense understanding.

Because the opportunity for further consideration of issues is more likely in an open climate, downstream work decisions are more likely to be more effective as well. It is this collective subjectivity that constitutes the common sense of the organization and must be rational to those charged with the practical applications. A command decision can sometimes be a relief when consensus seems elusive, but even though a command decision may be welcome, the lack of effective translation and understanding can reduce the odds of success.

Gaining the favor of chance

In preparing ourselves for chance's fickle favors, there are several basic and necessary steps. One should try to:

1. Identify all the factors that could affect the outcome.
2. Determine as best as possible how these factors are likely to affect the outcome.
3. Take steps to strengthen the supporting factors and reduce those that are potentially harmful.
4. Develop one's skills to a high level.
5. Husband the execution diligently.

When one has assessed these aspects of a possible action, things still may not work out as hoped, but they will work out as best as one can reasonably expect. Getting the odds in your favor defines what proactivity is all about. And, when rationally pursuant to proper purpose, that is what quality is all about. To the extent that these steps are not pursued, one moves from management to gambling. The process of optimizing the odds adds a more compelling rationale to much of the advice of improvement consultants. Employee involvement now can be appreciated as a means to obtain needed input (the more one knows the better one can improve the odds) and follow-through (the more one controls the application, the more one improves the odds). Probability provides a utility and operating context for quality tools, such as force-field analysis, and shows why it makes sense for managers to walk around.

The first and fifth steps reflect one of the most important understandings that a manager must have, which is that a decision does not begin when a question is put nor does it end when answered. When Michael Eisner makes a newsworthy decision at the jillion dollar level, tens of thousands of Disney employees are determining the daily reality of Disney through countless common sense decisions. A decision is executed by translation through myriad other decisions, interpretations, and standards and is effected at different paces and schedules, resulting in a number of different penalties and payoffs as it becomes someone's specific work. If the execution is superb and the purpose is sound, then any reasonable decision will probably do. On the other hand, if the decision is brilliant but the execution poor, it might as well be a poor decision.

Dialog of reality

Common sense itself, however, is not a constant thing. While our observations and abilities to respond can be strengthened by technology, the meaning we give to these observations and the responses we pursue are behavioral. Still, the primary focus of management may be on the technical at the expense of the behavioral. A recent advertisement for Fujitsu notes that "the gut [is a] big decision maker often forced to make decisions about stuff it doesn't understand." It goes on to note that Fujitsu spends $3 billion a year on R&D. While the ad makes a point, it misses the essential point about the decisional gut. Decisions are enriched with the good information and new alternatives that technical R&D can produce, but the human mind itself is strengthened only by better conceptual understandings of reality and the discipline required to process information using these concepts, not technology. It was their discipline and management paradigms that led Fujitsu management to invest $3 billion on technical research and development.

Hewlett-Packard spends $2.5 billion on technical R&D, but they spend even more in customer research and internal discussions to direct and employ the fruits of that research. In a recent interview about the Hewlett-Packard strategy for success, CEO Lewis Platt devoted one statement to technical R&D and the bulk of his remarks to people and organizational management. Great technical companies spend a great deal on technological innovation and development, but they also invest heavily in the decision-making abilities of their organizations.

When one says that people are not particularly good at calculations, unlike computers which are very good at them, but that people are good at patterns, whereas computers are not so good, they are talking about the human conceptual ability to create things from observations and to give meaning to experience. Meaning, in the human experience, is everything, and these conceptual realities are the basis of those business decisions that give utility to technical processes. Fujitsu and Hewlett-Packard, while each having its own name for their strategies, recognize the value of effective dialog to translate purpose to practice. Effective quality companies do not allow employee participation and training; they require it as part of being on the team. They understand the difference between a rational investment and a mindless cost.

For managers, rationality is a practical test of whether one is doing what one wants. Because there is no purely objective rationality to be had, organizations need to find ways to engender a practicable rationality in their operations with criteria for assessment that include performance in terms of organizational intent. This varies in practice with the general assessment resting on the authority of the manager — that is, authority-based management. This is not to say that the manager is not important, for such is certainly not the case. It is, however, to say that the role of a manager in decision making should be to ensure that systems bring in the best information before a decision and give the most accurate realization to it, with appropriate and timely adjustments.

Rational organizational decisions

Every decision is but a part of the translation stream from purpose to application, and a highly rational translation requires that those involved in making the decision a reality be involved in crafting the decision itself. That is why, when top management makes the decision to exempt itself from the changes required of others, it sows confusion and mistrust throughout the organization. The truth of this is so compelling, even obvious, that one wonders why demonstrating the desired change by doing it first is so much the exception and so rarely the rule. Actually, it *is* a rule in some of the better performing companies.

Much has been written here about the Hewlett-Packard way which involves all of its functions in assessing customer satisfaction and then in finding ways to provide that satisfaction, with the ultimate purpose of maintaining customer loyalty. What keeps the HP organization of open communications and cross-functional activities from flying apart is the flywheel of common values and purpose. This allows HP to translate continuously and more effectively the "meaning" of customer information for each person's work. The other factor that keeps the HP employee involvement process from evaporating, as it does so often in other organizations, is that it is part of the normal (learned and practiced until natural) decisional process, not an occasional afterthought that burdens managers from time to time.

The decisional process of Harley-Davidson created by CEO Richard Teerlink is a system of cross-functional and cross-hierarchical decision-making management teams, or "circles" in Harley jargon, one each for product ideas, manufacturing, and the creation of market demand. Representatives from these circles comprise a 20-person steering committee that reports directly to President Richard Bleustein. These circles meet monthly to generate, share, and decide upon ideas for improvement. The biggest ideas go to an inner circle of Bleustein and representatives elected by the other circles. These decisional circles have almost unconstrained authority.[4]

Another example is the significant cultural changes at Sears brought about by new CEO Arthur Martinez who established new job definitions, operating structures, reward systems, and communications patterns "to place decision making closer to the customer and make it more customer friendly." Sears is attempting to create "an environment where people can get energized" by breaking down the separation of managers from their decisions by having them put in significant time on the sales floor where the decisions are realized.[5] Such companies can involve their employees without the fear of being accused of making wrong decisions or wasting money because they understand the difference between hard-nosed and hard-headed management.

Steadfastness and constancy are generally considered virtues in managers, but they are not the same thing as blindness and inflexibility. The steadfastness must be to the purpose, but the flexibility must be for the pursuit of that purpose in changing circumstances that naturally occur as one moves. Those flexible adjustments can be reasonably comfortable adaptations when, as Sears' Martinez knows, they are made close to the place of impact.

Rational is as rational does

For all practical purposes, decisions *are* management. Management systems are essentially the guidelines and constraints on decision making by the participants in that system. These established decision opportunities structure the organization, provide the crucible of rationality, and manifest the translation of purpose to action. Organizational rank can be defined as the relative ability to make decisions, and departments can be defined by the areas in which decisions can be made. Management style refers to the way an individual makes decisions, and corporate culture refers to the typical way decisions are made throughout the organization.

For managers who want to improve their decision-making abilities, there are books and workshops available. Most of the techniques offered are good decisional disciplines that march a person through a rational decision-making process. Moreover, most executives and many of the managers of the major companies have been trained in some formal decision-making techniques. It is difficult to find a company or a public agency of any size in which managers have not had at least some training in this and many other management skills and quality improvement techniques.

At the same time, it is difficult to find an organization where anyone actually uses these techniques to make their decisions, at least with any frequency or for very long. One of the reasons that these techniques, all quite rational, are not used is that decision making serves many purposes other than making decisions in the ordinary sense of the word. The organizational ideology pursues activities for different purposes and assigns them different values. For example, depending on one's ideological focus, the activities in Table 1 can have particular meanings in the corporate culture.

When discipline fails

That most decisions are made on the basis of intuition, preference, or mutual agreement seems to work out just fine, or at least okay, which is "good enough". For one thing, people are not stupid and generally know more about their particular business than anyone else. They therefore tend to keep

Table 1 Cultural Meanings for Decision-Related Activities

Activity	Cultural focus			
	Formal focus	Human relations focus	Political focus	Symbolic focus
Planning	Set objectives; coordinate work	Promote participation	Air conflicts and re-align power	Signal responsibility, negotiate meetings
Decision making	Rational sequence to produce correct result	Open process to produce commitment	Opportunity to gain or exercise power	Provide comfort and support until decision happens
Meetings	Formal occasions for making decisions	Informal occasions for involvement, sharing feelings	Competitive occasions to win points	Sacred occasions to celebrate and transform culture

Source: Adapted from Bolman, Lee G., and Deal, Terrence E., *Reframing Organizations: Artistry, Choice and Leadership,* Jossey-Bass, San Francisco, 1991, p. 323.

things more or less on course intuitively. Second, no one makes a bad decision on purpose; they make decisions they believe will work. Finally, many decisions, even poor ones, can look good at first. Things will go as they are supposed to until the full implications of the decision begin to unfold and then the problems will become telling.

What fools us is that, when an authoritative decision is made, organizational resources begin to move to make it work, and it generally does to some degree. As people struggle to accomplish their charge and encounter continuing difficulty stemming from initiating an unwise decision, problems are now in the execution rather than the decision. While hindsight may identify a decision as "wrong", it usually faults the judgment of the maker rather than the process by which it was made. Management then brings in a consultant to implement some new program to "fix" the problem of the organization, an effort that is doomed to failure and frustration unless the program starts with top management and encompasses the entire decision-making process.

In most situations, decisions are generally a manager's to make, and bringing other people in is often not a good option for a variety of reasons, ranging from a fear of looking weak to preclusion by corporate culture to limits of time. Sometimes the manager wants to keep his options open and does not want to be committed until he sees how things work out. Often a decision is about a technical matter and has the appearance of being a technical imperative, although many of these are really decisions based on the human operating system and reflect deals with other managers or employees. The great bulk of decisions are simply adjustments of ongoing activities, and a formal, explicit process seems burdensome and unnecessary. Even in teams, with a high level of interaction, there is always the question of the decisions one can make and those requiring the involvement of others.

Formal decision-making techniques are rare among those managers who are heavily reliant on authority. A formal process usually involves other parties, and the conclusion of such a process may not be the "right" decision. Often, efforts to get others to participate in some formal process are met with resistance and even criticism. Practical people want to discuss things, which often means to make their point, and a formal process seems restrictive. As an added burden and cost, formal processes usually require a skilled neutral facilitator, which is more than managers want to be bothered with.

Most activities, from conducting meetings to dealing with individual performance problems to making technical decisions, do not seem to require high formality, and systematic processing is neglected. The loss is not so much the rigor for that decision, but of discipline in the decisional process. After bypassing and short-cutting processes for awhile, things get back to a seat-of-the-pants or let's-just-do-it mindset, and the quality improvement effort is over. The quality of the decision is found in its full application where, for poorly made decisions, the law of unintended consequences takes a particularly costly toll. If staff finds it necessary to conspire against their own management to do a good job or if too much extra effort is required, absent stronger pressures by authority, the effort will likely be abandoned. It is no wonder that so many improvement programs peter out after an initial surge.

Endnotes

1. Parkinson's laws, while written in a humorous manner, were meant seriously by the economist author; see Parkinson, C. Northcote, *Parkinson's Law and other Studies in Administration*, Ballantine Books, New York, 1957.
2. Related by Thomas Pyzdek in his *Pryzdek's Guide to SPC*, Vol. 1. *Fundamentals*, ASQC Quality Press, Milwaukee, WI, 1990, p. 28.
3. March, James G., *A Primer on Decision-Making: How Decisions Happen*, Free Press, New York, 1994; the author argues that, because of the ever-present limit on a person's understanding and information, everyone will have a "limited rationality".
4. See Stewart, Thomas, Tools that make business better and better, *Fortune*, December 23, 240, 1996.
5. The changes at Sears are reviewed in Dobryznski, Judith H., Yes, he's revived Sears. But can he reinvent it?, *The New York Times*, Section 3-1ff, January 7, 1996.

Part III

Structural impediments to improvement

Chapter nine: Budgeting and organizational rationality
How traditional budgeting and cost-cutting undermine organizational excellence
Perhaps the greatest structural impediment to organizational change is the traditional budgetary system. This tends to separate power and decisions into inappropriate activities and, thereby, work against collaboration and process integration. Cost decisions or benefit assignments are often made without reference to each other or to the rational purpose of the organization, an irrational condition.

Chapter ten: Framing the organization
Why managers often try to manage the wrong things
Technical expertise, the chief preparation of most managers, can cause management to misunderstand the realities of a dynamic organization. People see what they look for and they often miss the organization for what it is, i.e., a complex behavioral dynamic. Efforts to control an organization inappropriately cause more problems and, ironically, a loss of real control.

Chapter eleven: Routine as rut and groove
Why the attack on "routine" misses the point entirely
Many writers decry routine, which actually is the very essence of an organization. Ironically, change is inherent in every effort to maintain routine. It is this natural transformation process that is management's challenge and opportunity.

Chapter twelve: Hierarchy and organizational learning
Why hierarchy is necessary and why the problem is really in how you do it
While the purpose of an organization is to translate strategy to action, that process may require a number of translation steps between high strategy and particular application. Moreover, strategy must be translated for many different specialties in addition to incorporating the inherent differences of opinion that abound among people. There seems to be a need for some sort of hierarchy, but not necessarily the traditional authoritarian structure.

chapter nine

Budgeting and organizational rationality

How traditional budgeting and cost-cutting
undermine organizational excellence

> *Follow the money.*
> ∾Deep Throat

Invariably, when working with managers and supervisors in quality improvement efforts, I hear them complain about being overworked. At times like this I sometimes lie and tell them that if any of them could clearly and convincingly demonstrate the value-add of their work, the CEO would double their salaries. So far, no one has called my bluff. Then, I tell them the story of the farmer and the mule.

One Saturday at the market, a farmer was talking with another about the high cost of feed for his mule. The friend advised him that if he were to put 10% sawdust in with the mule's oats, the mule would not know the difference and would work just the same. Over the period of a year the farmer could save several hundred dollars. The farmer thought this was worth a try and began adding sawdust to the mule's feed. Sure enough, the mule continued as before. Seeing this, the farmer thought he might save more money by adding more sawdust to the feed, and he did. Over time he continued to increase the amount of sawdust until it was more than half the mule's feed.

The mule seemed a bit sluggish and had some difficulty in bodily functions, but still did an okay job.* The farmer was quite pleased at his cost-saving program and began to increase the amount of sawdust even more. Then one day the mule died. If one thinks of the farmer as a manager, the mule as the organization or its people, and the sawdust as work added or resources cut without appreciation of the effects, the story is an allegory of many organizations. The mule dying can be compared to quality failures, turnover, employee morale, safety problems, and the like.

---

* As we have noted, "okay" is usually "good enough".

Management knowledge vs. accounting

A characteristic of every organization I have ever observed is that everyone is "very busy". That this business stems from a general failure to set and keep priorities, to solve problems rather than patch them, to deliver information where and when needed, to develop and use adequate technical operating methods, and so on does not lessen the conditions of being nearly over-whelmed with work. Much of what keeps everyone so busy is, in fact, nonproductive work that contributes to the cost but not to organizational accomplishment. This causes pressures to reduce costs, not by improving the systems but by reducing staff, a move guaranteed to make things worse.

Top management may be convinced a plant is overstaffed, while the plant management sees itself understaffed. There is, however, no rational way to decide on appropriate staffing needs merely by the numbers of present staff. Rationality requires that such decisions be made in the context of desired purpose and needs to accomplish that purpose. Often staff reduc-tion measures are irrational, such as the present trend to reduce clerical positions such that professional efficiency is reduced and critical information becomes lost. Outside the truncated context of cost accounting, such deci-sions make no sense and only feed the basic problem of poor organizational control.

One cannot fault anyone for not knowing their value-add or even true costs because few organizations have such knowledge. In fact, organizational budgets and accounting systems are generally structured along traditional lines that do not reflect the real organization or its work. Often, a company has no way to determine accurately how much a particular product or service really costs. This is one reason why, for all the talk and effort aimed at quality improvement, management still finds itself in a mode of detect-and-correct. If one does not know what work processes are really costing and what one is getting for the money, the best option may be just to follow the funds and take the problems as the come.

If decision making determines the control structure of an organization, budgetary control is its most common and powerful form. Invariably, one of the key concerns expressed by managers is cost control. This is, of course, a proper and necessary part of management, but, by itself, it tends to cause great harm; perhaps the worst decisions are made under the rubric of cost-cutting. "Cost" is an accounting function derived arithmetically, i.e., by adding and subtracting. But companies are not in the business of saving money; they are supposed to be making it. For this purpose they invest capital.

Cost vs. waste management

When management confuses the concepts of cost and investment, it can cause problems. A good example is the banking company that is presently pursuing a twofold strategy: (1) go after only the bigger, more profitable personal accounts, and (2) save costs by cutting back on trust officers. As a result, the bank is generating a lot of new large accounts — for its more service-oriented competitors!

The real concern should be *waste*, which is an entirely different matter. How to eliminate waste is a judgment based on an understanding of what one is about and how to do it most efficiently. This is a management function determined mathematically — that is, as a function of relationships among respective values. Keeping workers poorly trained may reduce the costs of training but will greatly increase the cost of production. The managers who limit themselves by focusing on costs are no longer managing but are accounting. They begin to make technical decisions by trying to add and subtract costs while losing sight of the management role of determining the best use of resources to accomplish one's purpose.

Cost-cutting occurs so often because it is so easy, in a truncated and simplistic way. And, like the mule, things at first seem okay. It fails, however, to take into account the relationship of these numbers to other values that are critical for moving from just okay to excellence. It requires little work or brains to order a 15% across-the-board cut. It makes a manager look frugal and hard-nosed, and the complainers can be called whiners. Sometimes the justification is that times are truly desperate, although the blame is rarely on those who have been running things (unless there has been a recent succession), or that there is a need to get the fat out of the organization. The fat invariably turns out to be staff, training, spare parts, salary increases, and other "low-priority" items. It does not often involve executive perks and bonuses.

The problem of cost-cutting is worse than simple organizational anorexia, however, because it creates a mindset that reduces everything to its cheapest condition. The result is that any investment, other than some hardware purchases, requires more of an effort than most people are prepared to give or more risk than they are prepared to take. Still, any new value-adding activity requires some initial cost, even if only to take someone off a job to set it up.

Irrationality of cost-basing

Except for some dire financial emergency, it seems irrational for managers to focus on costs without regard to benefit. Organizational funds should only be spent as an investment in the furtherance of the organization's goals. Conversely, benefits without regard to costs would seem irresponsible. There is much of this going on, as well — primarily in the area of management rewards and perquisites — which also comes with unfortunate effects. When one cuts costs, it is simply a matter of spending less. When one eliminates waste, however, it requires a whole set of understandings and assessments about the enterprise. Waste is that which costs but does not add value and is, by its nature, an inappropriate expenditure. Moreover, by calculating a cost-to-benefit ratio, one is able to look at relative costs and values such that expenditures are not only smarter, but they are also wiser. This assumes, of course, that one is not too narrow and myopic in identifying related values such as community support and staff development.

Cost-cutting can seriously harm an organization's ability to function by denying the staff, training, materials, tools, and communication opportunities required for an efficient, quality operation. Management is often attracted to cost-basing because it seems an easy way to reduce operating costs. While cost-basing can give the appearance of saving money, it generally reduces spending by reducing operations. As a result, it often adds to the actual costs and reduces the quality of a product or service. These problems, however, usually become evident later as someone else's and are seen as separate and different problems. Cost-basing focuses on the negative, on not doing something, which is contrary to the whole idea of an organization, which is to do something. Negative management is the ideology of detect-and-correct, which often becomes patch-and-pray.

Eliminating good preventive maintenance, effective training, and adequate staff can result in significant costs in one way or another. The alternative to training is learning by trial and error, a wasteful strategy at best and a rather risky one for most organizations. Consider the following case of an organization that has been put into turmoil because of mindless cost control:[1]

> Valves are major problems, and much of their expense stems from operator training and maintenance. Pump operating life is shortened by poorly trained operators. Operating problems due to inadequate resources are probably the cause of having to fly in filtering sand at a cost of $80,000, chemical spills by overworked staff who were not able to keep check on levels or the accuracy of the control system, and $325,000 worth of materials being over-ordered and nonreturnable.

> The cost of the blending operation has not been calculated, but it is probably substantial both directly and in product "giveaways" when the product must be pumped out anyway. The plant invested tens of thousands of dollars in the computerized maintenance-parts inventory system but denied funds for adequate staff and training to use it properly. As a result the system is only marginally used and maintenance efficiency is impaired, as is that of operations.

As each area focuses on local and immediate concerns, avoiding any expense other than the barest minimum to avoid a serious problem, there can be little thought of the overall process or of working problems out of the system. The problems feed upon themselves, as each element struggles to make its particular section work without regard to this, causing problems for the other elements. This can further impair quality in a particular unit and in those that feed from or support it, and so on until the precipitating unit itself suffers.

Blind hope

To squeeze an organization in the hope that only the fat will ooze out and not needed muscle is an act of faith that is rarely validated.* Everyone cuts those things that hurt somebody else and rarely have any real rational basis for cuts other than cut where you can, meaning where it will hurt the least now. Later, they will worry about "later". When later does come, perhaps then it will be someone else's problem. In many cases, the primary reason for failure in quality improvement efforts is that the company has debilitated its operations through unwise cost-cutting. Despite advice by consultants, management is often reluctant to invest in those very areas it has cut to improve the cost picture.

The nature of an organization's management is revealed by the manner in which it seeks to reduce costs. For example, many managers try to squeeze out the more experienced people because they cost more. If an organization can do this without a loss of productive capacity, then clearly those people have been overpaid, as, in a rational organization, there would be a clear and compelling linkage between reward and contribution. When the reward systems are not in good order, you can bet that the other systems are suffering as well. And, where systems are not good, the informal relationships among the experienced people are pretty much the organization.

It is not uncommon for organizations to lay off their veteran workers only to hire them back as consultants because the systems are incapable of doing the work otherwise. It is not surprising that several studies have found that companies that just cut costs often do less well than those who focus on more effective use of existing resources. Put another way, the more rational the operation the more likely it is to be successful. "You can't shrink yourself into prosperity," advised Terry Ivany, CEO of Canada's VIA Rail.

---

* This seems to reflect the definition of H. L. Mencken, who defined faith as "an illogical belief in the occurrence of the improbable."

Irrational incentives

While cost-cutting can mislead managers striving to eliminate non-value-adding expenditures, actual costs are critical information. The question is, the costs of what? Cost control goes astray from the start when the accounting question about how much is being spent on vehicles is not imbedded in the management question of why. In a chemical plant with a wide area of storage tanks, operators were given gasoline-powered minitrucks to get around. Because of poor vehicle maintenance, poor traveling surfaces, and high use, the minitrucks began to have a number of mechanical problems.

The maintenance manager, who was concerned about the impact that repairing these vehicles had on his budget, blamed the situation on the employees' driving. He convinced the plant manager to replace all the minitrucks with battery-powered golf cars and bicycles. These vehicles were much slower, they added to the burden of the already understaffed operators, and they increased the risk of material spills, accidents, and costly operator error. Still, the maintenance costs were much lower.

A primary expectation of the maintenance manager was to stay within, if not under, his budget. Thus, the purchase was an isolated event with consideration only for the cost for okay quality, and the service was provided by a manager who, with his isolated departmental budget, was rewarded for minimizing his service. Operations was responsible for operating the equipment but not its repair or maintenance. There was no accountability for unplanned equipment downtime. When equipment broke down, it was accepted as a normal situation resulting from usage. If something gave the problem greater significance, such as an injury, failure to meet deadlines, or exceptionally high costs, there would be some finger-pointing. The situation in which critical management decisions are made based on isolated accounting principles is a source of trouble for many companies.

A commonly used system of determining pay is based on the number of subordinates and size of budget. This may exemplify the best thinking of the traditional approach, but it poorly suits the needs of quality improvement. The fundamental rule of rational expenditures would seem to be that anything adding value is an investment and anything that does not is a waste. Using that rule, the basic costing unit would seem to be the activities, materials, and equipment of the value-adding work process systems. As the above example illustrates, traditional budgeting and costing, however, are strongly established and interwoven with other institutionalized practices and provide the framework for so many other organizational values and structures, such as rewards, performance expectations, and authority. As a result, any change in budgetary structure becomes a radical change in almost everything else.

Managers often attempt to reengineer or reinvent their systems and talk about radical change while making virtually no change in their budgeting and costing structures. Traditional budgeting is the chief vehicle for hierarchical authoritarian-based management and, as such, shares its apparent virtues and hidden vices. It can be a major anti-quality element in an organization, the antithesis of customer service, as budgets are spent and defended on a different basis than the rational pursuit of optimally accomplishing organizational goals.

Traditional budgeting can create situations where people seek savings that can be dysfunctional. For example, engineers under-specify equipment, the parts department understocks its inventory, maintenance under-services, purchasing under-orders, management understaffs, and so forth. The purpose of an organization is to add value, not to maintain equipment or to train or to purchase or to do any of these things. Maintenance, or any other department, is like the human respiratory system: It has no purpose other than to support the overall system's efforts. Maintenance costs are only information and, in the words of James Aubrey:[2]

> Data are not facts.
> Facts are not information.
> Information is not knowledge.
> Knowledge is not truth.
> Truth is not wisdom.

Focus on costs creates a cynicism among workers when management seems, in the words of Oscar Wilde, to "know the price of everything and the value of nothing." What management is after is, indeed, wisdom, the highest form of common sense. This requires excellent knowledge, which, in turn, requires that information be timely, meaningful, and in a form suitable to one's needs.

Budget and control

It is only by changing cost structuring from departmental silos to comparing process costs and benefits that management can effect radical and fundamental change in its operation. This is the one area in which the metaphor of Phoenix and ashes is truly compelling. The intricate tangle of power, rewards, hierarchy, accounting traditions and standards, departments, physical layouts, ideology, and budgets is a formidable challenge to any real organizational change. Even the disruptions of massive layoffs and large-scale computerizing will only be a temporary unsettling until everyone can get back to the traditional way of doing things.

One of the reasons that structural innovations have difficulty is that they are essentially outside the budgetary structure and mean additional cost, but little glory, to department heads. Breakthrough teams, for example, are "loaned" from departments and may even have some funds of their own, garnered from these departments. What they recommend, however, can have a significant impact on departmental budgets. Since control over expenditures is the heart of organizational power, and probably the most fun part of being a manager, budgetary innovators face a managerial antipathy and task similar to separating a grizzly bear from her cubs.

The cost-cutting mentality usually leads to discrete element budgeting and costing, where each expenditure is an isolated event rather than part of a strategy for turning purpose to practice. This balkanizing of the organization is also a natural outgrowth of authority-based management and, like other authority-based decisions, often fails to control effectively because of the paradox of overcontrol. It suffers for the same reasons, such as complexity and poor control when attention is elsewhere, which it often must be.

Like authority, traditional budgetary control gives the appearance of management control, and taking it away creates a state of high anxiety and befuddlement to managers. Discrete element budgeting also has a perverse logic to it because the flipside of "that's too much, so don't do it" in regard to any given purchase is "that's not too much, so it's okay." The right questions for quality are more like, "What does it cost and how does it help us?" or "What does it cost us if we don't get it?"

Discrete element spending also allows irrational non-performance values to accumulate, such as "rank has its privileges" and "its Joe's shop so let him do it". Rank and responsibility do not, *ipso facto*, reflect contribution and may be antithetical to it. The case of the manager who used much of the travel and entertainment budget to enjoy fine meals and trips with little business value, while denying travel and expense support for others, is not unusual. Another typical problem is the executive who requires a secretary that enables him to get more work done but denies that kind of support to entire departments. In an authority environment, the costs that need to be controlled are those of others. This may be assumed for convenience, of course, but maintaining high rationality demands that such assumptions be validated periodically.

Activity-based costing

Assuming that management is prepared to change its budgetary strategy, the rising alternative is activity-based costing, which provides, in the opinion of super-guru Peter Drucker, "the information executives truly need."[3] The use of activity-based costing is uneven to date, being rejected by some, employed by some, and used as a parallel to traditional budgeting by others. In all fairness, it has not been until the past few years that information technology and its uses have facilitated shifting to activity-based costing. The value of activity-based costing depends on several critical factors, such as how one determines what activities are included and why, how expenditure decisions are made and reviewed, and how costs are defined and calculated.

The true cost of producing an item must include all of the activities required to produce that item, such as the support services of human resources and maintenance. Activity-based costing, in its most sophisticated form includes activity-based management, process analysis, value-added analysis, target costing, and a host of new ways of relating expenses to organizational performance. Unless activities-based costing is used properly, however, it will serve little better than traditional budgeting. When an operating unit, for example, is required to use in-house services regardless of comparative costs and quality, then activity-based costing serves poorly because the costs do not have a proper relationship to benefits. In this case, all costs over what would be charged for similar services by an outside contractor are non-value-adding costs, which is to say waste. Activity-based costing seems to be a considerable improvement over conventional costing methods and provides a basis for a rational budgeting and costing system.

Because costs are, or should be, a measure of expenditures against budget, the question is not really cost but the basis for allocating funds. Likewise, one is not interested in activities for their own sake but for their value-add. The ideology of management should not be to not spend, which takes no special genius and deserves no special rewards, but to spend wisely. A budget system that does not help management identify and separate value-adding investments from waste is inadequate and irrational. Perhaps a better term is process budgeting, referring to any identified value-adding process and its required support services.

Top companies, as a necessary part of their quality improvement efforts, are finding the need for more effective costing strategies. An example is Harley-Davidson, which has shifted toward actual process costs, the use of nonfinancial measures of performance, and strategic cost management in its accounting systems.[4] Tom Epley, CEO of Paradyne Corporation, notes that a "workable cost structure is critical" to corporate turnaround.[5]

Integrative budgeting

Process budgeting is to process management what discrete element budgeting is to traditional management. While effective process budgeting requires constant review to maintain viability, it is a reasonable efficiency and convenience to assume that ongoing budgets are valid and incrementally increased for a time. This assumption, like the higher benefit for higher managers, should still be validated periodically with such fundamental questions as:

- What needs to be done?
- What is the value added?

- What is the level of quality required?
- What does it take to accomplish that?
- How much does it cost?

Each of these questions is a bundle of issues, of course, such as whether one should do one thing or another, how quality will be measured, how costs are to be assigned, etc. Nonetheless, this establishes a more rational management condition and provides such otherwise elusive things as a true assessment of training needs and a basis for measuring the ROI on that training. Management, of course, often asks these questions as a part of the budgeting process. It does little good, however, if they then structure budgets and, importantly, cost expectations along traditional departmental lines.

The effect of process budgeting is integrative, whereas discrete element budgeting is isolating, creating an array of mini-wholes, or one might say, many holes. Process budgeting allows a truly effective assault on organizational wastes as process management moves upstream through the value-adding process and compares contribution to cost of each element. Process budgeting is cost-tracking, but it is also performance based. Technology is available to marry process management to budgetary management, giving both a true cost picture and a rational systems of control.

Using many of the existing tools, such as cycle-time reduction, managers can know where to look and what to do with costs. They can avoid being forced into the traditional quality mutilations of buying the cheapest, squeezing suppliers and employees, cutting training, and having inadequate safety programs and poor maintenance. The area where process budgeting would help the most, however, is in providing a cost-benefit picture to support the free enterprise principle of pay for performance.

Paying for performance

Companies, even government agencies, are exploring new ways to reward their employees, and many of these efforts seem to have been successful.[6] Success is more likely when such efforts are in recognition of the importance of an appropriate rewards system rewarding other improvement efforts rather than as a stand-alone effort. Indeed, the success of any improvement program rests upon an effective reward component. Paradyne's Tom Epley believes that an effective organization today requires a "truly entrepreneurial culture; a high degree of focused energy and a workable cost structure are critical." Central to this point is the "practice of rewarding those who step up and perform and not rewarding those who don't." That is what many reward systems purport to do but really don't. Often this is blamed on the employees, who are said to be in favor of across-the-board raises, a policy that employees actually tend to resent.

One survey of 4700 employees found that employees approve merit pay and, indeed, would appreciate the opportunity to have their work judged on merit. The problem was that they did not trust management's willingness or ability to judge fairly and reward without favoritism. That is not surprising, as most of the surveys I have done about performance appraisals find that the number one problem is that "my supervisor does not know what I do." In such cases, fair appraisal and the assigning of rewards is impossible. That is why most companies seem to simply give across-the-board raises and why only 10% of American workers felt that they would benefit from quality improvements, compared with 90% of the Japanese workers. The reasons why management does not pursue true pay-for-performance have been discussed elsewhere,[7] but they remain one of the biggest obstacles to quality improvement.

Free enterprise ideology

The single most important ingredient in generating proper motivation is a clear connection between one's efforts and one's rewards. A common condition in command management is that employees not only find their rewards separated from their work, but they also find themselves separated from their work by the rewards system. They are connected to their supervisors and rewarded by them, although one is not so much rewarded for doing good work as punished when in disfavor.

True pay for performance is unusual and can only be done when the organization has a culture that strongly emulates free enterprise. Absolute free enterprise does not exist anywhere where there is acceptable social order. Still, the principles, applied in a well-managed environment, are nonetheless a proper driving force in high performance for all those who are able pursue the rewards of appreciated contribution.

Management already uses free enterprise as its basic strategy for translating purpose to practice for its top managers. Some companies pursue this same thinking throughout their organization even, as in the case of Starbucks, for its part-time staff. Logic suggests that if the principles are sound at that level they should be explored for applicability throughout the organization. For example, customer focus would hold a much stronger incentive if it were a major part of the criteria for pay for performance. This, in turn, would help guide management in its efforts to provide effective enablement. Actually, it could provide a rationale for entitlement to resources required to do one's job well, rather than the kind of beggar or serf status that many employees find themselves in when it comes to use of organizational resources.

An entrepreneurial or free enterprise approach immerses an employee in the work and integrates performance and rewards. This, in turn, requires the kind of open system that enables free enterprise and cooperative work, including some reasonable involvement in the determination of rewards which might then be seen as internal profits. Managers often state the view that all employees want is more money, but what they really want is to share in the profits of their labors. This is evidenced by the union at Saturn voting to keep the "risk and reward" pay program rather than the higher and more assured base pay of General Motors' other employees.

Ownership and frugality

When there is meaningful involvement for employees in economic issues, they are quite responsible. There are many examples of involved employees seeking to reduce costs and even staff, such as VIA Rail. There are other models such as GE Business Information Center (GEBIC), which has been visited by Ford, 3M, and Honeywell, three companies with impressive quality programs themselves. Aspects of the GEBIC program — which has saved millions of dollars, doubled productivity, and improved customer satisfaction from 94 to 99% — include letting the employees take responsibility and rewarding and recognizing accomplishments. The true value of an entrepreneurial culture doubtless lies in the countless little things that are done that can render, in the aggregate, high savings and customer satisfaction. One such example is Sterling Chemical, where maintenance workers have found ways to improve scaffolding availability from 57 to 97%. That may not sound like much until one calculates all of the costs of not having scaffolding available, such as wasted time, extended downtime, extra work, etc.[8]

Actually, "rewards" is not the correct term for the way most people are paid. Employees are generally paid at a rate to placate them. Managers, on the other hand, often get bonuses no matter how business is doing or what bone-head things they may have done. The situation of Michael Eisner's $114 million dollar mistake with Michael Ovitz is well known. Less well known is Eisner's obtaining $58 million of concessions out of the Writers Guild in 1987. This did not affect (except to enhance) his remuneration that year of $63 million. There is also the case, actually many cases, of sales people having their commissions capped or their territories split because they were making more than their boss. A decorating company actually reduced the base salary and commission rate for its sales staff after they had a banner year and made too much money.

Companies can be stingy with pay for overhead activities, which, if truly nonproductive, should be eliminated. On the other hand, if they are critical, they should be given proper support. By separating employees from value-add processes, management fails to appreciate its social assets or "intangibles." This is residue from the Industrial Age when capital bought factories and equipment, and cash flow paid for ongoing costs such as people. Increasingly, companies operate less with tangible assets than with the know-how of their employees. Changing the tax structure and that of other institutions to social capital value may take awhile, but it must come. In the meantime, management can reassess it human resources as assets and how these assets should be rewarded.

Budgeting as knowledge

While the challenge of tangibles and intangibles may be around for awhile, the option of process budgeting is not so formidable. The maintenance manager does not have to manage a traditional department but can manage the maintenance function or (better yet) the physical plant reliability function. Indeed, there is little interest in maintaining something but great interest in ensuring that everything is operating as it should be. The maintenance manager would no longer be rewarded for shaving maintenance work to save money (or at least to appear to be saving money) but instead for helping optimize value-add performance. Operations would no longer be the enemy but would be a colleague, as both maintenance and operations have an interest in cross-training, operator abilities, and preventive maintenance.

Perhaps the clearest and most significant knowledge that employees have about their company and their work is what management is prepared to invest in and reward. Actions speak louder than words, and this is the loudest action of all. Consider the micro-example of a construction company that was concerned about the condition of its tools. On any morning, workers would find some of the tools stored the night before to be inoperable or in poor condition. The cost was not just the tools but a bigger problem of disrupted work schedules that could cost thousands of dollars daily. The company had been trying to solve the problem in the traditional way, i.e., threats, more rules, and increased supervision. When the tools were the "urgency" of the moment, there would be a flurry of interest and some improvement. When the heat was off, however, things quickly got back to where they were before.

As a part of instituting a new incentive program, I suggested that the company give each supervisor a promissory note for $2500, redeemable at the end of the project less the cost of replacing and repairing tools in their area's tool box. At the end of each week the supervisors were given a report of how much of their $2500 they had left. The attention given the tools was now careful and constant and the supervisors even began an informal competition about it. Because all bonuses were calculated on the total project's success, however, they still cooperated in sharing and caring for tools.

Of the three elements of an enterprise — i.e., purpose, system, and effort — discrete element budgeting and decision making focus primarily on the effort, usually on an *ad hoc* basis and generally through the exercise of authority. Enlightened management, on the other hand, seeks elegant control by focusing on the systems that facilitate effort and seeks to optimize rationality in terms of the purpose being pursued. The most critical system in an organization, and the one that determines an organization's ability to reach excellence, is the one that determines the value-add goals and the required cost of accomplishing them. Management can work either from an established goal and then determine the costs of getting there or from available money, determining what reasonable goals the money might support, or some combination thereof.

A rational justification of costs is always the same, i.e., how does it affect what you are trying to accomplish? If one is simply trying to accomplish staying within budget, then not spending is intrinsically good. While the practice is so ingrained that we have come to see this as an act of managing, it is hardly managing in the sense of using resources to accomplish work. The proper management questions are "How is the expenditure more enabling?" and "How is curtailing the expenditure impairing to the value-add process?" These are not accounting questions that can be answered by looking at costs but are critical management issues of cost-benefit. The determination of true cost-benefit is the pursuit of excellent knowledge.

Endnotes

1. Edited excerpt from a proprietary client report.
2. Audrey, James A., *Love and Profit,* William Morrow, New York, 1991, p. 89.
3. Drucker, Peter, The information executives truly need, *Harvard Business Review,* January-February, 54–62, 1995. An excellent description that began serious interest in activity-based costing is Cooper, Robin, and Robert Kaplan, Measure costs right: make the right decisions, *Harvard Business Review,* September-October, 96–103, 1988
4. Sadowski, Susan T., Changes In Management Accounting Systems With The Adoption of a Total Quality Management Philosophy and Its Operationalization Through Continuous Process Improvement at the Level of the Firm: A Case Study of the York Manufacturing Plant of Harley-Davidson, Inc., Ph.D. dissertation, George Washington University, 1994. This dissertation is an example of academia following the writings of practical consultants, a point made in Chapter 2.
5. Quoted in "Technology turnaround: how to win in today's explosive marketplace" in *Inter@ctive Week,* December 9, 23, 1996.
6. Of companies trying innovative incentive programs, 75% thought them to be "fully successful" in one study; see "American companies turning to nontraditional pay" in *Industrial Engineering,* August, 9–10, 1993
7. See, for example, English, Gary, Tuning up for performance management, *Training & Development Journal,* April, 56–60, 1991.
8. The GEBIC efforts are reported in Wilfore, John, Employees draw their own road map for cultural change, *Industrial Engineering,* June, 40, 1993. Sterling Chemical is reported in the same journal; see "Quality improvement program finds disappearing scaffolds" in *Industrial Engineering,* June, 25, 1993.

chapter ten

Framing the organization

Why managers often try to manage the wrong things

> *People think that reality is obvious, but*
> *reality is the hardest thing to assess.*
> ⁓Henry Kissinger

Much of modern management writing urges management to do more systems thinking: to see the big picture, to think longer term, and to understand the broader effects of immediate actions. Few people argue against any of this, but nonetheless it seems difficult for most managers to do. Part of the reason is that much of the literature talks about management but not about the thing that needs to be managed. To have breakthrough teams, reengineered processes, and behavior-based actions is all well and good. We cannot really understand the full implications of such actions, though, unless we have a grasp of the behavioral environment in which these things take place, what we call an organization.

Looking and seeing

When I was visiting the studio of a scenic photographer in the eastern Kentucky foothills, one picture seemed to stand out for its compelling and serene beauty. The view was across a meadow with an old hay rake about midway and behind that an old barn. The area was called Blue Lick, a valley framed by misty layers of the Blue Ridge foothills. The photographer, noting my interest, told me that this picture had been especially popular with his customers. One day, out of appreciation, he presented a print of the picture to the 80-year-old woman from whose back steps he had taken the photograph. Upon seeing the picture, the woman exclaimed, "You know, I've lived here all my life and never realized how pretty it was until I saw your picture of it." She had looked at the scene for years but, until it was framed for her, she never really "saw" it.

This story illustrates two points. One is that the difference between an artist and a layman is that while anyone may look, the artist sees. What is true for artists is also true for professionals, who, in their area of expertise, simply see things that the layman does not even know are there and, even when they are pointed out, might not fully understand. Like the view from the back door, much of our world has always been there but we are no more aware of it than a fish is of water. Until someone provides an intellectual device to frame its existence for us, we might never appreciate its being. It is ideology that keeps it hidden from us and science that attempts to bring it forth. The search for excellent knowledge requires us to understand how we see things.

Managers (artists) are measured not only by their insight but also by their control of the medium by which they express their insight. For managers, the primary medium of endeavor is the organization, which they ply with whatever insight and common sense they have. Many managers do not see themselves as *professional* managers practicing their art through the medium of an organization because (1) they do not see management as a profession, and (2) they have difficulty seeing an organization at all. They are more likely to see themselves as bankers, engineers, or soldiers unless the word "manager" is somehow in their title, such as a plant manager.* Many other professions, such as marketing, have the same problem in that one is "in computers" or "in marketing" or "with IBM" but no one is ever a "marketer".

To say one is "in management" is a statement of status rather than profession. While management may not have some of the neatness or recognition of some professions, such as law or medicine, it nonetheless has a number of qualities of a profession. These include such things as a body of specialized knowledge, a career path based upon competence and understanding, standardized procedures and practices, advanced and ongoing learning — techniques that are transferable to most any milieu — and the manager gets paid for doing it.**

As with the other professions, those who do not keep up with their field find modern management difficult. Viewed another way, those who do not have adequate knowledge and skills are not professionals at all but rather

---

* Even a human resource manager uses the term "manager" because something is needed to go with "human resource" to make it a title. Human resources are actually managed by just about every other manager in an organization *except* HR people.

** Americans get tired of always being compared with the Japanese way of doing things and, because the general Japanese culture is so different from ours, they are not always good models. It is nonetheless interesting to note that, while the Japanese careers also stem from technical specialties, their management track is quite professional. Management is an area to be studied and mastered, with ongoing development through *dontotsu* or seeking and learning the "best of the best" practices. American managers seek new and better ideas, but this is more likely an *ad hoc* response to a problem or a contemporary corporate program rather than part of a management development system.

amateurs trying to operate in a professional league. Worse, they do not know they are amateurs and muddle along blaming others for the problems that they have caused. It has been a truism for decades: 90% of business failures are attributable to management failures. Or, as Philip Crosby noted, "The business desert is layered with the bones of those who felt they understood completely and stopped learning."

Misplaced expertise

Sometimes our rationality is corrupted by misapplied strengths. There are three major areas of management expertise required to make an operation go well: the business (the acquisition of materials and selling of products and services), the technology (the applied technical knowledge that transforms ingredients into a product or service), and the organization (the instrument that makes the first two happen).*

Most companies have good expertise in their business and technology. Indeed, expertise in these two areas is usually the platform for entrepreneurial enterprises and the basis for career success, at least initially. The third area, organizing and managing the human facet of the enterprise, is where most operations run into difficulty. While the temptation is to use the paradigms of business and technology in organizational management, they do not transfer easily and can even be a handicap.

A weakness, it has been said, is but a strength misapplied. Technical experts, such as engineers, are especially prone to view human behavior with simplistic mechanistic paradigms. Those with financial or accounting backgrounds may try to kill the goose that lays the golden eggs by reducing available resources to the point where the organization cannot function well.[1] They often see management as something anyone can do with a little common sense. This is true, but the better one's common sense is fortified with appropriate models and knowledge, the better one is enabled.

As one oil refinery manager remarked, "Managing is just getting people to work together and do a good job, isn't it?" Of course it is, and refining is just turning crude oil into jet fuel, gasoline, and petrochemicals. Ignorance in what one is about, however, leaves the manager with few tools other than trying to push with authority. Except in those rare occasions when action must be immediate and unreflecting, reliance on authority is symptomatic of a failure in intellect, spirit, and energy.

---

* There is also a set of activities of corporate maintenance to cover those functions required to meet governmental elements such as OSHA and ADA and taxes that affect an organization's ability to exist at all. These are becoming increasingly important and, while they are not treated in this chapter, can be viewed as essentially another technical system together with marketing and conversion. Environmental matters could be considered either corporate maintenance or conversion activities, but probably this would be where both functions would intertwine.

When life was simpler, both management and organizational structure could be formed around closely held expertise and resources. Frederick Taylor and his efforts to make human workers more machinery-like seems less of an innovation than a natural development of those times. Today, however, no manager has all the expertise required for success. The volume and complexity of work are beyond what any one person can know, competition requires more flexibility and responsiveness than one person can have, and technology puts major decisions in the hands of hourly workers. Today, the general pace of work and change have served to make the old "span of control" a nearly useless concept.

Primitive models

At one time, the organization was a key focus for management studies. Planning, organizing, directing, etc. were the elements of management, and division of labor, span of control, and "bureaupathology" were aspects of an organization. Recent management thought, however, seems to have focused more on non-organizational factors, such as individual behaviors (leadership), business process (cycle time), and sub-organizational techniques (breakthrough teams) than the organization itself. Organizations seem to assume that reengineering or "management of change" will fix any organizational problems one may have. Team concepts deal with organization but in a way that attempts to deconstruct the organization as a dominant structure.

Some quality programs, such as aspects of TQM, key on the customer, while others, such as statistical process control, focus on conversion. The human relations approach focuses on the people in the organization and how they are treated, while others, such as Stephen Covey, focus on the leaders. While all of these things are essential elements of the whole, they are not the same thing as the whole. They are but aspects of the complex social medium management must master. Just as a human can be considered to be various organs and systems, so can a business operation be separated into component parts for purposes of more specialized knowledge and application. No damage is done, provided one does not forget that they are in reality vitally integrated with the total being and all its parts and dimensions.

In Africa in the 1950s, the U.S. Information Agency gave radios to remote villages so that they could receive broadcasts from the capital. The natives, who tended to explain things in terms of people and spirits, tore open the backs of the radios looking for the little people inside who were playing music and talking. For them, a mechanical device was difficult to grasp. Before getting too smug about the limitations of African villagers to see the reality before their very eyes, we might recall that, in the late 1800s, police tried using the newly invented camera to take pictures of murder victims' retinas. The idea was to capture on film the last image the victim saw and thereby have a picture of the killer. It seemed logical based upon the analogy that the eyes were like cameras and captured pictures. It was a logic, however, built upon a misunderstanding of how people actually see. It is true that cameras work much like eyes in that light comes through a small aperture and casts an image on the back wall. In a camera, the film captures the image. Eyes, however, don't "see" anything. They merely send impulses to the brain, which then processes these impulses into the form of a picture.

An archaic, mechanistic view of an organization suffers in much the same way as the ignorant but plausible concepts illustrated above. The confusion of the behavioral with something mechanical has continued to plague American management perceptions. The behavioral realities of an organization are as elusive to the comprehension of some managers as electronics are to African villagers.

Models and management

When managers think of their organization, they tend to think of individual people or abstractions of people, such as managers or employees. They may conjure visions of an organizational chart, tangible resources such as trucks or buildings, or symbols such as logos. While these are manifestations of an organization, they are not the organization itself. It is difficult to manage what one cannot conceive, and some mental grasp of an organization is precisely what managers must have if they are to manage their operations effectively. Most every model has an internal logic that can be quite compelling and, if pushed with enough authority, can accomplish specific goals.

When people discuss their organization, they tend to describe aspects that, while suggestive of the organization, are not really descriptive. Most everyone agrees that the boxes and lines of the typical organization chart are not the real organization and do not really represent how an organization works. Organization charts typically represent little more than the relative authority and status among managers. Still, people have difficulty getting away from such a chart when trying to explain their organization.

What you see is not always what you get unless you understand what you see. To understand the true nature of an organization requires seeing one's operation. To look past the obvious — the people, the buildings, the equipment, and the products — is difficult, but these are only artifacts of the real organization. The real organization is found in how people behave. Moreover, the obvious is where understanding begins, not where it concludes. As Harold Nelson, a director of graduate studies at Antioch University observed:[2]

> "It is ... difficult to establish clear problem definitions
> that remain stable over a period of time sufficient for
> allowing solutions to take effect. The noise keeps us
> from seeing what is real in our experience of chaos in

> complex systems and what is phantom. It is difficult to
> discriminate between symptoms and root causes."

Or, in the words of Margaret Wheatley in *Leadership and the New Science:*[3]

> "We haven't noticed information as structure because
> all around us are physical forms that we can see and
> touch and that beguile us into confusing the system's
> structure with its physical manifestation."

Human affairs being what they are, even the most archaic or far-fetched models can seem to work, given enough resources and attention. But that is not what the smart manager is after. What managers need today are not organizations that must be overcome to accomplish work, but systems that facilitate, support, enable, and, in general, add greater efficiency and quality assurance to work. Some people like to reach back in time to find a manager who was successful using the techniques of old. That seems a good point, until one considers that Henry Ford and the others who displayed brains and courage in their times would have been unlikely to let the world of modern management thought pass them by.

Finding the organization

A pure dynamic is difficult to see. The nature of the action and activity are only manifest when put in some tangible form, such as a written policy or a product. These things represent behaviors, desired or done, but they are not the behaviors themselves. An organization is not its people, its facilities, or any of these things. An organization is a set of complex and ongoing social phenomena, the interaction of the people with these things and each other. Organizational charts try to capture an organization but generally fail, as do many of the metaphors, such as machine, giant person, team, political system, and so forth.[4]

To get away from the traditional organizational chart that generally fails to indicate what is really happening in an organization, Eastman Chemical saw its organization like a pizza, Pepsi-Cola used an inverted pyramid, and many other theorists and managers have tried various ways to put the organization into some graphic, more tangible form. Most of these efforts have reflected the technical business processes in which the organization is engaged, and, while this is a good beginning, it is certainly an incomplete picture.

Because managers come from technical backgrounds, and a systematic professional management development track is hard to find, it would be useful to delineate the differences between technical and human systems in order to establish the proper realm of endeavor. While human systems operate technical systems, the two are completely different and have completely different rules. If one kicks a soccer ball, the result is predictable, theoretically at least, according to the laws of physics. The weight and inflation of the ball, the force of the kick, the wind, and other knowable and calculable factors combine to put the ball at a certain spot. This is a complex event which, like other complex events, has patterns that allow a fielder to sense where to stand in order to have maximum opportunity to play the ball.

If one hits the ballplayer, on the other hand, the laws of physics still apply but they have little to do with the significant results of that action. The laws of behavior are the ones that really matter, and these are not only more complex but less known. People do not get physically kicked in organizations, at least not anymore, but they are virtually kicked with great regularity. Either way, one is likely to get one or all of rage, resentment, and desire for revenge. Technical systems are mindless, soulless, and devoid of feelings, no matter that we name the family car Matilda or a hurricane Ralph. A machine may stop, even explode, but it will not get emotional. One can drive a mechanical device until it falls apart, but pressuring people to do better or more while frustrating that effort with a poor system is like, well, a kick in the pants. They will figure ways to deal with you.

Social and technical systems[5]

Technical systems are essentially mass, that is, hardware and materials. They exist objectively, although their utility is subjective. Social systems, i.e., organizations, are essentially energy, specifically, people working together. They exist conceptually, that is, in the minds of those who participate. A technical system is operated through technical knowledge and skills with the goal of changing the physical form of materials or knowledge itself. Human systems are managed, one might say led, through focusing, facilitating, and encouraging preferred behaviors.

Operating a technical system generally affords quite predictable and limited results, but the system is absolutely passive. An organization is a dynamic system in which every action affects the system either by establishing, reinforcing, or changing the interactions among its members, or any combination of these things. It creates its own limits and way of operating through countless decisions and determinations by and among its members. Table 1 indicates some comparisons between technical and human systems.

An organization forms around technical systems, for its purpose is to operate them, but it is an illusion of similarity. The difference between human and technical systems is like the difference between golf and computer golf.* The may have superficial similarities but are vastly different. A technical system or machine is designed to do certain things. When it does

---

* Perhaps boxing and computer boxing would be a more painfully realistic analogy.

Table 1 Characteristics of Technical and Human Systems

Attribute	Technical system	Organization
Significance	Use	Purpose
Proper condition	Ideal state	Not known
Working characteristic	Runs	Behaves, performs
Expectations	Designed	Created
Origins	Manufactured	Negotiated agreements
Terminus	Obsolescence, wearing out	Transformation, disbanding
Location of activity	With equipment	With people
Essential element/form	Physical/material	Energy/interactions
Governing principles	Physical	Behavioral
Control	Human set devices	Free will, common sense

those things, when it runs as designed, it is working. When it deviates or makes an unusual noise, it has a problem. Human systems, on the other hand, may have an acceptable performance but not an ideal state of operation. They are expected to follow and adapt prescribed processes to deal with events that are each slightly different. The organization is functioning whenever and wherever one or more of its members is thinking, talking, or in some other way concerned with company business.

Any perceived steady state is simply a snapshot or illusion of what in reality is an ongoing, constantly changing dynamic. Organizations exist in the form of countless interactions within, between, and among members and with numerous non-members who nonetheless influence what the members do. A technical system is inert unless it is being used in some fashion, and it is the same wherever it is used. An organization always reflects the locale and circumstances in which the interactions take place. Technical systems have characteristics but no character.

Organizations are not like plumbing, with mechanically controlled flows of material, but they are more like brains with communications synapses of messages and feedback. They are much like a symphony orchestra, which, while having a basic theme and sheet music, nonetheless may improvise as it plays along. Organizations are not only shaped by actions, but also by the expectation of actions. People operate on what they think is likely to happen as much as what has happened, if not more so. Acting on expectations produces the same result as if that which was expected was real, i.e., expectations are self-fulfilling. Therefore, an organization is largely tautological in that what happens is caused by the assumption of what will happen. For good or ill, organizations are essentially Pygmalion. Further, because the human system creates, operates, and adjusts the technical system, and indeed the operating environment, much of the work of organizations is in trying to keep up with its own handiwork.

Unlike technical systems, human systems are not built but are developed. They are not driven, but are pulled by a sense of purpose, energized through passion for that purpose and actualized through intellect and intuition. Organizations, therefore, are a collective form of common sense, an environment of shared understandings. One does not drive or extract from an organization; therefore, one evokes and elicits the productivity of its potential. When managed properly, this potential of individual and collective, rational, collaborative behavior works effectively and efficiently in pursuit of the purposes of the organization in what is called performance. This may be the great weakness of systems thinking in that, to the degree management sees the operation as a technical system, it misses the system that really does the work.

Management focus

Technical systems are easier to delineate in manufacturing or other environments with specialized hardware, but we can discern them in insurance, health care, or banking. For example, a hospital conversion system receives patients and discharges them (preferably in better condition than when they arrived), takes samples for diagnosis, administers treatment, and disposes of the waste in a manner that adheres to government regulations and professional standards.

A medical-care technical system consists of numerous technical processes that involve medical knowledge, governmental regulations and the procedures to meet those requirements, patient processing procedures, spatial requirements and materials, building cleaning and maintenance materials, and so on. Among all the equipment, materials, machines, buildings, memos, and office furnishings, however, are whirls and eddies of social intelligence and energy that give these inanimate things utility. All these materials and procedures have no effect until a group of people working together applies them in some value-adding way.

Ordinarily, people focus on the technical aspects of the daily press of business with little thought of the social system that operates it except when someone "screws up". This is as it should be, for otherwise the ordinary work would not get done. Most organizational activities are routine and require no conscious effort and, until something goes wrong, get little thought. The human operating system, however, is like a technical system in that, if neglected, there will be problems. An organization, unlike a technical system, is not a constant thing but a dynamic set of interactions. It requires, therefore, even more and better attention than technical systems.

Three basic errors

If the human operating system is managed properly, it will operate the technical systems properly. A common mistake is trying to do it backwards, that is, attempting to manage the human operating system by managing the technical system. Most managers are far more comfortable with technical processes than with the human operating system. They have spent most of their lives studying their technical field, and it has been the platform of their success. A major cause of failure in reengineering efforts, however, is precisely because managers have tried to use computerization to manage people.

In the absence of an agreed-upon set of theories, concepts, and body of knowledge in organizational management, a working manager often has little choice but to rely upon technical models or the common sense of pure feel. The temptation to use the wrong expertise in organizational management, including using technical explanations of behavioral phenomena, is powerful. One of the reasons for the remarkable success of the seven habits of Stephen Covey is that they provide a manager with a set of personal rules of behavior to deal with a world in which clear rules and understanding are often elusive.

Unfortunately, a manager with perfect character and competence still must work the organizational medium, which, according to Deming and others, causes 85% of his operation's problems. Technical remedies often make things worse. In a health-care setting, nurses may be given stricter procedures, even though problems they already face include conflicting orders, inadequate information, or unclear priorities. Factories are inspected for safety hazards, even though almost every accident can be traced to a behavioral rather than an environmental problem. It is like trying to control the speed of a car by manipulating the speedometer.

The technical system is the chief focus of management because that is the primary purpose of everyone there. It also fits nicely with the mechanistic model by which managers tend to perceive human activity. Further, technical processes are generally measured throughout, e.g., checks or forms are filled out correctly, evaporator temperatures are within the appropriate range, or the order is delivered on time. If the process measures are okay, then okay performance is assumed. For the human operating system, the outputs are measured, but the throughput performance is rarely measured, rendering the organization something of a "black box" to management.

While working backwards is a major mistake, an even greater error is trying to manage the human operating system by managing individuals. That is like using liposuction to lose weight in that it only deals with the appearance of the problem, not the problem itself. Worse, ordering improvement from someone who is probably only conforming to a flawed system might cause managers to feel that they have somehow dealt with a problem and need to pursue the matter no further. Unfortunately, they are trying to solve a problem by delegating its solution to a person who is more victim than perpetrator.

The organization is a technology and therefore has a cause/effect interaction with its users. An organization is the product of all its users working together but it is also the obverse, i.e., a critical behavioral influence and limitation on each member. People are told to get organized when most of their work is scheduled and prioritized by others, or to be nice to customers when they are forced to treat customers in ways and circumstances determined by the organization. People address the ever-present communications problem with such stillborn prescriptions as establishing meetings without changing the underlying forces that discouraged or precluded the meeting to start with. Such meetings usually take place once, maybe twice, before they fall into either a hollow mockery of compliance or people simply return to their old ways.

Endnotes

1. A discussion of numbers that look good but cover serious organizational problems can be found in English, Gary, Management review: an important part of due diligence, *The Journal of Commercial Lending*, February, 19–25, 1994.
2. Nelson, Harold G., The necessity of being "un-disciplined" and "out of control": design action and systems thinking, *Performance Improvement Quarterly*, 7(3), 22–29, 1994.
3. Wheatley, Margaret, *Leadership and the New Science: Learning about Organization from an Orderly Universe*, Barrett-Koehler, San Francisco, 1994, p. 104.
4. G. Morgan identifies eight different metaphors for organizations in his *Images of Organization*, Sage, Beverly Hills, CA, 1986.
5. This human operating system is sometimes called the "social system". In addition to that term's not reflecting the operating purpose of a business organization, I have found in practice the term "social" tends to depreciate the activity and to separate human activities such as teams from the "real work" of the organization in people's minds. The view of there being a social and technical spheres which interact to determine human progress is not new and may be best represented in the works of C. P. Snow, who said, "Technology ... is a queer thing. It brings you great gifts with one hand, and stabs you in the back with the other." The idea of "socio-technical systems" has been proposed as a new field of study (but has actually been around for more than half a century) and as a management change approach for several years. For more information, see Twist, Eric, The evolution of socio-technical systems: a conceptual framework and an action research program, *Occasional Paper No. 2*, Ontario Ministry of Labor, June, 1981.

chapter eleven

Routine as rut and groove

Why the attack on routine misses the point entirely

> *Habit is thus the enormous flywheel of society, its most precious conservative agent. It alone is what keeps us all within the bounds of ordinance.*
>
> ⌒William James

If there is anything that gets some gurus hot under the collar more than common sense, it is routine. Warren Bennis, in answering his own question about why leaders can't lead, argues that "routine work ... smothers to death all creative planning, all fundamental change." An article in the *American Journal of Nursing* is entitled, "Beware of Routine Procedures" and *Flying* magazine warns of perfunctory preflights. Hammer and Champy, of reengineering fame, made their reputations by arguing for discontinuous thinking, their term for starting over. Peters, still searching for excellence, seems to have turned Jacobean as well, calling for permanent revolution and creative destruction of established organizational processes.[1]

There is little question that organizations can develop terrible, irrational habits. They can become hidebound and encrusted with useless rules and activities, which we label with the pejorative "bureaucracy". These results are typified by situations such as the state government whose staff must wait up to six months to get travel reimbursement. It is also true that people going through critical routines may put things on automatic and just go through the motions, having lost sight of the purpose for the routine in the first place. This can certainly be a dangerous practice when done not only by nurses and airplane pilots, but by others as well.

One can sympathize with those who are frustrated by routine, but those who summarily condemn routine miss the mark. For all practical purposes, routine *is* the organization. The quality of an organization does not come from an absence of routine but from the quality of its established work practices. To condemn "routine", however, is like condemning the worm for its wiggle, for routine is the very essence of organization.

Routine not the problem

If organization is a form of discipline, then "routine lies at the heart of discipline," according to Dave Thomas, founder of Wendy's:[2]

> "Routine is what keeps us focused on the main things in life. ...Discipline means keeping things and people in their proper places ... discipline helps you keep track of your own thinking and also keeps such thinking simple and to the point."

The whole idea of an organization is to systemize, arrange, coordinate, and plan work — in other words, to make staff performance routine. Routine is simply the ordinary, typical expected way of doing things. A checklist is nothing but a job aid for ensuring the completeness of the routine. Only when work is structured in a predictable way can flexibility have any meaning or can there be any real control, elegant or otherwise. The value of organization is that it creates a condition in which simple controls can cause complex operations to happen.

The story of management is told in the nature of those controls which, in turn, determine how adaptive and well-focused the routines are. Flexibility affords adaptability, which allows the organization to avoid decreasing returns on its efforts. Stability and constancy, on the other hand, provide for the increasing returns that sweeten the payoff for highly productivity.[3] The problem with the assembly line was never that it was a poor idea. It was the treatment of people like interchangeable extensions of the machinery, rather than as critical craftsmen whose handiwork was enhanced by the equipment, that was the problem.

In sports, plays and the systems that prepare and enable players to execute these plays are but routines. They may be highly flexible, creative, and adaptable, but they are routines nonetheless. Every play is a routine, and every player's role is a complementary subroutine that molds individual and group discipline such that everyone can work together for maximum effectiveness. How much a player can improvise on a routine depends on the nature of the game and the situation at hand. Similarly, the degree to which an employee should improvise on a work routine depends on the nature of the work and the work circumstances.

Paradox of routine

One might recall the earlier example of the chemical plant safety program, where orientation was required but was essentially ineffective. On the one hand, it is good that the company requires everyone to go through its safety orientation before they can go into the plant. By having a standardized program, they can be assured that (1) certain things are included, and (2) a number of people can learn it and become instructors. And, even though much of the program was useless for the visitor in the plant, the exhortation to be careful and not to take chances alerts a visitor to the potentially dangerous place being visited. On the whole, however, the program fails because there is a disconnect between practice and purpose.

Like most routines, it was rationally designed by experts. They knew the dangers and knew the proper responses. This program was rational in its design and was modeled after that of another company with a good safety record. On the surface, everyone was satisfied that what could and should be done was being done. Still, the program failed to prepare visitors for emergencies. This safety orientation program is typical of many of the problems in instituting and maintaining any quality effort:

1. The measurement of value-add was only that the activity itself take place; there were no results measured.
2. The problem was solved at a technical level because that was the safety director's job, rather than through true managerial problem-solving.
3. The problem appeared to have been solved because a good safety program has a safety orientation and the information was pertinent.
4. The response was rational and based on a best-practice model.
5. The model was based on the best judgment of the resident expert.
6. Management was quite satisfied that the program fulfilled the safety requirement. This put the burden of proof to the otherwise on the person who would like to change the program. In other words, the plant was now in compliance with what they were expected to do.

It was assumed that such a program would prepare visitors properly, and that assumption was never questioned, let alone tested. To really prepare a person for a visit to the plant would have required some changes in the plant itself to inform the visitor where he or she was and where the emergency equipment was and probably would include some reminders and indicators about what to do when an emergency occurred. In other words, a results-oriented, customer-oriented program required a management perspective, not merely that of technical expertise. The experts did not know what it would be like to be a visitor in the plant without expert knowledge. The program, no matter how well done, would always be of poor quality. For the presenters, however, the program was excellent, and, besides, no visitor had ever been hurt after going through the program except, of course, in those cases where a visitor did something "stupid".

Poor routines and poor perspectives

Quality problems are rarely caused by technical ignorance or incompetence; most companies have the technical know-how and equipment they need to do good work. Nor are quality problems commonly the result of stupid or uncaring people, because most people are neither. Rather, quality problems occur when people are working hard, striving to make the best of the situation in which they find themselves. Quality problems result from good people who operate with mental models that fail to provide them adequate understanding and guidance in their work, at least in regard to the human operating systems.

As this example of a safety program illustrates, the real harm does not come from being wrong, but from being right in an inadequate context. When people's thinking is confined to their limited perspective, it is virtually impossible to convince them they should do something different. When one expands that context with quality thinking — say, for example, by starting with the desired outcomes and working back to appropriate actions — the orientation program is a poor one. It fails because it is not based on excellent knowledge and, therefore, cannot produce quality. It is compliance, not results, focused.

As we have discussed, the pitfalls of the language that lures us to quality shortfalls, the blaming and separating nature of traditional management ideology, and the separation of purpose and work practice from authority and hierarchy all combine to fool managers into thinking they are doing quality when they are merely complying with minimum standards. That is the problem with establishing effective change in most organizations, and that problem shows up most often in routine work that fails to assure quality or provide the appropriate efficiencies.

Resistance to change

Routines are difficult to alter, at least radically, because of four characteristics:

1. Routines represent profound management choices; therefore, small changes can seem profound.
2. Routines, for all their power over people's work, are largely invisible.
3. Routine is learned as a part of acculturation into the organization.
4. Routines have seemed quite effective in the past.

The most profound aspect of a routine is not what and how something is done. Rather, it is the vast array of other things that have been rejected, ignored, or are unknown to those who pursue the routine. Management determines that it will sell kitchen appliances and not bathroom fixtures, or that it will repair its own brand but not others, or that it will make circuit boards but not chips, or that it will have stores in major malls only, or that it will manufacture in Mexico but not Hong Kong. These decisions focus everyone on certain kinds of activities at the expense of all others.

Work routines represent the defining decisions of an organization and they are supported by an array of passive dynamics that sustain and empower the routine. Just as the arms and legs of a gymnast are constantly and subtly adjusted to enable a gymnastic routine, so too do all the parts of an organization adjust to support and further established work routines. That is why changing shopfloor practices to reduce cycle time often runs into problems stemming from reward systems, supervisory review, maintenance, and purchasing "requirements." Organization do not tend to be simply sets of routines, but rather *tangles* of them such that the changing of any one, like a spider's web, reverberates throughout. When the organization is the traditional authoritarian hierarchy, these reverberations can bring out a flurry of vested people ready to bite whatever is disturbing their own established ways of doing things.

Aristotle said "we are the things we repeatedly do" for they reflect our true beliefs and character. These qualities are ordered in the form of social roles that tell us who we are and what we are about and define how we should behave and toward whom. We tend to pursue those roles and aspects of those roles that reward us with pleasure and satisfaction. Humans are social, psychological, and biological beings, and our experiences occur on several levels. There is the immediate enjoyment, the memory of the enjoyment, and the complex of relationships that intertwine that enjoyment with other aspects of our lives. There is a redefinition of self, based on when one has succeeded and when one has failed, and even a change in biophysical brain chemistry that can become addictive.

Even the most utilitarian routines, even those that are distasteful, over time are integrated into our personality. One develops an emotional attachment to them and the people with whom we work them. Kurt Lewin found that reinforced behavior becomes a tactic of choice and, eventually, becomes a habit. As the practices and interactions become an integral part of our lives and memories, associated with those fond times, they become institutionalized and acquire an emotional value above and beyond their utilitarian purpose.[4] We become fans in a way that is difficult to explain or share; it can only be felt. The memory of institutions tends to be selective, even unrealistic, making its grip both less observable and stronger at the same time.

The invisible paradigm

The most common way a person learns to work in an organization is through on-the-job training (OJT). This is often a misnomer, because while it may be on the job, it usually involves little training.* Managers like it because it seems cheap and effortless. Whatever problems develop from the resultant poor worker abilities are deemed to be that person's fault (thank the Peter Principle or damn the personnel department). OJT does not teach innovation but rather adherence to existing routine; it limits rather than stretches worker effort. It is not purpose oriented ("get these trees to the customer in good condition") but is activity oriented ("load those trees in that truck"). When a novice asks why this and not that, the answer is likely to be that's how they do it here or, even less rationally, that's the way the boss likes it. Paradoxically, OJT is often done so poorly that employees are forced to *ad lib* their work. While that forces people to be more innovative and adaptive, it is rarely the kind of rational creativity a company wants.

When routine is properly focused, it is both the product and producer of organizational learning as people master the skills that comprise the routine and become capable of adapting it to meet situational needs. As Peter Drucker, in his *The Effective Executive*, noted:[5]

> "A recurrent crises should always have been foreseen. It can therefore either be prevented or reduced to a routine which clerks can manage. ...[A] routine puts down in systematic, step-by-step form what a very able [person] learned in surmounting yesterday's crises."

The goal of learning is to make the new skill a natural part of a person's repertory of performance. One can envision the process and practice and prepare, but when the time comes to perform, the focus must be on the task at hand. The master manager knows this, but the amateur thinks only of swinging at the ball, unaware of the learning and practice required for excellence.** In every strength, however, lie the seeds of weakness. In Greek tragedies and modern companies, it is often pride that blinds people to the need for renewed effort.

Even for the humble, there is the paradox that skills, to be effective, must slip beneath the conscious level to the natural subconscious. When this is

---

* OJT, as a rule, is indicative of the general poor conditions of most organizational human resource development systems. This is discussed in a book now in preparation, but there is a good example to illustrate the point. On one occasion I was discussing with a client the prospect of training a group of representative staff to review incidents in the company, such as accidents, employee complaints, or production failures. I mentioned that this had been done in another company where, after an accidental release of SO_2, OSHA had ended up congratulating the company on its excellent investigatory work. The client replied that he was training his staff to do investigations "by doing them", a process that sounded a lot like no training at all.

** This brings to mind one of the most significant differences between sports and management. In sports, one cannot talk about being the fastest or best; one must demonstrate it. In management, excellence is often decided by simply being able to say it is so.

done, common sensibilities becomes highly intuitive and inferential, and the person can perform quite well. On the other hand, this same process of habituation hides the process and separates it from the product. Performance routines may become better executed when subconscious, but, in a literal sense, they become more mindless.

When the routine is focused properly, it can then be efficient and reliable. The purpose of routine work is to allow performers to focus on the technical aspects of work rather than to worry self-consciously about their technique. That is why people with high skill levels often make poor teachers. To them, things just seem to come naturally. Ordinary routines are less subjected to scrutiny and, therefore, are most likely to contain hidden inefficiencies and quality failures. Routine typically becomes visible only when something is wrong, meaning either that a performance did not satisfy the expectations of the routine itself or the desired outcome of the routine was not produced.

The larger purpose of a routine, while at first clear and usually rational, over time becomes assumed and eventually can be lost entirely. The routine becomes self-justified and perpetuated, even institutionalized, until its lack of contribution, perhaps even its dysfunctionality, can no longer be ignored. Even then, the myriad of interactions constituting the human operating system may go unappreciated as management focuses either on the technical process where the problem occurred or on individual performance. The temptation for management to try to cure problems with technical or narrow *ad hoc* solutions is almost irresistible. Because the real source of these problems is the unseen system, however, most particular problems are merely manifestations that will recur unless the system itself can be fixed.

When good routines go bad

One of the things that obscures management's observation (and one of the reasons for new paradigms and reinvention) is that these routines, which now seem off track, were once the very engines of corporate success. Previous successes validate present practices, causing management to lose sight of the quality failures and inefficiency that are wasting money. Activities that were initially "make-do" become established practice and then tradition. Unless there has been an open and effective dialog among organizational staff, information that would have warned management may never have gotten through or had any credence. Success ties us to the past, and the groove can imperceptibly become a rut as the organization seems to harden and get fat at the same time. Costs rise, but there seems to be less capacity to respond to new needs and opportunities.

Managers always seem to be struggling with urgent but marginal things without reference to the big picture. Organizational activities are no longer purposeful but become the center of attention in their own right as people fall into the activities trap where winning is simply getting through the day. Activity-centered management loses its sense of priorities when everything is a top priority, such that nothing is really a priority except that which is immediately urgent. Activities themselves can become almost sacrosanct, and people, in the words of George Santayana, "redouble their efforts while losing sight of their goals." Common sense suffers as absurdity displaces rationality.

In such circumstances the likelihood that the organization will wander from the productive path and lose its goodness of fit with its goals is great. A company then becomes less competitive, which, in today's world, can be quite harmful or even fatal to even major companies such as IBM and Eastern Airlines. Eventually, there will seem to be a need for major changes, and the temptation to make drastic changes in the organization becomes great. At some point, when things seem to be going poorly, or at least suboptimally, management is pressured to find a more effective fit with the market. This has likely been preceded by great pressure on the workforce to somehow make the old ways work better.

The traditional mechanical view is to start over with a brand new model (created by an *au currant* change program) or to rebuild, both of which are likely to mean staff reductions or turnover. The realistic view, of course, is that you can do no such thing. One cannot realistically dismantle or rebuild a human system, for it is a dynamic of common sense relationships, and the operative model is not an engineering one but a horticulture one. One can fashion and design, but things grow within that rubric according to their natural inclinations. For human beings, whatever develops is at some point purposeful and volitional.

Except in the more dire emergencies, where any cost is acceptable, abrupt and radical change that severely threatens an organization's work streams would seem attractive only to the irresponsible or blindly hopeful. After all, the primary purpose is to control chaos, not create it. Routine allows an ordinary person through ordinary work to join in the process of achieving large-scale and complex things. Ironically, the radical changes that some advocate can only be implemented as new routines, such as statistical process control to eliminate variation in routine. Anything that requires a sustained, self-conscious, and exceptional effort that cannot be incorporated into routine within a reasonable time will be dropped. Eventually the new way will become lost as the pressures to produce pushes the organization back to its old ways.

Inherent resistance to change

People and their organizations are inherently conservative, their changes being primarily variations on a theme, a tweaking of routine. While revolutions may be sometimes necessary, a revolution is only destructive until the new institutions have been established and systems set in place for their maintenance, i.e., routines. As mentioned earlier, business turnarounds are not accomplished until the organization is stable and ready to meet its newly defined challenges.

Organizational bloat is usually a function of poor systems being patched by throwing people at the problems, not a function of middle managers somehow magically reproducing themselves. People get caught in the squeeze of change, especially when change rests upon a one-trick pony that only puts pressure on people but fails to bring the entire organization around to support them. Practices that have been so rewarded and seemingly efficacious are suddenly invalidated, leaving people stunned and confused.

It is a common belief that people don't like change. Actually, people like change where they see some improvement and it is done in a way that makes sense. Resistance to change may be a problem not so much of willful resistance but more of being enmeshed in a largely assumed and invisible world that is not as easily adjusted as the glib promises of the consultant would suggest.

When one notes that a person is enmeshed in ways of doing things, that is not a light statement. Perhaps it can be illustrated by looking at why it is so hard to quit smoking. If it were only the nicotine addiction, one might be cured by a patch. If it were only habit and addiction, one might find relief from nicotine gum. But the real hook is the psychological reliance, the sense of control and definition of self that smoking provides. Watch any cigarette smoker in a situation where he or she is self-conscious or anxious and you will see the hand go toward the pack. While most of us do not know what to do in such situations, the smoker always does.

Like organizational change, the change from smoker to non-smoker must be a comprehensive effort that removes all the hooks. If one substitutes in the above observations "seat of the pants, autocratic manager" for "smoker", the observations still hold. To argue that a quality improvement program must overcome corporate culture is like saying that to change the way people behave they must change their personality. It is true, but essentially tautological. Corporate culture and typical practices are, like personality and typical behaviors, the same thing. These things cannot be overcome but must be adjusted through systems that enable, reward, and, yes, penalize one toward the desired behaviors.

Camels and straws

A major problem in change efforts is that top management demands the changes of the organization in addition to maintaining or even increasing present productivity pursued through established routines. Improvement efforts are stacked on top of what is already seen as too much work with too few resources. That much of this work may not be productive does not matter to the people who are trying to do it and are now choking on the additional load. Sometimes organizations need some sort of beachhead of time and staff to begin a change process that can develop and an organization that is capable of advancing that process. Often times consultants are forced to initiate change activities even though the organization is clearly unable to do so, often because of the pressures from the same top management that is pressuring for greater efforts under the very system that is to be changed.[6]

Not only does a new program threaten success with the work already assigned, but there is also great unpredictability in all great changes caused by the law of unanticipated consequences. This law refers to the difficulty of understanding the hypercomplex interconnectedness of the real world and that every effort we make somehow changes things. Sometimes things work out for the better, such as federal safety and environmental requirements that prompted greater efficiency and productivity in chemical plants. But most times, the law is cited when things go wrong, such as river levees that caused a river to accumulate mud to its bottom, which raised the level of the river and prevented the overflow from receding back into the river after a flood.

Inherent dynamic of change

The difference between a groove and a rut depends on how you feel about it. When two people are given the same job, one may feel in luck and the other may feel stuck. To a dancer, discipline represents an opportunity to perform, but for a prisoner it is a miserable constraint. The difference is that the dancer is able to interpret, to truly perform to the best of her ability, to make a statement by doing and by being a part of something larger and laudatory. For the prisoner, the object is to comply, to conform, to be in a condition where the purposes only use him, where his best effort only serves to avoid punishment, and where he is in something but not really a part of it.

Organizations need dancers who are disciplined by the urge to perform well, but they often create prisoners who are restricted by authority. One recent book argued that employees, indeed, have more restrictions than prisoners.[7] Authority-based systems, which attempt to control by threat, are themselves easily threatened. They are threatened by dialog among employees, sometimes to the extreme of being afraid to have employees meet for a United Way campaign. Curiously, managers seem especially threatened by the prospect of having a dialog with employees. They see that as somehow compromising their power when, in truth, it gives them real power, not to mention a bit more knowledge in its exercise.

Everything is being simultaneously affected by two seemingly opposite forces — those of change and those of stability. These two forces are what enables something to move and to stay the same at the same time. For a mechanical device, the divergent or destabilizing forces are less obvious but, as any technician can assure you, they are occurring. More scientifically, it may be expressed in the Second Law of Thermodynamics, in which things have an inherent tendency to attenuate. But this requires one to recognize that things have form to start with and, as they lose one form, they take another. Similarly, all organizations are in the constant process of simultaneously becoming less organized and becoming more organized, of structuring and restructuring.

The convergent force is toward conformance, which is to reduce variation in process and product. That, indeed, is Philip Crosby's definition of quality. As one moves up the organization, however, where the issues are more general and less technical, decisions are more concerned with transformance, rather than conformance. The goal is more toward new goods or services, new markets, or better ways to find goodness of fit with market potential. The organization is constantly in a dynamic of seeking to resolve divergent energies with convergent ones, to translate transforming information into conforming applications of technique and technology in order to reduce variance in work.

Every act of conformance for changing situations and conditions is transforming, and the trick is to ensure that such changes are in rational pursuit of proper purposes. Given effective leadership, an organization will naturally adapt to its environmental demands and opportunities, provided the organization is unimpaired and in full communication with itself. The organization as a stable but adaptive community of practice and learning will form itself around organizational purpose unless authority-based actions interfere and debilitate this adaptive process and weaken the dialog. The command approach "dumbs down", makes an organization rigid, impairs the development and employment of dedicated craftsmanship, and, consequently, loses potential value-add from its human resource.

Sports analogies are not always appropriate for management because sports are comparatively simple and more easily controlled. Still, even with that comparative simplicity, they are quite complex, and, if one is mindful of the differences, there are valuable lessons to be learned. For example, on paper every football play (routine) is a touchdown play, yet touchdowns are infrequent. The reason is that in their execution a number of factors combine to thwart progress. In the same way, management schemes designed to accomplish some business purpose and issued with great optimism tend to encounter difficulty in the execution. In football, a good team continually reviews what has happened and makes appropriate adjustments around its existing repertory of possible actions.

A good coach knows to add new techniques to the team's strengths and to incorporate them into what the team already does best, making adjustments as appropriate to optimize team performance. After all, there is a schedule to be played. According to Tom Epley:[8]

> "[T]he secret is in identifying what the company is doing right and taking swift, immediate action to streamline process and business, capitalizing on core strengths, and preparing to build on those strengths."

Endnotes

1. See Bennis, Warren, Why leaders can't lead, *Training and Development Journal*, April, 35–39, 1989; Lilley, Linda, and Robert Guanci, Beware of routine procedures, *American Journal of Nursing*, October, 18, 1995; Berrenson, Tom, Perfunctory preflights, *Flying*, June, 105–106, 1995; Hammer Michael, and James Champy, *Reengineering the Corporation*, Harper Collins, New York, 1993. The comments from Tom Peters were notes taken from the televised seminar, Meet the Minds: Lesson in Leadership, sponsored by *Fortune* magazine (see the September 13, 1996, issue).
2. See Thomas, Dave, and Ron Beyman, *Well Done! The Common Guy's Guide to Everyday Success*, Harper Collins, New York, 1994.
3. Arthur, W. Brian, Increasing returns and the new world of business, *Harvard Business Review*, July, 100–109, 1996.
4. Lewin, Kurt, Group decision and social change, in *Readings in Social Psychology*, Newcomb, T. and Hartley, E., Eds., Holt, Reinhart & Winston, New York, 1947.
5. Drucker, Peter, *The Effective Executive*, Harper & Row, New York, 1966, p. 41.
6. See also Forbes, Lincoln, What do you do when your organization isn't ready for TQM?, *National Productivity Review*, Autumn, 16–18, 1994.
7. Holoviak, Stephen J., *Golden Rule Management*, Addison-Wesley, Reading, MA, 1996.
8. Quoted in "Technology turnaround: how to win in today's explosive marketplace" in *Inter@ctive Week*, December 9, 23, 1996.

chapter twelve

Hierarchy and organizational learning

Why hierarchy is necessary and
why the problem is really in how you do it

> *It's the wrong war, at the wrong time, and in*
> *the wrong place, but it's the only war we've got.*
>   ◯∿U.S. Army colonel in Vietnam

Much of the effort at organizational improvement has been in the form of an attack on middle managers in an effort to flatten the organization. Because the area in which the U.S. is least productive is its white collar operation, and because a great deal of that work is "rework" anyway, reducing the "bloat" in the middle makes a lot of sense. Organizations are often too layered, such as the small town that has 150 employees and six layers of authority from city manager to hourly worker, with one supervisor for every three people.

Hierarchy is an organizational feature currently out of vogue and often equated with inefficiency and resistance to change. There are many advocates for flattening the organization by reducing the number of hierarchical layers. There seems to be a tendency for organizations over time to stack up, primarily because adding people seems the easiest way to deal with whatever was a current urgency. Flat organizations, however, like non-competitive sports, just never seem to really catch on.

"Flatten" can have more than one meaning, of course. It can also refer to laying an organization low by taking away its ability to operate. This has also been the result of such efforts and the problems can be profound. I have worked with at least two companies that eagerly flattened and downsized by getting rid of its senior staff and middle managers only to find that much of its abilities and organizational memory were gone. Many of these people were then hired back as consultants, making more money and double dipping. Before one starts getting rid of people, tearing up operating systems, and, in general, throwing away social capital, it might be wise to pause for a moment and reflect upon the full implications of such actions.

The new hierarchy

The concept of hierarchy generally prompts visions of cascading orders moving through descending levels of authority and, perhaps, something called feedback from below. In simpler times, when organizations were some version of the plantation model, this picture was essentially accurate. Even the most sophisticated version of this model, the assembly line, did not change things much. The arenas of knowledge were fairly simple and limited, as was the focus of the organization. The chief knowledge variable was the amount one had, which was essentially particular. Very little information had to go down or up the operation, and every day was pretty much like the others. Control of these organizations was not through knowledge but through the power to inflict punishment.

Work processes have, of course, changed radically. The typical workplace today involves a vast array of knowledges and skills, and no one can master many, if any, of these. Most people find it difficult to keep up with even their own specialties. Consequently, when one talks of the information-based workplace, one is talking of a world where differing kinds of knowledge must somehow be blended and fit together to deal with a complex and rapidly changing world.

In the modern information-based workplace, which can be reengineered through information technologies, it is essential to understand the relationship between information or knowledge and organizational structure and dynamics. One of the chief problems in modern management is to apply the right knowledge at the right place and time. The role of an organization in translating the languages of different technical and functional interests, say marketing and production, is generally well known and understood. Multifunctional teams are one of the modern tools for this purpose. What is not so appreciated, however, is the role of organizational layers in translating conceptual (general management) and particular (technical) knowledge in a way that makes sense to everyone.

Hierarchy of knowledge

As discussed earlier, every operation requires two kinds of knowledge to operate. One is the high-concept knowledge, such as marketing and value-adding strategies, and the other is a set of particular tricks of the trade to accomplish technical work. Between global strategies and particular working knowledge, however, is a vast conceptual chasm. Reason tells us that grand strategies and particular work tricks, involving many specialties and roles in work processes, must be translated in a manner that provides the right mix of concept knowledge and particular knowledge in any given organizational situation.

Common sense usually requires varying degrees of both particular and conceptual knowledge, the degree which is appropriate depending upon where one is literally and figuratively. The technician requires mostly particular knowledge, some of it obtained through training, but much of it through simple trial and error. At the loftiest of organizational levels, particular skills are almost irrelevant. Lee Iaccoca operated through a highly refined conceptual knowledge of markets, finances, and production, although he may not have understood the particulars of these very well at all. Top management controls the general organizational course through concept, although that may be surrendered in a variety of ways. In the trenches, hands-on technicians control their work through particular skills as they give injections, fix engines, transact deposits, answer telephones, and so forth.

A custodian may never be able to grasp the full nature of Hyatt's marketing strategy, but he or she can understand the value of customer satisfaction in that plan. Similarly, Hyatt executives may not have a clue about getting gum out of a carpet (although that would be good preparatory experience), but they must still understand that this has to be done if the customer is to be really satisfied. The custodian's view of his work and the view of the executive must be of the same mosaic, although one looks more at the pieces and the other more at the patterns. The more conceptual knowledge of organizational purpose and activities must be translated into more technical or particular knowledge. Similarly, strategic concepts must be realistic in terms of technical practicalities.

Since the chasm between grand strategic knowledge and highly particular application is likely to be great in an organization of any size or complexity, the translation of one to the other requires some intermediate steps where knowledges can interlock in a meaningful way. Such knowledges include those of architects and designers, purchasing agents, human resources personnel, technical support, maintenance, and so forth. The custodian generally learns from direct supervisors as well as from the staff, training, equipment and materials support, and reward systems, all of which reflect upper management's true values. If there is any justification for hierarchy today, it is that it serves the purposes of translation and organizational learning.

The goals of zero defects, being a customer's preferred supplier, and putting the customer first must become translated into specific work and relationships, which will determine just how "first" the customer is. While top management must support an improvement effort and the measure of success of such efforts is to be found in the work of technicians, the real battleground for improvement is not at either level but rather in critical connectivity between the two — that is, in the vast middle.

As we have seen, much needs to be done to a general statement of goals and objectives, the product of top management, before it can be turned into a practical application throughout the organization. As Quinn's study of large corporations concluded:[1]

> "[A] pragmatic compromise emerges [as] top managers ... provide a framework of broad goals for their subordinate units. They then encourage lower level managers to make proposals that respond to these goals through planning, budgetary, and *ad hoc* processes. This brings a kind of *collective wisdom to bear.*" [Emphasis added.]

Top management relies on the organizational layers and components to translate general goals and objectives into ever more appropriate action terms. Even sports teams of any size have a hierarchy of coaches whose special knowledge is beneficial to the performance of specialized players. It is difficult to think of an outstanding team that is self-coached, regardless of its talent. Middle management and hierarchy seem to retain the critical role in translating grand purpose to an ever more particular technical application in most organizations.

Clash of paradigms

As Peter Drucker observed:[2]

> "The problem ... is that the important and relevant outside events are often qualitative and not capable of being quantified. They are not yet 'facts'. For a fact, after all, is an event which somebody has defined, has classified and, above all, has endowed with relevance. To be able to quantify, one has to have a concept first. One first has to abstract from the infinite welter of phenomena a specific aspect which one then can name and finally count."

When one analyzes the communication problem that every organization seems to have, it is not due to a lack of skills by the parties but rather a clash of the situational paradigms through which they are seeking a common sense solution to whatever problem they are facing. One can argue that data and statistical process control can make the workplace more democratic, but only if the knowledge which gives meaning today has a democratic frame of reference. This is a big "if".

How important is this frame of reference? Consider the proposition of fishing from the point of view of the fish, the worm, the fisher, and the cook. Management too often positions itself as the fisher, the customers as the fish, and the employees as worms. As a result, the contention of paradigms is horrific. Reengineering or some other such technique, especially when glee-fully pursued in the hopes of reducing staff, only serves to make it worse. The object of good management is to make everyone feel like fishers who partici-pate in the sport as players, not as expendable supplies.

Muddle in the middle

One of the most misunderstood parts of an organization is middle manage-ment. They are seen as an organizational dinosaur and a major impediment to change. According to one study, middle management was blamed for 79% of the resistance to quality initiatives. One woman told me of a recent experience at a professional meeting where the presenter pointed his finger at the audience of middle managers and said "soon there won't be any jobs for you people." An FMC executive expressed the need to reduce the ranks of its middle management because they are burdensome on the "operations people in the field who were actually doing the company's work." One observer concluded that 40% of middle management time is spent moving messages through organizational layers modified to suit the needs of the middle managers."[3] Anyone who has dealt with a government agency knows that the worst part of the bureaucratic knot is in its middle management. Efforts by government to reduce middle management, however, are driven by essentially the same reason as most corporations, i.e., to reduce labor costs.[4]

With middle management coming under so much fire it is easy to over-look how critical it is in making an organization work. After all, there was a reason why they were there to start with, and, while their role is clearly changing, they become more important as their numbers decline, not less. One needs to look at the replacement of people by technology (or nothing at all) in proper perspective. When a person's work is multiplied by technology, the impact of that individual on the success of the organization is much more important than any one person was when work was more labor intensive.

In the same vein, as operations become more complex, intense, and rapidly changing, the critical role of middle managers for channeling infor-mation to the executive suite, moving work structuring to the front lines, and holding the organization's diverse areas together is likewise more critical. One observer felt that a key problem for South Korea's competition with Japan was that it lacked the necessary expertise, "especially in the middle management sector."[5]

Built-in contentions

There is no doubt that hierarchy is a serious problem in many organizations, for this is where the broad visions of top management are intricately reformulated into practical realities, where the goals and needs of one set of people are converted to those of others. But even this simple view fails to account for the forces of contention that push and surge throughout even the most focused and committed organizations.

For example, departments are often typified by certain personality types which can be so in conflict as to require direct interventions. I worked with one company whose computer staff could not work effectively with their internal clients to utilize fully its fourth generation information system. The personality tendencies of this group, as well as those of their internal customers, such as accounting and marketing, were exacerbated by the departmental isolation that so often typifies traditional organizations. After some training and opportunities to discuss their common goals, however, there was a marked improvement not only between the computer staff and its clients but among accounting, operations, and marketing, as well.

Hierarchy itself is a source of contention among top management, middle management, frontline supervision, and hourly employees as each attempts to make a common sense determination of what work assignments mean to their situations. Even within each individual, moreover, there is a constant stream of contentions that require a decision, such as whether to spend a little more time on a task to do it better or to let it go and get more tasks done. Sometimes the answer is to go on to the next task, and sometimes the answer is to shut down the production line to get this one right.

Even if the person is committed to quality work, one often has to choose among "quality is job one" and "that's good enough" or "aw, what the hell". The object of management at every level is to ensure that all self and group dialogs are focused on the organization intent and that they construe a rational action from among these diverse views such that the operation of the organization is nonetheless consistent and constant.

Role of middle management

At one time middle management was called the lynch pins and transmission belts of an organization — a decidedly mechanistic view, but one that recognized its critical role. Middle management, ranging from department heads to frontline supervisors, is where conceptual knowledge is translated into appropriate tasks and where the organizational implications from particular work challenges are formulated. Middle management is the articulator of action to, from, and among organizational members. As such, it is the primary locus of organizational coherence. In other words, middle management is what makes the organization run. It is not so much that middle management is strong in their numbers, but rather that they occupy most all of the conceptual space between the highly abstract top management and the highly particular front line. (See Table 1.)

Table 1 Middle Management, the Conceptual/Abstract,
and the Particular/Concrete

Abstraction	Knowledge	Organization/rank
Assets	Highly abstract/conceptual	Top management
Ranch		Upper middle management
Livestock		Lower middle management
Cattle		
Herefords		Supervision
Bossie		
Milk	Highly concrete/particular	Front line

Creating the blend of knowledge

It is in the cascade of translating decisions between the abstractions of top management goals and the tangible realities of particular work that organizational common sense is determined, and it is middle management where one finds the blend of conceptual and particular knowledge that holds the organization together. It is not surprising that Peters saw the critical role of middle management and called for reconceiving the role of middle management as one of his 45 prescriptions. Crosby argued that top management must rally middle management to be successful, and Deming saw middle management as being the key to change. Without an effective translation, there can be no real change or even intentional and controlled improvement.

Middle management is part technician, part manager, and often wholly schizophrenic about what it is supposed to do. It is the middle manager who, under pressure from top management, is expected to put himself at risk by empowering subordinates without delegating any of the responsibility (read: blame). The situation of the middle manager has become so difficult that there are even gurus for them offering advice on how to survive in the workplace.[6] The same cascade of decisional and interpreting power constitutes authority or, at least, the appearance of authority. As William Bullock, Vice President of Operations for Lockheed Aeronautical Systems, noted:[7]

> "In large organizations, all employees tend to listen to the people that they work for. They pay attention to, and are responsive to, the people they report to. Things that come to them from other areas are sometimes listened to but become somewhat academic."

The muddle in the middle determines what a strategy will look like when translated to action and also serves as the critical gatekeeper for upward information. Top management, often frustrated by the translation process and always looking for ways to reduce the cost of labor, has enthusiastically gone along. Top management, of course, is what determines what middle management will look like and have to work with. A critical point to bear in mind is that management is a function which can be performed by a variety of means. It does not have to be a person or even a fixed structure.

Middle management alternatives

If one is looking for a place to live, there are two basic options. One is to find an existing structure or design and to adapt to it. The other is to build a dwelling based on what best suits one's needs. It is the same when looking for a way to operate collectively, which often goes under the collective name of teams.

Efforts at team management often fail because they are not rationally conceived. They begin as ideal, even ideological structures and are stuck into the organization as a hot-house flower.* This begins the long and painful process of trying to make the team work. Sometimes little progress is made because the discussion centers around the team rather than the work. At some point, the team system goes through a renewal process, which is essentially an effort to get the organization back into some more productive mode and to alleviate the hard feelings that have built up.

The proper way to establish teams is first to understand the function, then to structure the work to accomplish that function. In that process of review, one will be able to determine who needs to do what when, etc. The requirements for information sharing and coordination become clear. If there is a supervisor, his or her role and responsibilities can be outlined in terms of work need, not positional prerogatives. In other words, the formation of a team should not start with empowerment but with (1) what it is to do (purpose), and (2) what is required to do it (enabling systems). Using this rational process is quite different than (1) establishing a team according to some model or other, and then (2) trying to find a way to make it work.

Teams properly fashioned can be quite effective as management. Indeed, one of the basic problems with teams is that they are usually thought of as groups of employees working together. A better way to conceptualize teams is as a collective manager, a group of people who together perform traditional management functions such as coordinating, planning, analyzing, etc. Viewed from this vantage, teams are not radical at all but are rather a more elegant form of management.

---

* This is something of a simplification regarding the creation of teams and why they seem to have so much trouble, but it does get to the heart of the matter in my mind. Other factors, such as departmental budgeting, inadequate systems support, and the failure by top management to understand the nature of organizational behavior are discussed elsewhere in this book.

On one occasion, a client was having difficulty with one of its packing houses. An initial assessment suggested the problem was the packing house manager. Subsequent assessment made it clear that the packing house manager needed to be replaced. Because experienced packing house managers were scarce, the client thought perhaps a bad one might be better than no manager at all. Having worked with the four area supervisors in the packing house, it seemed clear to me that they could run the packing house quite well by themselves if they worked as a team. The packing house manager was terminated, and the four supervisors developed a system of meeting three times a day to coordinate their work. The packing house quickly became the cleanest, most productive, and most preferred place to work in the organization.

Alas, the story does not have the happy ending of the team running the packing house happily ever after. The supervisors kept facing the problem of not being able to prepare their plant for the fruit runs because top management consistently failed to tell them what fruit was to be run. The supervisors learned what was to be run only when the trucks arrived for unloading. This often meant that the plant had to hurriedly re-gear from running, say, grapefruit, to running tangerines.

Under such firefighting conditions, a centralized authority is often the only thing that could pull the operation together, so a new packing house manager was hired. Fortunately, this one was quite good and appreciated the way the supervisors worked as a team. Over time, however, staffed changed and the operation reverted to its plantation style of management. When last I heard, the packing house was for sale and the company had filed for Chapter 11. Perhaps more team work at the top would have spared the company such trouble. Certainly, it would have spared them the need for an expensive packing house manager.

Since the tuition for this experience has been paid, one might look for the lessons. Two lessons that could be gleaned are*

1. Good management in the middle requires good management at the top.
2. Poor work processes require authority to work.

Inherent diversity of opinions

Teams will not cure the failures of upper management nor will they eliminate the contentions and conflicts inherent in any human enterprise. Rather, they can serve to utilize and channel the energy of diverse opinions into a focused and powerful goal-achieving force. As discussed in Chapter 8, the process of

---

* As discussed in the following chapter, authority-reliant management undermines quality work processes and, therefore, requires more authority to work.

converting ideas about the future to realities of the present requires a common effort, but it will always be the stuff of opinions as diverse as the people involved. Still, these opinions must be merged, blended, and adjusted to create a workable amalgam of shared, common sense effort.

Decisions, according to Peter Drucker in his *The Effective Executive*,[8] do not begin with facts but with opinions. Unless there is a disagreement of opinions no decision is called for. Further, he observed that decisions rarely involve situations where one course of action is right and the others wrong; rather, it is a choice among alternatives. People tend to vary and, hence, disagree, in their perception, assessment, judgment, and action because they apply different qualities of intellect, intuition, integrity, and passion to the issue at hand. Sometimes the goals themselves are contradictory, such as long-term growth and immediate profits. People can disagree in good faith and even disagree with themselves when they second-guess their own earlier decisions.

Common sense involves perception, assessment, judgment or selection, and rational action in the application of values to real-life situations. As such, it is the stuff of conflict and disagreement. While scientific management techniques can improve information processing, they will not change the highly judgmental way in which actions and their genesis and outcomes are viewed. Consider the deliberations of a city council as to whether to apply for a federal grant for the city. All save one advocated that the city apply, observing that the money was available and if they didn't get it, someone else would. The hold-out argued that he thought a major problem with the federal government today was that it was granting money it did not have, and by participating in the program the city became a part of the problem. Which position was the more rational? Which made the more sense? The answer could be either, depending upon the configuration of one's values, focus, assessment of impact, and primary concerns. One person's passionate conviction is another's lack of integrity and failure of intellect. Disagreement of opinion is so built into human affairs that we often disagree with ourselves, wishing today that we had acted differently yesterday.

Translation and organizational change

No organization," observes Quinn,[9] "no matter how brilliant, rational, or imaginative — could possibly foresee the timing, severity, or even the nature of ... events." What is required are

> "Successful strategies [that] constantly reassess the future, find new congruencies as events unfurl, and blend the organization's skills and resources into new balances of dominance and risk aversion as various forces intersect to suggest better — but never perfect — alignments.

> The process is dynamic, with neither a real beginning nor an end."

Quinn further states:[10]

> "Rarely [does] the total solution to a major strategic problem suddenly appear full blown, like Minerva from the brow of Jupiter. Instead early resolutions [are] likely to be partial, tentative, or experimental."

In such circumstances, the organization is in a constant state of adjustment of trying to maintain its existing commitments in the face of change and trying to adapt to the new strategies. A bedrock set of corporate values and a viable management ideology are necessary for the organization to adjust effectively. Translation, therefore, is not simply a matter of explaining management intent to staff, but of allowing staff at different levels the freedom and means to adjust in the most efficacious manner to the constant stream of changes they must deal with. Authoritarian management is absolutely at a loss even to understand this challenge, much less deal with it. An enlightened management would seem less likely to thrash an organization with ill-considered change programs than an authoritarian one that operates through a narrow and archaic framework.

Management often says that people are the most important asset, often just before the ax falls for downsizing or just plain cost-cutting. It has become something of a joke, much like the "check is in the mail" or "trust me". What is becoming more the consensus is that innovation and adaptation result from organizational properties, rather than technical ones or even the work of a few bright people. Innovation, in that it is properly focused and utilized, seems to be the product of an innovative culture that is also facilitative and enabling which translates organizational purpose into both strategic and situational actions in the face of changing needs and opportunities.

Based on an analysis of corporate innovation, an article in *Fortune* magazine observed that R&D expenditures were not the key to innovation. Instead, they concluded, that:[11]

> "[I]nnovation is a style of corporate behavior that's comfortable with, even aggressive about, new ideas, change, risk, and failure. And it must permeate a very wide swath of an organization in order to make a difference."

Factors such as technology, market access, and natural resources traditionally have been considered the primary competitive advantages, but in the modern world this may not be enough. Professor Edward E. Lawler, III, after a comprehensive study of organization effectiveness in the face of changing conditions, noted that the organization itself can be the critical competitive advantage. Modern management systems and work processes enable a company to perform in a way that traditional bureaucracies cannot.[12]

The challenge of management today is change, but not just change. It is finding ways to turn the natural dynamic of change into a constant stream of improvements while, at the same time, maintaining a daily operation. In the effort to establish and maintain organizational excellence of knowledge, there is the need for an ongoing review of new challenges and opportunities in terms of the present. The learning process must constantly address five questions:

1. What does accomplishing our purpose require that we do not have?
2. What are we doing now that is of a cost-benefit for accomplishing our purpose?
3. What are we doing now that is not cost-beneficial for achieving our purpose?
4. What do we need to change and what is the best way?
5. What do we need to do to optimize what we are doing now that we want to keep?

Change management focuses on the first question, but excellent knowledge must address them all. An open organization that effectively translates intent into action does not stem from a manager merely saying "tell me if you hear anything" but rather from a constant dynamic of interactions which make common sense determinations about what is observed, what is needed, and what will be done by all parties of an organization. The manager needs to participate as a coach, keeping authority in his or her pocket as much as possible in order to optimize employee value-add through effective translation of purpose to practice. In that way, the organization can constantly adjust and adapt itself to pursue its intentions and avoid the twin plagues of organizational rigidity and organizational creep. In that way the organization can maintain a an effective fit between its efforts and the market.

Need for new concepts of hierarchy

Undoubtedly, middle management is the key to successful improvement and, undoubtedly, many organizations are overstaffed in this area. On the other hand, flattening an organization poses considerable risk by seriously impairing the organization's ability to connect strategy and practical, ordinary action. That most organizational problems can be attributed to this very failing ("We have a communications problem!") does not obviate the fact that eliminating essential capability will hardly improve things.

The understanding of conceptual and particular knowledge provides a basis for management to take appropriate actions, such as training and orientation, so that the remaining layers can make the necessary translations from the ideal to the pragmatic, whatever the organizational design. And, whatever the design, it is doubtful that an organization will exist for long without an effective hierarchy of translation and decisional authority.

On one occasion, I was asked to assist a chemical plant with its team-management system. The system had been established about 5 years prior and was designed by the workforce. The roll-out occurred one day when all of the supervisors were asked to leave the plant and the employees took over. The supervisors were told to find something productive to do. As one might imagine, there were 5 years of grief such that at one point more than 40% of the employees were involved in the employee assistance program.

The new president asked me "to find out what the hell is going on and some way to make it work." While there were problems aplenty, a fundamental one was that there was no hierarchical structure to connect the organization to itself. The teams had no official leader, only a person they would send to meetings to report back. The different plant areas (operations, maintenance, engineering, and administration) had no coordinating bodies for their proper management, nor was there anybody to coordinate the several areas into a plant-wide operation.

The new organization design involved establishing team leadership which, in turn, comprised area councils to coordinate the work for each area and make area-wide decisions. These area councils, in turn, formed a plant-wide council which operated under the authority of the chief operating officer. It could, therefore, make those decisions that were plant-wide. Thus, while there was a clear hierarchy to organize the work of the plant and to make appropriate decisions at various levels, there was no "boss" in that every person, in a real sense, worked for himself through the elected and appointed team leaders.

There were a number of particulars to the structure, but the main point is that there are a number of ways to perform hierarchical functions. They need not be autocratic, isolating, and stultifying but can be dynamic and serve to integrate the organization. The guiding principle should be form follows function, not form gives function fits.

Performance-based design

If the muddle in the middle is a sort of Bermuda Triangle for management intentions, it is usually because top management has failed the first rule for organizational leadership: "The team starts here." In most hierarchies, the complaints and frustrations of people at every level sound amazingly just like those expressed at every other level, which demonstrates that threats run downhill, among other things. The product is fear, and the product of fear is defensive posturing and curtailment of communications, the product of which is irrationality of operation.

The paradox may be that, with the advent of e-mail and increasingly uninhibited communication throughout the organization, some sort of hierarchy may become even more important to ensure the needed quality of information, decision making, and assessment of effort. This cannot be done by old-style authority, however, but only through leadership and systems that provide the necessary forums for organizational dialog. Decisions made throughout the hierarchy must be performance based, i.e., rationally optimizing work to achieve the organization's intentions, rather than being authority based.

Performance-basing is when decisions are made on the basis of how their outcome will accomplish the organizational purpose. Optimum efficiency, and likely effectiveness as well, occurs when decisions are made at the closest competent level. Authority-based management tries to raise the level of the decision, while performance-based management strives to enable competence at the closest place to the action. Management has created the proper organization when the management hierarchy is not a rigid order of feudal lords, suspicious and fearful of their vassals, but rather a fluid community of coaches and players who are committed to helping their teams achieve excellence.

Endnotes

1. Quinn, James B., *Strategies for Change: Logical Incrementalism*, Irwin, Homewood, IL, 1980, p. 257.
2. Drucker, Peter, *The Effective Executive*, Harper & Row, New York, 1966, p. 16.
3. Larkin, T. J., and Sandra Larkin, *Communicating Change: Winning Employee Support for New Business Goals*, McGraw-Hill, New York, 1994.
4. See, for example, Walters, Jonathan, Flattening bureaucracy, *Governing*, March, 20–24, 1996.
5. Clifford, Mark, How far will South Korea go?, *World Press Review*, April, 50, 1988 (from *Far Eastern Economic Review*).
6. Maurer, Rick, *Caught in the Middle: A Leadership Guide for Partnership in the Workplace*, Productivity Press, Cambridge, MA, 1989.
7. Quoted in Caroselli, Marlene, *Total Quality Transformations*, Human Resource Development Press, Amherst, MA, 1991, p. 213.
8. Drucker, Peter, *The Effective Executive*, Harper & Row, New York, 1967, pp. 143–165.
9. Quinn, James B., *Strategies for Change: Logical Incrementalism*, Irwin, Homewood, IL, 1980, p. 53.
10. Quinn, James B., *Strategies for Change: Logical Incrementalism*, Irwin, Homewood, IL, 1980, p. 115.

11. O'Reilly, Brian, The secrets of America's most admired corporations: new ideas and new products, *Fortune,* March 3, 60–64, 1997.
12. Lawler, III, Edward E., *From the Ground Up: Six Principles for Building the New Logic Corporation,* Jossey-Bass, San Francisco, 1996.

Part IV

Management, leadership, and organizational performance

Chapter thirteen: Leadership, coaching, and quality
What effective coaching and leadership must have
Leadership style and leadership substance are essentially the same thing. The key to understanding leadership, however, is found less in personality inventories than in what others require of a leader — specifically, honesty and the ability to help others succeed.

Chapter fourteen: Leadership and motivation
Why leadership, motivation, and organizational excellence are essentially the same thing
Leadership and motivation operate in three areas — purpose, systems, and effort. These are also the basic aspects of any enterprise. Managerial leadership is successful when it motivates people to discipline themselves for the energetic pursuit of the organizational goals.

Chapter fifteen: Common sense management
Why common sense is the essence of good management
There are many forces that can pull an organization away from the effective pursuit of its goals. Organizations become irrational when they are no longer in optimal pursuit of these goals and fall into a struggle over urgencies rather than a striving to fulfill priorities. Only when the purpose is clear and compelling, and the systems rational, can people have the focus and generate the emotional energy required for high performance.

chapter thirteen

Leadership, coaching, and quality

What effective leadership and coaching must have

Great thoughts reduced to practice become great acts.
          ◡William Hazlitt

There is no single element in an organization as important as its leadership. Anyone who was in the military can remember the difference that a commanding officer made in the morale and quality of the unit. The tone and climate set at any level essentially sets it for the organization from there on down the hierarchy and to tangential elements as well. Because this importance is recognized, although not always fully appreciated, much attention has been paid to leadership in general and top leadership in particular. A great deal of this attention has concerned leadership style, management style, behavioral style, personal style, etc., all of which mean essentially the same thing. Whatever the instrument used, whether it is looking for Driver-Expressives, Intuitive Thinkers, Investigative Realists, or Analytical Pragmatists, they measure some typical responses by a person in given situations based upon some set of behavioral categories. The defining nature of such inventories invariably finds a plausible, self-validating place for everyone in their categories.

Leadership style and all that

There is much discussion of management style and behavioral style, but the terms are unfortunate because, like most pop jargon, they seem to trivialize the subject. Style is not an aspect of managing, it essentially *is* managing. "Style" is another name for personality, that is, how a person typically behaves. A person who has a listening style opens up communications and is much more informed. Someone with a coaching style coaches. Sometimes people confuse a style with a technique which, when used with regularity, becomes a part of one's style. For example, a manager who asks each department head at the end of every staff meeting what he or she has done in the past week to improve operations moves the organization toward a continuous improvement posture. This technique is ludicrous, however, if the manager does not listen to the answers given or yells and screams about issues. When styles are not consistent with techniques used, one will be judged as having a cynical style.

Style theory holds that people have preferred styles, and they choose the kind of work they do because it lets them operate in a certain way. Groups of attorneys, accountants, engineers, human resource managers, computer programmers, and, yes, even management consultants seem to have many personality traits in common. It is not surprising, for example, that on the Kirton Scale operating managers tend to be adaptive (maintenance oriented), as is the average population, while consultants tend to be innovative (change oriented). These findings make sense since the great bulk of the work of most managers is to keep the process flowing, while that of consultants is to look for things that can be changed, preferably for the better.

One cause of vocational unhappiness is when the nature of the job and one's favored way of operating are not in harmony. Technical people can go crazy when concrete problems are discussed in other than technical and pragmatic terms, while systems- and process-oriented people may see the focus on mere technical problems as missing the point. Human resource people may seem too "touchy-feely" for some, and intuitive feelers sometimes can't get away from being fascinated with the vision itself rather than how to realize it.

People who are predisposed to change things and have a more modern view of the world are also inclined to try quality improvement activities. In one instance, when a group of managers from a manufacturing company visited Milliken, those who were predisposed toward improvement found much at Milliken to support their ideas, while those who were less inclined to change expressed that "Milliken is different from us" and it "won't work at our place."[1]

Style inventories, such as DISC and Myers-Briggs, help people understand their own styles and that of others. In that these inventories and related exercises help people understand and respect their differences and enable them to operate better with different kinds of personalities, they can be powerful developmental tools. To the extent that they are offered as an organizational development approach, however, managers should be wary. While being made aware and being appreciative of the legitimately different ways we think about things is a beneficial part of a development program, the primary focus for quality improvements must be on the work processes and their systems, of which individual personalities are just a part.

What leaders must *do*

Leadership training, while useful, tends to over-promise as well. The skills and traits that instructors attempt to inculcate into aspiring leaders, such as being organized, honest, nice, and a good listener, etc., are certainly pluses for anyone who works with people. But that is the point — they are good for *anyone* who works with other people and are not particular qualities of leadership. And, while it is true that leadership is a relationship, it is a special relationship that involves special expectations among the parties. In their book, *The Leadership Challenge*, Kouzes and Posner reported on their survey of 1500 managers that asked them what they looked for in leaders. The top four qualities that they wanted in a superior were (in order of response frequency) that they be honest, competent, forward-looking, and inspiring. There were 221 other qualities, but the scores fell off dramatically after these top four.

The idea of being forward-looking and inspiring relates directly to an ability to provide an effective vision. The role of a leader in providing an inspiring purpose becomes increasingly important as each leader moves up the organization. Each elevation brings broader and more general responsibilities and, commensurably, the need to provide more general statements of purpose and translation of that purpose for increasingly diverse constituencies. One of the tests for promotion should be an ability to articulate a broader purpose and what it means to those who work with more particular or tangential applications. According to Walter Bennis,[2] people want four things from their leaders:

> "They want *direction and meaning* — a sense of purpose, a sense of vision — a set of beliefs and convictions. They want leaders to be purveyors of hope and optimism — they have to get people to buy into the future. And finally, they want *results*." [Emphasis added.]

"Results" means "competence" and has to do with an ability to engender effective and rational systems. As responsibilities become more general, the expectations of competence increasingly concern one's abilities in regard to human operating systems rather than the technical system. The need for competence increasingly refers to managerial skills and leadership rather than technical prowess. Indeed, continued reliance on high technical involvement becomes a form of overcontrol and usually results in poorly developed subordinates. In an open system with a team-like atmosphere, colleagues will usually help one another (including superior managers when they are seen as colleagues) in areas of competence, assuming the elements of shared purpose and trust are in place. In a more restrictive authoritarian environment, however, information that would have been helpful is often cut off, and management competence problems are not as easily corrected.

Honesty first

More than anything else, however, people want honesty, without which they will give little credence to a person's supposed beliefs and convictions. In a study of employee attitudes about recognition programs, Disney World found that what employees really wanted most was sincerity in any recognitions.[3] Honesty is so important as a quality of leaders that it was rated one half again as important in the Kouzes and Posner study as competence. People can be forgiven a great deal if they are seen as a good-faith colleague and honest broker when forces contend for favors and spoils of profit are to be shared.

Where honesty is suspect, however, trust suffers, and consequently the entire organization is impaired. Jack Welch, CEO of General Electric, believes that the only way to create trust is by "laying out values and then walking the talk." Dave Thomas, founder of Wendy's International, stated that honesty is the first ingredient among those that he feels are necessary for success. Other studies validate the insights of Welch and Watson and the findings of Kouzes and Posner. A study by the American Institute for Research found that one of the key elements for success in quality initiatives was "walking the talk" by "providing commitment through action."[4]

Honesty, however, is not something that someone has but rather what someone does; it is a way of dealing with oneself and with others. Like so many virtues that seem simple at first glance and are often treated simplistically, honesty is the product of other qualities such as courage, determination, hard work, and reasonable competence. A person who lacks courage will not hold the proper line when under pressure, a person who does not work hard will constantly find himself in positions where all the choices involve betraying someone who trusted him, and a person without competence is likely to let people down eventually. One might think honesty to be the easiest of the qualities to display, but it apparently is one of the most difficult.

When trust is a problem in an organization, questions of management's competence, character, and caring are the cause. To the degree that trust is lacking, an organization cannot be optimally managed. The reason is simple, but not obvious: In a complex, fast-changing, and wide-ranging world, much of what goes on in an organization must be taken on faith. The rational linkage between practical applications and proper purpose often has to be taken on faith because it cannot be directly or fully observed.

Without trust there is no faith, and without faith people redefine practicality in self-serving terms rather than in the best interests of the organization. Faith tells us that we can take communication at face value, while mistrust moves us to look at the real meaning behind every statement or action for an explanation that is plausible and satisfying to each person's common sense assessment. People begin to move away from a shared common sense toward other directions and into defensive positions. Rationality begins to dissipate, and organizational ligatures begin to dissolve. More authority is required to move an ever more passive-aggressive workforce, and, despite some occasional promising results, quality and efficiency evaporate.

Honest demands

Once they trust a leader, people can be inspired by being challenged to meet a worthwhile goal in a way that tests their abilities. That is what makes for interesting work. People tend to be proud of what they can do and want to show it off. The also expect some recognition for their work, even if it is only recognition as a member of the team, as an adult, and as getting a fair share of the earnings. The diesel mechanic is not much different than a professional ballplayer in this regard. In discussing Peter Drucker's metaphor of a CEO being like a musical conductor, jazz musician Gary Burton gave examples in support of the similarities. He noted that:[5]

> "[T]he best jazz musicians wanted to play with Miles [Davis] because they knew he could get them to go places musically that they wouldn't be able to go to otherwise. He would sign up the biggest stars to play with him, encourage them to do their best work, and be strong enough himself to bring them all together and meld them into a cohesive group. *As demanding and intimidating as he was, it was worth it.*" [Emphasis added.]

Good people rise to a challenge when they can get a fair test of their abilities, especially when working with someone from whom they can learn and with whom they can achieve greatly. That is why Robert Crandall, CEO of American Airlines and called "the Darth Vader of the airline industry, the nastiest guy in a nasty business," steered his company into one of the few profitable airlines in the early 1990s, just as has Herb Kelleher, CEO of Southwest Airlines, who, in contrast, has been called "the closest thing to a hero."[6] These two airlines, with so different a leadership (Herb Kelleher seems much more huggable than Robert Crandall), continue to be ranked the top two airlines by both customers and competitors.[7]

Some of the most successful sports coaches were men who were known as being tough, such as Bear Bryant, Vince Lombardi, and Mike Ditka, or who were gracious and soft-spoken such as John Wooden of UCLA. Some had serious personal problems, such as Billy Martin of the New York Yankees, but still led their teams to success. There is no doubt that, all things being equal, a person who rated high in all of the personal qualities and human relations virtues would have the advantage over most of the rest of us lesser beings. But all things are not equal, and people will forgive a great deal if they have trust and confidence in a person. The path for normal people to being good leaders does not require sainthood to proceed nor does it require training by people who may not really have a clue about what leading people is all about.

If someone wants to know how to be a good leader, then one might do worse than to emulate the principles of good coaching. People may not be committed to leaders personally, but people will commit to the enterprise, to its purpose, and feel good about doing their jobs. It is precisely by denying this opportunity for commitment and satisfaction in meeting that commitment, by frustrating efforts through irrational management, that morale problems are caused. Crandall is a competitor, as is Kelleher, and they promise that their team will win. That they go about it differently, like Vince Lombardi and John Wooden, does not mean they are not effective leaders.

Coaching to win

Coaching, in management, has come to mean either dealing with employees who are having trouble or has become so trivialized as to mean not using a master-sergeant style. It is easy, therefore, for serious managers to overlook what coaches actually do and how it is similar to what managers should do. Consider the tale of two different basketball coaches. One coached for a basketball powerhouse that was now losing. During the coach's Sunday television review of a loss the night before, the show host asked the coach what went wrong. "They just didn't do what I told them to do," declared the coach. "And what did you tell them to do?" the host asked. "I told them," the coach replied as everyone leaned closer to hear to words of basketball wisdom, "to go out there and *win!*" In addition to being ridiculous, this is a classic example of Deming's anathema of "exhortation".

In contrast, a more useful and Deming-like example of coaching is that of John Wooden, one of the greatest basketball coaches of all time, who was asked during a television interview if he put a lot of emphasis on winning. His reply was that he "never emphasized winning because that is something you can't control." Rather, he emphasized performance and worked to "get the players to do the best they are capable of." The critical role of coaches is not to scream at players and officials and throw their hats and towels, although that may be what most comes to mind. The coach's job is exactly like that of managers — to translate the purpose of the team (winning, however defined) into appropriate effort (performing at one's best). No coach in his right mind would waste player talent by not using them fully or be satisfied with compliance rather than whole-hearted effort.

When the game is truly understood and winning is the aim, each person is expected to do his or her best, and systems are set up to do that. It is this challenge for excellence that makes sports fun and, indeed, ennobling. The advice that a manager's job is to set the goals but not tell people how to do them is gratuitous, facile, and, indeed, irresponsible, which is why managers tend to ignore it. Empowerment as a concept fails because no manager wants to be in a position of helplessly watching employees get off the track. When taken in the context of coaching, i.e., translating purpose to action, one can see the object is not to let go completely, but rather to *work more closely* with employees.

Coaches do not try to make people productive because that is how the entire system is measured; instead, they try to get them to perform at their best. They don't empower players; they enable them through decision-making authority, equipment, training, plays, teammates, and in all the other ways that support performance. They don't think about quality, although they use the word a lot like everyone else; they look at how each player and activity is a value-add in terms of the team's purpose.

The essential job of a coach is to pursue effective strategies and develop players by example and instruction. Chip Bell,[8] in *Managers as Mentors*, observes, "Most leaders are conditioned to drive the process of learning." He warns, however, that "mentors who attempt to hold, own, or control the process deprive it of the freedom needed to foster discovery." Imagine a coach who fails to debrief players during and after a game, takes advantage of their insight, and changes his or her own way of performance as necessary. What are the winning prospects of a coach who spends all the training money on himself rather than on the players?

Su Hua Newton, CEO of Newton Vineyards, recognized that the work of those who had the hardest and dirtiest jobs, such as pickers and barrel cleaners, were the key to good winemaking. She gave her workers samples of the best wines and some of the worst to show them what they were trying to accomplish. She knows, as a manager, that "your dream must become their dream ... something to take pride in."

Fidelity's Edward Johnson and Microsoft's Bill Gates are two CEOs who have been styled as a rare combination of nerd and predator.[9] They both have a tough competitive spirit and a thorough knowledge of the game, two qualities good coaches must have. Keeping the purpose in mind is important for a coach, and the players for that matter, but no less so is knowing the game. They study it, think about it, even enjoy it in their spare time, and inspire the players to do the same. It is the same for managers and the game of organizational performance. The coach and manager who already know it all are likely on the path to losing through accumulated ignorance. Being prepared, even eager to learn, takes a genuine self-confidence that comes across as courage and honesty. It is also a necessary ingredient to help others succeed, for every teacher is a learner in the process. Failing to teach, on the other hand, only reinforces one's own limitations which, over time, become a form of ignorance.

Price of power

Common sense tells any true leader that there is always the fiddler to be paid for the dance. Managers can choose to pay up front for quality through organizational rationality or later for quality failures because of insufficient rationality. Many small businesses are still family owned and managed, and the biggest obstacle for them to move into the realm of effective modern, professional management is the feeling that "it is my company, everything here is mine, and, therefore, I should be able to do what I want." One would have to agree with these statements, but the point one needs to recognize is that there is a cost to this benefit. One should not expect things for free in their operation that can only be purchased by practicing self-restraint, letting others feel a part of things, and establishing the conditions for rational management. Managers need to recognize that what they see in their operation is a reflection of what they have done, and, in that regard, an organization is like a giant mirror.

To change the image requires not a change in mirrors but a change in what one projects by what one does. That is another, if not the most fundamental, problem in quality improvement programs — managers want everyone else to change but not themselves. The payoff in such cases is often cynical compliance and passive aggression, not operational optimization. It is management who must be the first to change, to demonstrate what kinds of changes are expected, to be honest and lead by example. Moreover, management may have to demonstrate these changes for quite awhile to show that these changes are here to stay and are not just another program. This, of course, means that management must really be prepared to stay its course. If management were merely to do this one thing, to demonstrate what it wants rather than just preach or demand it, they would see the organization respond quickly and profoundly as people begin to trust in their competence and character.

The way that managers demonstrate these things is by (1) following an articulated purpose with (2) rational systems. The employees will then provide the proper effort because leadership has provided them the opportunity to accomplish their purpose. Lest one think that this is Pollyanna-ish, it is important to remember that one of the most critical systems is performance management. It is the absence of an effective performance management that causes employee disenchantment, not its use. Expectations are often not clear, pay is not on the basis of performance, good feedback from supervisors is rare (and then it is mostly negative), and performance problems are scanned for blame not causes. This, of course, is the antithesis of quality. When I interviewed disgruntled union members in a northern manufacturing facility, the chief criticism was that management was not doing its job because good performers went unrecognized and poor performers got away with it.

Responsibility and power

The first thing that managers need to do is to empower themselves, which requires two things. One is to dedicate themselves to the craft of management, striving to learn its modern subtleties and complexities. Being a professional means dedication, study, hard work, and high standards, whether coaching, managing, or engineering. This means learning the paradigms of modern management and growing away from the old simplistic, mechanistic, and flat-Earth ideologies. As Robert Fritz observed in his *The Path of Least Resistance:*[10]

> "One of the fundamental principles is that there is a direct connection between what occurs in your consciousness and what occurs in your external life, and that if you initiate change internally a corresponding change will happen externally. You go through life taking the path of least resistance. The underlying structure determines the pattern of least resistance. We can change fundamental underlying structures of our lives. ...Everything has an underlying unifying structure. Even though you may not consciously think about structure, you presume. You presume that a building will be structured with walls, floors, ceilings, windows, corridors, stairs, elevators, lighting, etc."

In management, the primary underlying structures are behavioral.

The second critical step a manager must take for self-empowerment is to avoid blaming everyone else for problems and take responsibility for them. Disavowing responsibility for which one is supposedly charged is the mark of a poor leader, such as the supervisor who complained that he had "a guy who works for me that has not been worth a damn for the past six years." By accepting responsibility and fault and recognizing that the problems one faces stem "from what I have done or failed to do," one can make things different in the future by doing something different now. As Ernest Hemingway in his novel, *Green Hills of Africa,* said after missing an easy shot at game, "Every damn thing is your own fault, if you're any good."[11]

It is Zen-like, but one is thus empowered and unbound by the charge of responsibility. The courage to accept fault moves the blame-taker from whiner to winner; it puts the person in a position of handling rather than having problems. It is an act of courage that is not only a test of a manager's character, but is also the *sine qua non* of quality improvement in an organization. Many of those who advocate particular approaches to management improvement recognize this critical element in management. Most are familiar with Deming's 14 points, but even lesser known approaches argue for this requirement, such as cycle-time management, which notes the need for management to keep its promises, to be willing to stick it out when it runs into trouble, and not to "avoid blame with CYA memos."[12]

Managers must lose their fear of employees and focus more on success and less on avoidance. One can only earn trust by trusting, and managers must overcome the fear of being taken advantage of. As James Autrey, speaking at an ASQC Quality Forum, noted:[13]

> "Of everything I have discussed, trust is the most dif-
> ficult. Managers are fearful that if they trust people,
> they will be taken advantage of — that their trust will
> be abused. *Well, of course it will.* But if that is your worry
> as a leader, then you're not a leader, because to move
> from manager to leader requires you to let go of your
> ego. An employee who abuses trust won't last long
> anyway. Don't waste your time trying to be in the
> police business, defining the job of management as
> waiting for someone to goof up so you'll have some-
> thing to do."

One can observe that the fear that one may be taken advantage of can reach almost pathological proportions as managers attempt to write intricate "gotcha" rules for such irritants as, say, misuse of sick leave. If such problems are widespread, then rules will not save the situation, for there is a more pervasive and pernicious problem in the organization. Usually it is a few employees, and, rather than deal with the malefactors directly, management tries to impose rules that do their job for them. This blindness to the general level of employee performance almost qualifies as an individual pathology and, by treating all employees as the worst ones, serves to create an organizational pathology. Common sense, however, would suggest that, while some people (including the suspicious manager) may take advantage of the company in some way at some time, one should not shoot oneself in the foot because of it.

A more healthy and productive approach is that of Hewlett-Packard, which deals immediately with problems. Lewis Platt, CEO of HP, notes that "people don't make it here because they don't have the right attitude, ... dedication, ... [or] don't fit into our culture." In general, however, HP operates on a different principle from most:[14]

> "If you create an environment with a fair amount of
> freedom, employees usually become more committed
> and responsible. ...[E]mployees are not going to take
> advantage of it. As you give more freedom, employees

usually become more committed to their jobs and often
take on new responsibilities."

The key, according to Platt, is mutual trust and understanding.

An often-expressed concern of managers is how to motivate employees. This is appropriate considering quality is a function of the care and diligence of how the work is done which, in turn, is a function of how workers work. As Dr. Su Hua Newton observed: "The executive suite can dream, but at the end of the day the rank and file have created the reality; what people do is the only thing that matters." Walt Disney expressed the same judgment on several occasions: "You can dream, create, design, and build the most wonderful place in the world ... but it requires people to make the dream a reality."[15]

The best effort, however, is hardly given by a compliant person, only by a motivated one, and getting that best effort is the job of management. It seems that everybody wants to go to heaven but nobody wants to die, and wanting motivated workers is not the same thing as being prepared to do what is required to motivate them. Actually, people do not have to be motivated, because it is an intrinsic part of just being alive and sentient. The proper question is how to get this motivation focused, energized, and constantly applied to suit the needs of the organization. To address this question requires an understanding of the relationship between motivation and leadership, a subject to which we now turn.

Endnotes

1. Related in Drensek, Robert A., and Fred B. Grubb, Quality quest: one company's successful attempt at implementing TQM, *Quality Progress*, September, 91–94, 1995.
2. Bennis, Walter, Leadership matters, *Human Resource Executive*, December, 23, 1996.
3. Smith, Vernita C., Spreading the magic, *Human Resource Executive*, December, 31, 1996.
4. See Tichy, Noel, and Stratford Sherman, *Control Your Own Destiny or Someone Else Will*, Doubleday, New York, 1993; Thomas, Dave, and Ron Beyma, *Well Done! The Common Guy's Guide to Everyday Success*, Harper Collins, New York, 1994; American Institute of Research, *Winning Competitive Advantage: A Blended Strategy Works Best*, Zenger-Miller, San Jose, CA, 1995.
5. Schrage, Michael, The Gary Burton Trio: lessons on business from a jazz legend, *Fast Company*, December-January, 110–113, 1997.
6. See Petzinger, Jr., Thomas, *Hard Landing: the Epic Contest for Power and Profits That Plunged the Airlines into Chaos*, Times Books, New York, 1995.
7. See, for example, "Americans are more finicky than ever: industries ranked from best to worst in customer satisfaction" in *Fortune*, February 3, 108–111, 1997; "Where companies rank their own industries" in *Fortune*, March 3, F–1f, 1997.
8. Bell, Chip, *Managers as Mentors*, Barrett-Koehler, San Francisco, 1998.

9. See "A quiet passion for performance" in *Time*, September 30, 53, 1996.

10. Fritz, Robert, *The Path of Least Resistance*, Stillpoint Publishing, Salem, MA, 1984, pp. x and 6.

11. Hemingway, Ernest, *Green Hills of Africa*, Touchstone Books, New York, 1996.

12. See Northey, Patrick, and Nigel Southway, *Cycle-Time Management*, Productivity Press, Portland, OR, 1993, p. 88.

13. See Autrey, James, Love and profit: finding the balances in life and work, *Quality Progress*, January, 47–49, 1996.

14. Quoted in an interview by Karen Bemowski, Something old, something new, *Quality Progress*, October, 27–34, 1996.

15. Su Hua Newton, speaking at ASPC Quality Forum XII, October 3, 1996; Smith, Vernita C., Spreading the magic, *Human Resource Executive*, December, 28, 1996.

chapter fourteen

Leadership and motivation

Why leadership, motivation, and organizational excellence
are essentially the same thing

> *A dwarf on a giant's shoulders sees the farther of the two.*
> ∾George Herbert

Managers today are constantly admonished to exhibit leadership in order to better motivate the workforce. On the whole, managers try to be leaders, and most I have talked with think they are leaders, although others may not share that opinion. Certainly, most managers are constantly concerned about motivating the workforce, and no sensible manager would do anything designed to demotivate people, although that, in fact, is probably the problem that most plagues managers today.

Leadership has been the focus of study for as long as there has been language to talk about it. It is usually defined, when reduced to basics, as getting people to go along with some group effort. Also, leadership is almost invariably linked in some way to motivation, because if no one is following then one is not leading. While the linkage between leadership and motivation is assumed, it is not always clear. The belief that leadership is motivating or that motivation comes from leadership is, at best, an act of faith* and, at worst, begs the question. Leadership has been essentially defined as what a person does that motivates others to certain actions.

Managers, not really seeing the connection between the two, easily succumb to the more expedient exercise of authority. This is especially true when their own boss is arbitrary and authoritarian. Indeed, it may be required. They have seen it work in John Wayne or other action-hero movies, as an influential force that should not be underestimated. Many managers have also found that their best bosses have been those who were firm and decisive, attributes which can too easily become the crutch of authority-reliance with all of the problems it brings.

---

* Here, "faith" means strong hope by managers, not the strong belief of some writers.

As one manager said, after a discussion about the leadership training at his corporation's university, "Sometimes you just have to pound it into their heads!" Here was a bright person, well schooled in all of the latest theories of leadership and motivation and wanting to do the right thing. Still, he thought that to really get the job done you had to revert to issuing orders backed up by threats. Clearly, this manager had neither the faith in nor true understanding of the linkage between the prescriptions for proper leadership behavior and the motivation of his workers. Had this intelligent manager understood the relationship between leadership and motivation, he would have better understood the relationship between his actions and their impact on his staff.

Motivation as a field of study probably began with Maslow's hierarchy of needs, moved forward with Herzberg's satisfier-motivator model, and today has become an avalanche of studies and ruminations. Most managers have been exposed to many of these studies or suggestions in college management courses, professional workshops, or in management books and journals. Sometimes managers use these principles and devise better ways to motivate employees, such as in behavioral-based safety programs. Just as often, however, when managers attempt to use these lessons in the workplace, they soon find themselves falling back on "pounding it into their heads".

Elements of motivation

Motivation is whatever goes on in a person's mind that causes them do something. It is a common sense response to that person's environment. If the response appears inappropriate to the stimulus, as most others perceive things, we think there is something wrong with that person. When a challenge is before us we consider a possible action based on:

1. Its desirability
2. Our confidence in doing it
3. The worth of the effort or cost-benefit

If it is desirable, we have confidence in our ability to do it, and if it is worth it, we will make an effort. If it is of little value to us, we do not think we can do it, or if it is not worth the effort, we will not do it or not do it very well. In other words, we are not motivated. Motivation is, of course, more complicated than that because there are many things competing for our attention. Work and social situations change, and we change in our interests, energy levels, etc. Still, these three requirements of motivation must be sufficiently met if we are to act.

If someone makes us do something by offering rewards we want or must have, penalties we want to avoid, or a combination of the two, we will comply to a degree and for a duration commensurate with our wants. We will give what we must and reserve all of the rest for ourselves. That is what Joseph Juran meant by his observation that "the major underemployed asset in the U.S. is the education, experience, and creativity of the workforce."[1] The object of leadership is not to be a nice guy but to acquire this available, but not employed, discretionary effort by the workforce. Leadership, from this perspective, is not an option of good management but a critical requirement if the company is to get its money's worth from its people.*

Management and leadership

If motivation** has the three aspects noted above, leadership must connect meaningfully with these areas. While motivation is a function of desire, confidence, and cost-benefit, leadership is an appropriate combination of:

1. Presenting a vision of a desired or preferred situation
2. Offering a promising and cost-beneficial means to realize that vision
3. Making available the incentives that make the effort worthwhile

One can immediately see the symmetry between leadership and motivation. Since leadership is usually defined in terms of motivation, this fit should not be surprising. To understand how they actually work together, however, we must look at the basics of any enterprise, which are

1. Purpose, i.e., what one hopes to achieve or even why the enterprise exists
2. System or process, i.e., how one is supposed to accomplish the purpose
3. Effort, i.e., how well and how vigorously one will use these processes to pursue the purpose

Formulating and inculcating commitment to the organizational purpose is what we call leadership. Establishing and maintaining appropriate and

---

* Here is another example of how our language helps and hinders us. We devised the concept of "leadership" to identify those elements that seem to be missing from much of the old plantation approach to management but, having done that, find it difficult to integrate it into the concept of management.

** Whenever one person attempts to influence the behavior of another, whether it is to get them to buy a car, loan money, go to the movies, or be more diligent on the job, it always involves the same principles of social psychology. Because the behavior is the same, studies of behavior in management, organizations, public administration, communications, marketing and consuming, and other areas of social interaction are based on many of the same basic concepts and methodologies. The division in these areas today is more the product of institutional academic vested interests than the organization of knowledge today.

Table 1 Symmetric Fit of Managerial Leadership and Motivation

Enterprise	Managerial leadership	Organizational translation chain	Workforce motivation
Purpose	Vision of desired new state	Strategic vision or purpose	Shared vision of desired new state
Systems, processes, including incentives	Means to accomplish Information Rewards, incentives	Translation Translation Translation	Confidence in means Knowledge Cost-benefit
Effort	Assessment of effort	Particular effort	Effort

effective systems and processes are what we call management. Together they comprise management's true job, which is *managerial leadership*.

One can now see the common elements begin to form, but there is one other aspect that must be added for any complex operation, that is, the organization itself. The basic function of the organization is to translate strategic concepts (in the form of mission and goals) to particular work (in the form of technical and particular knowledge). Excellent knowledge occurs when the conceptual knowledge of strategic purpose properly fits with the technical and particular knowledge to do excellent work at any given level and area of the organization. When this function is added, one has a model of managerial leadership in actualizing the enterprise as organizational performance. (See Table 1.)

Translation and common sense

There may be some dramatic decisional events, but the translation of purpose to action is an endless stream of essentially routine activity that occurs whether management chooses to make a decision or not. Rumors exist in the absence of good information, and improvisations occur in the absence of clear guidance for the work at hand. Decisions are actualized in the countless particular common sense determinations made by everyone in the organization. These, in total, determine what the organization does.

People are constantly being stimulated by one thing or another and constantly make decisions as to what the stimulus means, such as whether they will give it any attention, what they will do about it and when, and so forth. An employee's being late for work can serve as an example of how these faculties determine a work decision. If one employee is late frequently, this is an individual performance question. When the situation is widespread, however, it may be a failure of organizational common sense. For example, what is "on time" and what is "late"? Does "on time" mean being

Table 2 Common Sense Assessment of Being On Time

Intellect	They say be at your desk at 8:00 a.m., but a lot of people aren't here until 8:15 and no one says anything.
Intuition	If I'm at my desk at 8:10, no one will say anything — or — They don't really care if you are here at 8:00 or not.
Passion	I don't really care, because they don't appreciate it if you are here at 8:00, anyway.
Valuation	My job is to do what they say, and apparently they think it is okay to come in at 8:15. If the boss is satisfied, then I've done what I'm supposed to do. It is only right considering how they ... [go back to intellect for some rationalization].

at one's place and working, or being in the building, or being on the premises? Is still getting coffee okay? An employee might make the common sense assessment provided in Table 2.

There are many examples of this kind of thinking by employees for which they are condemned, even though they may be responding to management messages sent through management actions. The following are not uncommon:

- "Management talks about safety, but they want production."
- "Management talks about customer service, but, if I break some piddly company rules in the process, I am in trouble."
- "Management doesn't really care about employees. They want loyalty, but don't give any."

The centrality of purpose

All rationality begins with purpose, whether express or assumed. It is by our perceived purpose, our interpreted impact on the world, that we are defined. Employees are generally pleased by the purpose of their company and would gladly work toward fulfilling it if given a chance. Work divorced from productive purposes becomes justified by common sense assessments such as "it is what we do" and "that's what the boss wants", hardly a perspective for quality improvement. Moreover, all things have multiple purposes, e.g., mine, the team's, and the company's. It is the job of management and a function of leadership to make the organizational purposes clear and meaningful and to show employees how these purposes are to be translated into practice.

When we know the purpose of something we are more prepared to understand it, relate to it, and assess its utility. Utility, however, is not inherent in something; rather, we place the utility upon it. For example, a bee serves one purpose for the hive but another for a flower and still another for a hungry spider. The purposes of people are usually a part of their several roles, such as employee, accountant, colleague, supervisor, member of the quality team, headquarters staff, friend, minority member, etc. The people involved in each of these roles see the person differently. It is also through these roles that one becomes a person rather than just a biological organism. A beehive also has different purposes for the bees, beekeepers, and bears, although all involve honey. Likewise, an organization has multiple purposes which differ for each participant, whether staff, customer, vendor, or share-holder.

A group's purpose is the cohesive force that brings about that collective discipline we call an organization. Perhaps what separates our species most from all the others is our ability to envision some new or different situation and then to work toward realizing that vision. We can imagine and create new realities because we have the power to create our own purposes and definitions of our efforts. Leading scientists are those who offer seminal works that open up new possibilities of knowledge that others will explore.

Managerial leaders are those who provide new possibilities of accom-plishment which include a purpose and a way to get there. As their compa-nies make innovations in products, services, markets, or processes, corporate leaders can become industry leaders as well. That is the essence of leadership — imagining new possibilities and creating new realities. The fulfillment of purpose, be it a real estate development or a door knob, is to change the world in a way that it would not otherwise be.

Purpose and priorities

An organization's purpose, strategies to accomplish them, and the way in which each person's work fits into them should be discernible at any point in an operation. It has been said that an organization is holographic in that the whole system can be seen in any of its parts, and there is some truth in that. When the job of the loading supervisor is to make sure that those trees get to the customer in good condition, one knows a great deal about this supervisor and what purposes of the company are in his mind. One should be able to see the organizational purpose in every job; conversely, one should be able to anticipate the work of every person from knowing the company goals and values.

When the purpose, expressed as goals and values, is vague or absent things can get very messy. Study the focus of the engineering department of one company:[2]

> Without clear goals and objectives, priorities and strate-gies become meaningless and rational management is impossible. The problem of priorities can be appreciated

in the engineering department's efforts to service a large number of projects. Engineering has a list of 101 projects, according to one supervisor, and most of these are "number one priority". One supervisor's list was almost 85% number one priorities, and one half of these were "hot" number ones. Even so, they have not worked on many of these in months. An engineering supervisor argued that one "cannot have a priority for each project" so all have a number one priority.

With such as system, priority loses its meaning. The only purpose common sense allows is survival by dealing with the most urgent. This, of course, means whatever is most urgent to the boss at the time. Decisions have no rationality except to get through this situation and on to the next one, as one is forced to pick and choose the work based on the most immediate pressure. In this manner, the organization deteriorates until that is the only way it *can* operate; it is a problem that feeds on itself. In poorly managed operations such as this, everyone is incredibly busy but the job just never seems to get done. Everyone seems frustrated by not really being able to do anything well and some things never at all.

"There is always time to fix it," one often hears, "but never time to do it right." That is a warning that the organization is not focusing on its grand purpose (assuming it has been formulated), the organization is wandering, and rationality is dissipating. Each "problem" is an *ad hoc* situation to be patched as best one can, preferably without undue attention. There is little regard for the grand purpose or for feeding information about problems, only to get through the moment.

Organizational common sense

Without a clear and compelling purpose, there is no standard to guide and gauge activities, that is, to provide a basis for rationality. Without an agreed upon worthy purpose, efforts at organizational discipline can seem arbitrary and indulgent. Rationalization and self-interest reign. An example is the case of a major automobile dealership which was suffering from squabbling and poor cooperation among its sales, service, and parts departments as they pursued their own separate and often conflicting goals. When it was suggested that the key department staff meet for a day or so and formulate a common set of goals and purposes, the owner rejected the idea because "everyone knows we are here to sell cars." True, but the roles of the service and parts departments, operated as separate profit centers with different and often conflicting goals, were never made clear. A typical employee response was, "If they don't have any better sense than that, I'm going to just do my job and stay out of trouble."

One might reasonably assume that almost everyone in an organization ought to know why they are there, and there is truth in that. In fact, most employees do have a good idea of why they are there; therefore, the presence of a clear and compelling statement of purpose, while certainly beneficial, is not absolutely necessary. Indeed, that is why employees are so resentful of management actions which they see as contrary and counterproductive to the very goals they and management should pursue. It offends their sense of reason and fair play. When employees see management not being true to values it has urged upon employees, they see management as being hypocritical or inept and become cynical.

One of the primary purposes of an organization is to define good sense so that its members, managers, and employees will know what to know, what to do, and how to do it. The common sense of an individual becomes the common sense of an organizational member. Thus, individual common sense becomes a truly common sense through organization, and it is this collective common sense by which individual efforts are measured. Such efforts are judged by:

1. Their accomplishment as measured against expectations
2. The rationality of policies and practices

Management failures to optimize organizational performance are typically failures in providing a rational context for tasks that allows the work to makes sense to others. A task is the technical action; the context is everything else.

Management may think that it has provided a clear statement of purpose, and certainly there may be some documents that have such statements, but that is not the same as effective translation. For example, a major international company distributed its mission and values statement worldwide, with a great introduction to all subsidiary management. For the tens of thousands of employees, the mission and values just appeared on the walls in the working areas one day. As one employee responded when asked how his job fit within the provisions of the mission, "I don't know anything about them ... nice frame, though."

For most organizations, there is precious little connectivity between the lofty management statements of purpose and the everyday work of the organization. The employees who just don't seem to get it and are blamed for failing to understand management, although it is management that has failed to make its case.

Organizational quality as discipline

On occasion, one hears managers wistfully reflecting upon the virtues of beehives and their industrious workers, so busy and uncomplaining. Actually, a beehive is an excellent model for managers, but managers tend to miss the lesson it provides. If beehives were organized like most organizations, with separate departments and bosses for drones, nectar gatherers, entrance fanners, and the queen, they would probably be as inefficient as many of organizations. Also (and managers seem to miss this point altogether), beehives have no managers, only producers. The drones, of course, are tolerated only as long as they are producers and then suffer downsizing. Managers ruminating about the glory of beehives usually see themselves as the queen who is served by an ideal workforce. Actually, the queen is a key producer, not a boss.

A beehive is the ultimate self-managed team, because no one is in charge. This condition is enabled by a shared purpose among all the members of the hive, which is survival. It is not, as far as we know, a learned purpose but one that is engrammed in the bees' genes, what we call instinct. They do not fashion or contrive their organization but rather inherit it. Human organizations, on the other hand, are constantly being refashioned through creative adaptation. The focus, therefore, rests upon leadership to provide a cohesive and motivating purpose.

People are always assessing what they observe, and most always have choices, although not always good ones. This means that everyone is essentially self-managed and self-disciplined, and the purpose and activities of the organization must make sense to organizational members if they are to employee themselves fully. The lesson of the beehive still stands, because the key to effective organization work is a shared sense of purpose and belief that what one is doing will accomplish that purpose, i.e., a rational organization.

Where people with diverse but complementary professional and technical goals and standards work together in some established, disciplined way, one has organization. The more disciplined and focused the organization, the more effective it is likely to be. This discipline of behavior is based on what people are trying to accomplish. In reality, purpose and discipline are no more separable than laser and light particles or magnetism and ferrous molecules. Purpose and discipline are inseparable, because purpose without discipline is only a notion, and discipline without purpose seems meaningless and absurd, even neurotic. If an action does not make sense to people, they are unlikely to commit strongly to it, although they may comply if they feel they must.

All discipline is self-discipline that stems from a person's willingness to engage in conduct pursuant to some purpose. External threats of sanctions, which is what people often think of as discipline, will usually get compliance to the degree necessary to avoid harm, but effort is usually grudging. Acquiescence in such cases may give the appearance of commitment but not the kind of passionate commitment that makes the difference between okay and excellent. Indeed, if it generates enough resentment, one may get malicious compliance, in which a person finds ways to hurt the enterprise or supervisor in the act of complying. Sabotage is not unknown.

True discipline is adherence to a program of behavior to accomplish a purpose seen as worthy of the effort. While quality requires a discipline of commitment, compliance through authority can seem easier to get and, at any given time may be quite okay, which is why so many managers are satisfied with it. When organizations are run on the basis of externally imposed discipline, however, the internal regulators either never develop or atrophy. When these external regulators are no longer in place, there may be little self-discipline other than that required to beat the system. Under such circumstances, one can meet certain standards, but true quality is rare and continuous improvement unlikely.

This point, exquisitely demonstrated by the countries that were formerly a part of the Soviet Union, is certainly one of the chief hurdles that any quality improvement must overcome. Part of this may initially be people's testing whether management is really changing its commanding ways, especially if they have gone through all this before and management has reverted to commanding ways. Employees who may have been treated like children in the past are unlikely to have established effective ways of self-managing in terms of the overall organizational purpose, although they have learned how to look out for themselves.

The organizational leader is tantamount to a spiritual leader who provides the purpose that others see as worthwhile and keeps the organization focused. Lewis Platt sees his job as ensuring that the organization has a solid set of values to keep them from drifting. He does this by "working around" trying to "reinforce these values, making sure they are kept alive." Where management does not generally operate by leadership enabled by strength of purpose and rationality of action, management decisions are never questioned, the reasons for these decisions are never really understood, and the purposes of the organization are not always clear or even seen as the true purposes.

Purpose and common sense rationality

A common thread running through successful leadership strategies is that employees must understand a strategy's value, and be committed to the organizational purpose. If managers want people to think globally while they are acting locally, however, they need to ensure that some global perspective is a part of their ordinary work expectations. A proper vision satisfies two fundamental questions that define every member of the organization: (1) who are we, and (2) what are we doing here? Engineers, accountants, and professional secretaries have a definition of who they are and what they are doing as professionals, but what are they doing as a member of the organization? An organization seeks technical skills, but it hires people, and these people require some purposeful framework to provide a utilitarian value to technical skills.

Where an organization does not have a worthy vision or where that vision has not been properly translated for practical application, people find themselves caught in swirls of parochial and technical activities that may seem rational within their own internal logic loop, but are not rationally pursuant to the overall organizational intent. In such as situation, authority seems the only way to harness the organization. A grand purpose should not eliminate these more confined technical purposes because it is the quality of these technical standards and abilities that allow an enterprise to be successful. It helps these professional and technical specialties to become disciplined to the service of the organization and comprise harmonious and intersupportive performance systems. If the professional or technical standards of a CPA or a welder are at odds with those of management, then the organization's purpose should be reviewed to see why it is not being duly supported by a person using legitimate work standards.

Management must also show that these stated needs have rationality, which is an assessment of the goal achieving value of an activity. In other words, management must convince staff that the purposes of the employee can be achieved by aligning them with those of the organization, and that the activities of the organization are logically and reasonably pursuant to these purposes. In this regard, employees are little different from customers, and this is the reason that the concept of internal customers is so critical a model for dealing with external customers.

Quality and managerial leadership

In the midst of the daunting storm of rapidly changing markets, technologies, and new management theories is the silver promise of effective and powerful organizational control. The world is not all confusion, attenuation, and morbidity. There is a natural health about the world, a natural order, and a tendency for organization. The world is one of constant reform, not of absolute ends and clean-slate beginnings. The manager who can use these natural forces can garner effective control, because the very forces that pull an organization in different directions have within them the power to pull it together.

While there are many purposes among organization elements, there is generally a common purpose that embraces everyone. The technology of a given enterprise, the professions it utilizes, the nature of the market, the typical pace of events, shared self-interest and common investment, and even social sentimentality all serve to create a powerful organizational polymer. These forces are everywhere in every organization, and they will defeat or enable managers, depending upon their ability to use them. This, in turn, requires that managers understand and learn to use them. For some, this requires a radical shift, for others a little refinement, but for all who attempt quality improvements, an effective context in which to guide and measure their improvement techniques.

Table 3 Model of Managerial Leadership

Leadership (purpose and values)	Management (systems and processes)
Customer-driven quality	Fast response
Company responsibility	Management by fact
Leadership	Continuous improvement and learning
Partnership development	Results focus
Long-range view of the future	Design quality and prevention

The premier standards for quality in the U.S. are those of the Malcolm Baldridge National Quality Award. It should come as no surprise that these standards are virtually congruent with those of managerial leadership and organizational performance. The Baldridge standards are essentially standards for leadership (values and purpose) and management (enabling systems). The Baldridge core values and concepts include:

- Customer-driven quality
- Leadership
- Continuous improvement and learning
- Fast response
- Design quality and prevention
- Long-range view of the future
- Management by fact
- Partnership development
- Company responsibility and citizenship
- Results focus

These standards fit the model of managerial leadership quite well, as indicated in Table 3.

Quality standards, regardless of how realistic or appropriate, are not self-effecting. The difficulty for managers is not with the Baldridge standards themselves, which are quite logical and reasonable, but in implementing them. This is especially challenging in a world of high flux, high pressure, and hypercomplexity. Creating a quality operation in the face of daunting adversity is, of course, what managerial leadership is all about.

Endnotes

1. Juran, Joseph, and Frederick Gryna, *Quality Planning and Analysis*, McGraw-Hill, New York, 1980, p. 153.
2. From a proprietary client report, changed slightly to mask the identity.

chapter fifteen

Common sense management

Why common sense is the essence of good management

> *Nature gave men two ends — one to sit on and one to think with. Ever since then, man's success or failure has been dependent on the one he uses most.*
> ᴄ◡George R. Kirkpatrick

Being able to enjoy the additional margin of productivity and power of a positively motivated organization, rather than that of a merely compliant one, is what the quality movement is all about. The critical difference in the new Xerox and the old Xerox, which lost most of the market it created years ago, is that the new company enjoys a discretionary margin of genius and energy from its employees that was always there but had not been used well. In top-performing companies, everyone is there for the same purpose, and management exploits that by inviting employees to use their skills and brains to accomplish that purpose, a condition not easily found in poorer performing ones.

Peter Senge, in his *The Fifth Discipline*,[1] notes that the job is not how to make something happen in an organization, but how to "release what wants to happen anyway." Actually, that may not be enough. Like an apple tree, there is an inherent flow of activity in any organization that will produce a natural result. Certainly, a natural potential is always there, but potentials are vast and varied and include the products of poor control, such as bugs and blemishes. To achieve not just apples but *excellent* apples, therefore, requires a vision, knowledge, skill, and effort that are commensurably excellent.

Similarly, to achieve the excellent potential for any organization requires excellent management of that organization to wrest from it, not what it will do anyway but what it can do optimally. An organization will function on its own, but it will not achieve excellence without excellent management and leadership to mold an excellent common sense throughout.

Priorities and urgencies

John Kotter, in his *Leading Change*,[2] argues that the number one cause of failure for quality improvement programs is complacency, a lack of urgency for improvement. This is true, but a bit misleading. The situation in most companies is not that there is no urgency, for invariably there is a great swarm of urgencies. In a slap-dash environment of ever-shifting urgencies, the problem is an absence of priorities. A new improvement program will have virtually no priority in the workplace, other than it will help deal with some immediately pressing urgency.

The strategic plan that gathers dust on an executive's bookshelf is an old joke, but it is not funny. Management, as a deliberate effort to accomplish some purpose, requires planning, and that requires priorities. A priority is an initial choice that guides and measures all subsequent choices. It is a statement of relative importance that reflects strategic values. Urgency, on the other hand, is created by needs, i.e., the pressing exigencies of the moment. Whatever is the most pressing at any given time is the greatest need. That there may be a need for priorities does not mean that this need is the most pressing need or even that it will be addressed at all. That is why the first step in any improvement effort or definition of quality is to determine the strategic corporate values. These are what the vision statement, mission statement, or statement of purpose should articulate. Rationality starts with values and goals.

The primary cause of urgencies is poor systems which give rise to expediencies, i.e., actions taken for reasons of time or cost that bypass the system. Because expediencies undermine official management systems, they generally create more urgencies. Thus, poor quality feeds on itself as everyone is pressed into a standard of making do and moving on to the next emergency. When systems are so corrupt and impotent that people must conspire against them to do their jobs, quality and efficiency are only part of the problem. If people can conspire to do their jobs, they can also conspire for other purposes, and there are usually other problems, such as shrinkage, poor customer relations, discrimination, unionization, and abuse of position.

When people lose sight of the organization's strategic purpose or values, they will pursue other purposes. This does not mean they do not care, but rather they are pretty much left on their own to determine the values they will pursue. Some elevate technical or professional interests, leading to goal inversion, while some put their own interests or those of the work group first. To the degree that other interests drive the workforce, that organization is out of control. One can assess the degree to which an organization is driven by its strategic values and purpose or by parochial values by making the following comparisons (see Table 1).

The chief roles of management are to formulate corporate values (purpose) and to ensure that they are being pursued (systems) with quality and

Table 1   Management vs. Parochial Decisional Drivers

Actions driven by strategic values or purpose, i.e., management	Actions driven by parochial or narrow technical values or purposes
Needs	Urgencies
Eliminating wastes	Cost-cutting
Long-term	Short-term or immediate situations
Plans and goals	Situations
Excellence	Get by this one

vigor (effort). Unfortunately, it is management that is the primary cause of an urgency-driven organization. The failure to listen to employees, to involve pertinent others, to respect the time needs of others, and to follow its own stated goals are the chief causes of such an organization. That is what many writers mean when they refer to lack of management support. There may be a brief blush of interest in setting priorities by some managers, but these are put aside under the pressures of new management directives or initiatives (often commanded but without appropriate support), new environmental or safety requirements (known for some time but only authorized or ordered as the deadline is imminent), being instructed to ignore important major market failures (until drastic adjustments seem required), and so on.

Centrifugal and centripetal forces

Many managers today are frustrated in their efforts to control their organizations to ensure that the desired outcomes are produced. Where employees are knowledge workers, it is difficult to know not only what people are doing but also what they can do for the organization. For example, it is difficult to know when a computer person is pursuing some new breakthrough, is on some costly and irrelevant tangent, or is just plain goofing off. With the advent of e-mail, which has reengineered the grapevine, the organization threatens to become even less controllable, at least in a traditional way. The diversity of purposes and opinions, the separations through distance and technology, the flux of change, and the general complexity all seem to contribute to the seeming centrifugal nature of modern organizations.

Efforts to control these processes directly can make things worse because people often generate defensive and counter responses rather than productive ones. Organizations are too complex and changes too rapid to be controlled effectively through mechanical conceptual linkages, such as when departments are siloed and decisions flow from the top. For example, a petroleum company calculates profit by the relative prices of crude oil and gas at the retail stations. Marketing wants maximum flexibility to buy whatever crude is cheap on the spot market. An oil refinery, however, must be designed for specific crude properties. Maximum flexibility — being able to process a wide range of crudes and store a wide variety and large amounts of products at an oil refinery — is expensive to provide and costly to operate. The driving goals of the oil company's marketing and refining can be quite contradictory, even seemingly irreconcilable.

While there are numerous forces that serve to break down an organization, a manager's job is nonetheless made relatively easy because of the natural centripetal forces of any organization. Despite efforts to separate them, there is a natural unity among components of any organization that comes from shared perceptions, ideology, and the complex camaraderie of being fellow bankers, grocers, or cowboys. Much of what they share seems natural because they have learned to perceive the world that way through their common culture.

While this natural tendency of organizations clearly exists, management may use it poorly by simply coasting on this natural energy rather than working at real leadership. The natural deference toward authority is critical to good organizational management. It becomes dysfunctional, however, when this natural deference engenders an unnatural reliance by lazy managers. Because the organization has an inherent tendency toward strength and production, it tends to perform in the okay range no matter what management does. This often gives management the impression that they are managing well when, in fact, they may not be managing at all.

Natural elegance

The answer to living and working in a maelstrom of change is not to create a maelstrom of confusion inside our organization. Responding to everything is eventually to respond to nothing really, so an organization must be in control of itself first before it can control its interactions with a turbulent world. Management must be capable of guiding and delivering a studied, vigorous, and assured response, in real time of course, in order to take the wiser course. Sophistication, not complexity or disruption, is the answer.

One of the reasons given for IBM's decline of recent years was that its operation and management had become too complex.[3] While the world is indeed increasingly complex, and organizations must be capable of commensurably complex responses, the control of the organization cannot be. If control is too complex, no one can keep up with it, much less manage it. As discussed earlier, the answer to complexity is not simplification but elegance, i.e., actions that are simple but effective. Elegance is found in defining sets of activities by their essential qualities and then controlling them so that simple effort achieves complex but properly targeted response.

A modern organization, the primary medium for getting complex or wide-ranging work done, is a hypercomplex set of events that comprise the dynamic organization. To be effective, an elegant control must guide, enable, and measure each and every action of this complexity, orchestrating its activities in ways to make them intersupportive and harmonious.

Elegant control is exercised by helping people define what they are doing in terms of what the organization needs. Management does this by refining sets of activities into their essential qualities and then controlling them such that simple effort generates complex but properly targeted response. The simplicity of elegance stems from concepts that provide more effective *categories of events* which, when stabilized, become *systems*. The fallacy of inelegant overcontrol is that, lacking an effective understanding of the causes and true nature of events, it focuses on trying to control particular events without reference to their controlling, systemic contexts.

Not only does overcontrol usually fail to solve the real problem, it also provides no guidance for solving other problems. A truly elegant control is not situational but universal in that it:

- Is readily available
- Is something anyone can use
- Fits every circumstance
- Requires no extra effort
- Is realistic and practical
- Energizes people to action
- Is always a proper measure and guide
- Is accepted as valid and appropriate by everyone, i.e., it makes sense

Given the high flux nature of the operating world, the increased pressures and complexity of organizational operations, and the necessity of wider and more diverse involvement in decision making and work processes, the only strategic model that would seem to satisfy these criteria is organizational rationality. The test is whether, given the organizational purpose, the activity is properly in pursuance of that purpose. This assessment, in turn, can only be made by each person, at whatever level or organizational calling, through their common sense faculties.

Common sense, rationality, and purpose

Rationality, in the strictest sense, is an intellectual assessment. In real life, however, people make decisions about suitability and appropriateness based on feel (emotion), ideas about other options (intuitive review), and worthiness of purpose to any action (valuation). Rationality is a relative assessment, not an intrinsic one. A great effort, for example, is not rational if the purpose is unworthy. Because many improvement efforts do not pass muster when looked at from the full common sense perspective, they often fail in application because, despite their logical plausibility, they are not deemed practical.

Rationality requires, of course, a clear purpose against which to assess activities. Tom Peters argued that the key to organizational excellence and success is to have an "overriding and compelling vision."[4] This vision must satisfy two fundamental questions of every organization: Who are we and what are we doing here? The purpose must be compelling in that people are prepared to invest themselves in it. It must be overriding because every organization is swarming with a variety of interests that can misdirect activities if not guided by something grander.

The key to control is not to control what people do with their hands, but to guide how people think about their work. When one seeks to improve organizational performance, one is essentially trying to change the way people think about how fine, quick, and cooperative their work should be. Margaret Wheatley argues that the organizational vision creates a field that guides all behavior, Peter Senge urges managers to give employees a view of the system of which they are a part, and Stephen Covey suggests beginning with the end in mind.

Because people essentially self-manage through their choices, a clear and compelling purpose allows them to make the proper choices. Their common sense will align with the organizational purposes if it makes sense, seems legitimate, and gives their work and role meaning and value. This is why, after an extensive study of corporate success in a world of change, Edward E. Lawler, III, found that employee involvement was the most effective source of control. The traditional command systems impaired optimum employee value-add by denying them an understanding of the business, an understanding of their place in the value-add stream, and rewards commensurate with contribution.

Common sense and the aspects of enterprise

Understanding the purpose, however, is but one aspect of common sense motivation. Through their intellectual understanding, intuitive insight, determination of purpose, and energizing through passion, people makes assessments about what they observe. They determine, through their common sense processing, what the true meaning is for them. Purpose is only the guiding element in elegance and rationality, for people also make an intellectual assessment of the rationality of management systems to purpose.

Exhortation, which Deming sees as the nemesis of good management, is but trying to get people to do something by appealing to their sense of purpose. This is a quite reasonable and proper effort by management, but it is only one pillar of the common sense edifice. To exhort people to give greater credence, faith, and investment to an irrational effort, without providing appropriate support for that effort, however, is not rational and only prompts cynicism and defensive postures. In other words, management can exhort, but it needs to back it up with both example and supportive systems.

Managers insult rationality with actions that are not linked, or are even at cross-purposes, with the espoused organizational purposes. An excellent example of this is in safety management, an area where it would seem everyone could agree. Still, the first problem that must be overcome in launching a safety program is to get employees to believe that management is serious.[5] This disbelief stems from management's preaching about good safety but failing to provide proper support. This is why Crosby refers to safety as the precursor of quality. Support for safety and the environment is often minimally compliant with OSHA and EPA requirements, a leadership example and standard of performance that permeate the organization in other areas as well.

By failing to provide adequate training while sending key executives to seminars in luxury resorts, or failing to provide good equipment while enjoying a fine office and new company car, management breeds cynicism and skepticism throughout the workforce. One multi-millionaire company owner was known to drive to the office in a Rolls Royce and complain to employees about the number of ballpoint pens being used. Employees are not fools, and organizational society is more like a fish bowl than some realize. Office romances and management indulgences are often known to all, if not directly at least through rumor.

The difference between a sterile statement and an effective vision is the extent to which those corporate goals and values have been infused into every nook and cranny of the organization. As described by Max De Pree, former CEO of Herman Miller:[6]

> "[The] first responsibility of a leader is to define reality and then create a condition of reality which gives "reason and mutual understanding to programs and to relationships. ...A rational environment values trust and human dignity and provides personal development and self-fulfillment in the attainment of organizational goals."

It is not difficult to find evidence of irrational systems in any operation, although finding the full range of the system and the nature of its rationality takes some study. Here are some examples of easily observed evidence of system irrationality:

- A chemical plant control room, where operators are surrounded by computers, must keep several logs in longhand. Most of the logs contain the same basic information. The logs do not seem to be read by anyone, but they are kept just in case.
- The personnel office of a major university requires applicants to fill out five forms, each a different shape and color and all containing

basically the same information. The person who handles these forms for the office suggested putting them on a computer as a single database, but no one was interested.

- Twenty percent of the service work at a major auto dealer was returns for work that had not been done properly or for which spare parts were not available. The parts department did not keep the factory-recommended inventory, and no data were maintained as to what non-inventory parts were most in demand. Also, there was no data tracking or systematized service problem analysis, including one of costs.

- The president of a small church-related college was receiving a number of complaints about the actions of the Dean of Women, who had called female students names, had occasionally yelled and screamed at them, and on one occasion had thrown an object at a student. When asked what he intended to do, the president responded by saying that he had received a number of complaints about this dean, but how could anyone know that whoever replaced her would not be worse?

- In a fine restaurant, a customer had to request a clean fork to replace the dirty one he had been given.

- The receptionist was not quite rude, but not quite nice, and hurried through a rather long, scripted greeting. She did not know how to work the telephone system or where to refer the caller.

- A major automobile manufacturer spent more than a million dollars trying to create a more team-like culture at one of its largest plants and then hired a "kick-ass" manager to run it, thereby spoiling much of the fruit of its million-dollar effort.

One could go on forever with these kinds of observations because we see them all the time. These are precisely the kinds of actions that reveal the nature of a system and tell people what the real intent of management is. In her *Fad Surfing in the Board Room,* Shapiro notes that this is how the admonition of "quality first" becomes "get the tons out", "customer service" becomes "get the order however you can", and "innovate" becomes "don't screw up" to the workforce.[7] These are also the typical experiences of an organization where control is attempted through authority, as in a "kick-ass" manager. They reflect not only neglect by the limited attention of the authority-based management, but also the general disruption it tends to cause. These are the kinds of evidence that a consultant looks for in a systematic and rigorous way to identify system deficiencies that need changing for quality improvements. That is why consultants sometimes seem to be just giving back to the organization what they have been told by its members.

Emotion and rationality

Managers intuitively understand the importance of emotion but tend to use it the wrong way. While Deming argued that managers should try to get fear out of the workplace, many managers work hard to instill fear into the workplace. Examples abound, such as when a major automobile manufacturer downsized its engineering staff but left those remaining working among the empty desks as a demonstration of what could happen to those who did not want their jobs badly enough.

Another example is the paper products company and its marketing chief who told the heads of public relations and of advertising that only one would be kept and whoever impressed him most would be the survivor. The idea, of course, was to energize these two staff, and it did — to torpedo one another. Constructive work, however, suffered greatly in such a hellish environment where the raw emotion of fear dominated every action. Even the advertising agency was caught up in the turmoil.

Every aspect of life, no matter how coldly technical, has an emotional quality. ROI has a rational value that can be calculated, but it also has an emotional value that must be felt, the latter generally being the more influential. Value itself, while a calculation, is ultimately an emotional and intuitive judgment. Watch the eye-blink rate of a computer programmer working a problem or an engineer discussing a new design, and you will see intense emotion, although it may be cast in technical terms. A favorite argument of cynics is that people operate on emotion not reason. That is true in a sense, but it is highly misleading. People can be dominated temporarily by emotional flashes of anger or surges of pride, lust, or envy and do things they may regret later in more reflective circumstances.

When management "kicks" employees, they tend to shift their purpose away from that of management to something more suitable to their psychological needs. When a person uses reasoning for self-satisfaction at the expense of some seemingly higher purpose, such as stealing inventory or padding one's expense account ("everybody does it, and besides they owe me") it is rationalization. While rationalization is still reasoning, it is the use of the intellect in a self-serving and truncated context that stands reason on its head. Rationalization is us convincing ourselves that we are right or justified even though it involves something that we believe would otherwise be wrong.

People who are intoxicated, with mental controls debilitated by alcohol, may display protracted behaviors that reflect a high emotional quality. But normal people (by that I mean people who are reasonably sober and are neither psychotic nor highly neurotic) do not sustain that kind of emotional mode for any length of time. What occurs more typically is people are moved by an emotional surge to shift their purpose or the relative importance or urgency of a given purpose. Once a sent message is captured intellectually, our passion, intuition, and purposes provide a context that frames the issue. An emotion is "attached to each input before it is sent to be processed in our rational mind" and is a part of our "emotional intelligence".[8] These are the faculties that allow us to make leaps in our perception about what we are to do and how well we should do it. It helps us deal with such constant assessments as:

- Is it the right thing to do?
- Is it worth the effort?
- How good is good enough?
- What is its priority?
- What can I get; what can I lose?
- Is it fair (is the boss doing it, too)?
- Why should I care?

Based on our answers to these kinds of questions, we then make a common sense determination about what seems rational for us. If our faculties are in disharmony, we will rationalize our decision, no matter how self-serving. If one is asked to make a special effort because the team is facing a special problem, that is one thing. If one is asked to make a special effort because management failed to plan properly, one is being asked to do something quite different even though, on its face, the request is the same.

When politicians, sales people, lawyers, and managers appeal to emotions, they are trying to energize people into moving to a frame of reference that gives plausibility to the action sought. Lawyers strive to put a certain construction on events that effectively redefines reality, as happened in the O. J. Simpson trial when the issue moved from the evidence provided by the LAPD to the procedures of the LAPD itself. The advantage that politicians, sales people, and lawyers have is that they only need to move people once and their job is essentially done.

A manager must move people all day, every day, for years, and that requires a different strategy. On the one hand, that means that managers do not have to motivate people in the sense of charging them up, but it does mean they must avoid demotivating them by generating emotions that can shift employee purposes to those other than the grand purpose of the organization. If management would just eliminate the demotivators in an organization that push people into using their common sense defensively, many of its problems would evaporate.

At a recent ASQC Quality Forum,[9] Terry Ivany, CEO of VIA Rail Canada, said, "Quality comes from the hearts and minds of employees [including] everyone on the job." At the same conference, Hal Rosenbluth, CEO of Rosenbluth International, also noted that "one cannot delegate an emotion." Management still often fails to translate organizational purpose into suitable employee emotions. Many feel that a video of a sincere CEO and a statement on the wall should be enough to stir worker passions. Actually, these could well serve to stir employees, but only if they are supported by the constant stream of messages that surround employees in the organizational environment. It is this organization-as-message system that managers must master.

Endnotes

1. Senge, Peter, *The Fifth Discipline,* Doubleday, New York, 1990.
2. Kotter, John, *Leading Change,* Harvard Business School Press, Boston, 1996.
3. See Ramo, Joshua C., Act two for Big Blue, *Time,* November 4, 62–64, 1996.
4. Peters, Thomas, and Robert H. Waterman, Jr., *In Search of Excellence,* Harper & Row, New York, 1982.
5. This is an observation by Thomas Krause et al., in *The Behavior-Based Safety Program: Managing Involvement for an Injury-Free Culture,* Van Nostrand Reinhold, New York, 1990, which I have found to be true in many facilities.
6. Worth reading is De Pree, Max, *Leadership Is an Art,* Doubleday, New York, 1989.
7. Shapiro, Eileen, *Fad Surfing in the Boardroom: Reclaiming the Courage To Manage in the Age of Instant Answers,* Addison-Wesley, Reading, MA, 1995, p. 58.
8. Goleman, Daniel, *Emotional Intelligence: Why It Can Matter More than IQ,* Bantam Books, New York, 1995.
9. Telecast October 3, 1996.

Part V

Creating organizational excellence

Chapter sixteen: Strategies for change
Why effective change must be both strategic and incremental
The goal of change is to maintain a goodness of fit of an organization with its market. To do this rarely takes radical change, which can be disruptive and debilitating, but rather a guided incremental change which, in the aggregate, constitutes strategic but controlled changes. Organizational design should also represent a goodness of fit with the organization's rational strategies for excellence of operation.

Chapter seventeen: Quality and organizational rationality
How things we already know, but often forget, are the keys to organizational excellence
An organization is rational to the degree that its activities are pursuant to its purposes. To the extent that an organization is rational, it will "make sense" to participants and allow them to translate purpose to application. There are six basic marks and measures of organizational rationality: (1) a clear purpose defined by measurable goals, (2) a specific plan that guides and measures all activities, (3) a striving for the best in both craftsmanship and tools, (4) decisions based on data and analysis, (5) performance-based strategies, and (6) managerial control of the organization.

Chapter eighteen: The quest for quality
How management improvement is looking at ordinary things in a more rational way
Management and organization are dynamics and exist as people do things. Whether an organization is rational/performance-based or traditional/authority-based will determine its organizational quality.

chapter sixteen

Strategies for change

Why effective change must be both strategic and incremental

> *We know the good, we apprehend it clearly,*
> *but we cannot bring it to achievement.*
> ᕽ Euripides

Part of the problem managers have with quality is trying to define it in real operational terms. How will they know when they have achieved it? This is especially vexing as most management writers argue that it is ever receding, like the end of a rainbow. Quality often seems to managers like obscenity to the Supreme Court — they cannot define it with any certainty but they know it when they see it. Actually, we often do not know it when we see it because we are not really sure what to look for.

Quality, to be of any value as a management strategy, must be more than a neat idea. It must be capable of being actualized. While it can be defined as conforming to specifications or customer enthusiasm, neither of these provides a sufficiently complete map to guide and measure organizational management strategies. We have discussed how an enterprise involves purpose, systems, and effort. What we need is some formula for determining the relationship of the internal aspects of an enterprise with its environment. The degree to which an organization is effectively suited to what it is trying to accomplish could be called goodness of fit. Said another way, we might consider quality as excellent organizational goodness of fit with the market and other environmental elements.

Goodness of fit

One could look at the restructuring efforts of turnaround managers as attempts to fit the organization to the market. But it is more than a mere expedient fit, as urgent as that may be at the time. An organization can be said to have actually turned around only when it has the capacity to thrive in its new market position. Downsizing is dumb-sizing, unless it is right-

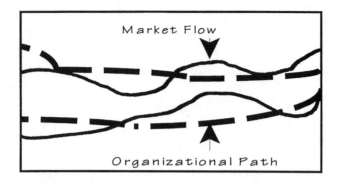

Figure 1   Approximate and varying goodness of fit between organization and market.

sizing, but even that misses the point. It is not the size of an organization that is important, it is its goodness of fit with its market. Tom Epley, turnaround CEO of Paradyne, looks "for companies that, at one time or another, were very successful, and then for some reason lost some of their luster."[1] In other words, the company has gotten away from its market.

To create goodness of fit, where purpose and organizational values and strategies effectively fuse, is the vision everyone keeps talking about. Peter Ivany, CEO of VIA Rail of Canada observes:[2]

> "It is prudent to match people to necessary activity ... throughout the organization. ... Once we decided what activities we should and shouldn't be doing, we had 1500 too many people. ... [W]e now have a *closer match of people to necessary activity*." [Emphasis added.]

If one considers the market to be something like a vein of mineral in the ground (see Figure 1) and the company as the miner, once one has the basic technology and an understanding of where that seam is, extracting that mineral is fairly easy and certain. The seam may wander underground, and the miner may have to dig up a lot of low-yield dirt, but essentially it all works. This may be okay until either the seam takes a surprising, radical change in direction so that the miner gets mostly dirt, or technology changes the economics of mining, or something else seriously changes the picture. Then, being suboptimized may no longer be good enough, and serious change becomes necessary.

Importantly, the market is not actually "there" as it has no physical presence. The market is a dynamic set of relationships formed around available goods and services, between customers and suppliers. Competition, newer products, better service, etc., change these relationships. Goodness of fit is a lively dance between a dynamic organization and a dynamic market. In this kind of flux, controlled change is the only healthy condition of any organization that would prosper. In such flux and complexity, management must find the combination that assures proper control of its operations through rational organizational processes. When organizations have gotten away from market fit and appropriate capacity, severe actions may be required. But such corrections are, like major surgery, another form of injury and impairment.

What often does require a radical change is management's willingness to accept responsibility for the present condition and for change. Like honesty, responsibility rests upon courage and, like honesty, it marks the only path to leadership. Turnaround artists are often necessary because former management would not accept the responsibility for what was happening to the company and, therefore, were not prepared to lead the change. They preferred to blame problems on a variety of things, such as unpredictable markets and new technologies, inability to get good people, government regulations, or some such.

Keeping fit

When the goodness of fit between the market and organizational capabilities gets too far off, new management may be deemed necessary to turn the organization around. Even then, however, it is not a matter of starting over, for, if things were that bad, the company would need an undertaker not a "turnarounder". Eliminating waste assumes the presence of some sinew that can be developed into greater capacity. If a company is to be turned around, there must be a core of basic residual strengths that can be developed into an effective market fit.

At Paradyne, Epley found a strong technological capability. "What was lacking," he observed, "was the ability to translate that technology rapidly into modern products and market those products in a dynamic and laser-like way."[3] Similarly, Ivany noted that VIA Rail "had high-quality service but it was delivered inconsistently." The value-add of the technical resources always relies on the quality of the human operating system. As discussed earlier, the organization is the key to quality and utilizing innovation, not the technology.

Oftentimes an organizational path seems to fit quite well with the market — that is, there is some profit being made or the cash flow seems good. Sometimes it may be off, doing mostly okay in the swings. Certainly, life is a matter of surges and lurches. Managers, therefore, are often able to take credit for the company's doing well and place credible blame when things are not going so well. And, because okay means that it is profitable (or, for government, it is being funded with not too many complaints), management clearly is doing a good job. Mediocre management, therefore, seems to be doing quite well because it is within the realm of acceptability, which is as good as excellent and cheaper.

The effect of this approximate fit is that there is generally a low urgency for change because acceptable is okay and in the same realm as excellent. To say that an organization could do much better and that it is operating at 60% of optimum only insults the manager who thinks he is doing well. What prompts many change efforts is not the desire for excellence but specific situation problems that are so pressing as to require some attention, such as loss of market share or unionization efforts. The weaknesses in an operation do not become apparent when things are going well, but only when it is under pressure, when management may suddenly discover, as did IBM, that it had 75,000 too many people on the payroll.

Fortunately, most companies are doing okay and should, with reasonably able management, continue to do so. The wise strategy is usually to move it toward excellence without unduly impairing its productive capacities. As noted before, most organizations do not require radical surgery, but rather better conditioning, modification, upgrading, and fine tuning to better utilize their present strengths. Organizations are already set up to do what they do best now. People mostly know how and generally have the resources to do what the organization presently does. This may not be where an enlightened manager wants to end up, but it is where one can start, moving forward with good control and utilizing whatever techniques best serve the organizations purpose until the organization is optimized, without burning it down or running aground in the process.

Even if management feels the need to make major changes, diving in dark waters with only a best-selling management book for a life preserver would seem a bit risky. Just as a good coach analyzes an athlete, management must find those areas of the operation that are not performing at their best, analyze the causes, and then ensure that optimal performance is facilitated. This is not to advocate complacency, for the days of a stable organization as defined in the past are doubtless over. Flux, change, surprise, radical new technological developments, organizational mergers, divestitures, growth and downsizing, shifts of global economics and markets — these are the stuff of the present and future for managers.

Stability and flexibility

The value of a highly flexible organization is that it can better adapt to the environmental shifts and thereby maintain goodness of fit. Effective flexibility, however, is not synonymous with disorder. Rather, it refers to a pliant and tractable structure that affords responsive strength and competence. There must be something to be flexible. Deconstructionist ideas such as dejobbing may be interesting to managers only when they support and further the organization, not when they dismantle it. It is curious that people who condemn the short-term thinking of managers may themselves be offering short-sighted organizational remedies. They, like some managers, are focusing only on the technical system but miss where the great bulk of problems and opportunities lie.

Machines operate according to design, but their operators give them utility through their purposes and skills. Further, while technical process may be quite stable and predictable, all human systems are constantly fluxing to some degree. Each task, each situation, each condition is always a little bit different even if it is only in the mind of the person at that particular time. When the entire set of organizational interactions are considered, there is a lot of adjusting going on. Sometimes one adjusts to satisfy customers and sometimes to satisfy bosses. Sometimes this is called variance (bad flexibility) or transformance (good flexibility). Unlike beauty, the difference is not in the eye of the beholder, but is in view of the purposes that drive the organization.

Quantum changes, however, come more as walks than leaps. Borrowing from another field, one could argue that the one-hand jump shot and the forward pass reinvented basketball and football. Certainly, these innovations did eventually change their sports substantially. The forward pass and the one-handed jump shot have come to typify their respective sports. These developments occurred at the same time that teams were using their best capacities to have a winning season. No doubt it was traumatic for many coaches and players who, having established reputations and positions on the basis of traditional performance, found themselves having to learn something new or give way to others. Change is not a choice, although there is a choice in change, as every action by every person either reinforces or alters the system. Further, every person or team either adapts to the new system requirements or gives way, in one way or another.

In reality, reinvention is a term that is either inapplicable or a form of hyperbole. Human systems are dynamic disciplines, and mechanical terms such as reinvention and reengineering must be used with great caution when applied to social behavior. The market, government regulations, and other environment factors constantly force organization to make adjustments. At the same time, such internal factors as changing values, people, technology, and size constantly rearrange the organization from within.

The problem is not making change so much as managing change. Moreover, change is never a zero-sum choice, for while changes affect the previous way of doing things, the new ways carry clear genetic similarities to what was done before. The one-handed jump shot made the game more fun, but basketball is still essentially the same. Even the Saturn automobile, which was an effort by General Motors to reinvent its business and seems to have been a successful effort to break the grip of corporate bureaucracy, has an unmistakable family resemblance to GM.

Incremental approach

A quite different approach from wholesale restructuring is advocated by incrementalists. The incrementalists take the position that wholesale changes are not only disruptive, but they also fail to get the job done because they usually have little impact on the people who do the actual work of the organization, at least not in a facilitative way. They argue that real change must begin with the work itself and, as one pursues problem causes, problems in the system and overall organization will be found and better remedied. In addition, as expressed by Robert Schaffer:[4]

> "Strategic thinking, probing and investigation require time and energy. ...Unless managers know that the day-to-day job is under control and the necessary improvements are being made, they will not have the time, the perspective, the self-confidence, or the good working relationships that are all essential to imaginative strategic thinking and decision making. ...There is no way [managers] can ignore the demands of current [work]."

The great bulk of improvement advice, however, does not come from the radicals, although they seem to get most of the press, or the incrementalists, who seem to get very little. Most advice is on techniques for doing things better, ranging from personal improvement (e.g., Covey), human relations (e.g., McGregor), behavioral modification (e.g., Daniels), systems analysis (e.g., Rummler-Brache), performance technologies (e.g., Mager), cycle-time management (e.g., Northey and Southway), process management (e.g., Deming), decision making (e.g., Kepner-Tregoe), and a host of other approaches to improvement.[5] Whatever the advocated approach, however, all are offered with the same admonitions:

1. If you get this one area right, all the rest will fall into place.
2. If you don't do this, all the rest will fall to pieces.

For the manager trying to choose a course of improvement, it is a daunting task to pass the shelves of management books each declaring itself to be the way. It is even more difficult because, in truth, each of these books offers sound advice, each has great promise to work, and some are downright essential to any real, lasting improvement. No single approach, however, whatever its claims and admonitions, is likely to do all that is required. A company cannot do them all, although some seem to be trying. Successful management of change really requires a chest of well-chosen action tools to deal with resultant changes that reverberate throughout the organization.

The choice from among the holistic, incremental, or technical approaches is a false one, however, because system and effort are, in essence, the same thing. While one needs to have a clear end in mind and to be able to select wisely from among the various techniques, any practical implementation must be relevant and efficacious at the front line of work, that is, at the incremental level. On the other hand, every situation or incremental action must reflect and support the system that drives it. An effective change strategy must address and integrate all three aspects of an enterprise, i.e., purpose, system, and effort.

Given that strategy, process, and specific application must all work in quality improvement, the question is where is the best place to begin an improvement effort. There are places to begin that are better than others, but the first action is only part of what must be a strategic approach. Research indicates, for example, that companies that had "the highest success rates with their quality efforts were those that adopted simultaneous quality, team, and process-management initiatives."[6] This means that management must first have an overall strategy for change that will allow it to select the most promising approaches for their organization and use them with an assurance that connects strategy, process, and incremental work situations.

A successful strategy must be well founded in the established flow of work that has become natural to staff, moving them toward optimization as gently as practicable. It is not surprising to see promising new quality improvement schemes rejected by an organization like so many foreign bodies. Many change approaches are foreign, even deliberately hostile, to the ecology of the existing organization. That these approaches frequently are seen to fail is not surprising.

Strategic incrementalism

The greatest ideas are realized in countless individual acts. In that sense, all things great are small incremental actions which, conversely, have meaning only in that they realize a grander idea that gives them purpose. Top-down, system-wide radical change efforts that fail to give due regard to individual actions in various situations can cause great disruption and expense. Like great waves, they tend to crash on the rocks of daily, incremental realities.

Incremental approaches, on the other hand, without guidance and measure by some strategic end in view tend to dissipate or become self-justifying activities that lose their relevance. Introducing techniques to change systems without a strategic perspective can foster self-encapsulated logic that is likely to be a difficult operational fit for an organizational body.

Personal improvement programs can help each of us but may make little difference where systems require different kinds of behaviors.*

Strategic incrementalism is not just tinkering at the margins. It is strategic organizational development, starting with situational applications and working through critical systems in a test of their rationality measured by organizational purpose. When done properly, even the purpose itself is under constant assessment and refinement for suitability. This combination of clarified purpose, selected and aligned systems and techniques, and real, incremental applications focus can have powerful, far-reaching, and lasting effects.

These are the ingredients of effective translation, for which, rather than merely solving an immediate problem, there is always a view of what else is involved and the adjustments necessary at every level and area. This requires that people work in an open and flexible organization that brings together those who need to be involved like so many antibodies. If this work flow is an integral part of the managerial decision-making process, then one has, *ipso facto*, a strategic incremental quality improvement process.

Given an adequate opportunity, common sense leads people to the source of problem flow. Quality improvement comes as people not only solve these problems, but begin to adjust in anticipation of problems to facilitate appropriate outcomes. This, of course, is done by fashioning the kind of performance-oriented processes and systems that characterize a well-managed organization. Prevention can be done by authority-based management, although it tends to be limited and *ad hoc*, but facilitation can only be done by the parties acting in concert and enabled by authority.

Incremental holographs

Most every specific problem is the tip of a system iceberg, and any true solution will quickly find you at the heart of the way the organization is managed. This is what makes an organization holographic. A specific example will illustrate how individual work situations reflect the greater systems. A construction company was having difficulty determining why, with good planning and good people, things turned out wrong. To address this question, we assembled a team to determine why a concrete floor had been poured badly and had to be torn up and repoured.

The cost of the rework was determined to be $75,000 to $100,000, depending on what was included as costs. Fair enough, but at least we had a

---

* There are clearly benefits to be gained from the lessons of Stephen Covey, Situational Leadership, and other approaches to improving personal operating styles, but they seem something akin to ballet lessons to enhance individual grace and strength for athletes. Their final utility, for business purposes, must be in their interweaving and support of a general organizational improvement strategy, not in lieu of one.

minimum number that would have been profit had the problem not occurred or, put another way, how much could have been spent to avoid the problem in the first place. The cause of the problem, they all agreed, was that it was a government building, which meant that they were obliged to use a minority subcontractor who was considered not very good. They claimed to have had problems with this subcontractor before.

As they proceeded to analyze the case, however, a number of other contributing causes became clear:

- The wrong re-bar sets had been ordered, preventing the use of the laser leveler.
- The concrete was ordered from a vendor who was far away the work site but cheaper, resulting in the material's being overmixed when it arrived on the job site.
- There was no one from the construction company to oversee the work of the subcontractor, even though he was supposedly not very good.
- The on-site superintendent was not kept apprised of decisions being made by the manager at the home office, which made work scheduling difficult.
- The manager was not kept informed by the superintendent about situations on-site and continued to make decisions under outdated assumptions.

As it turned out, no one really knew what kind of job the subcontractor could have done because the whole job had so many problems that hardly anyone could have gotten it right. The wavy floor was the product of a poor management system that ranged from design and specification, to procurement, to managing subcontractors, to coordinating their own staff activities. To prevent these kinds of problems in the future required adjusting the management systems to facilitate work by all the those elements who had to perform well. It also turned out, as it usually does, that the cost of doing it right the first time would have been essentially the same as doing it wrong. "Quality," as Phil Crosby says, "is free."

Using what you have

What is also clear from this analysis is that most everything needed to do the job properly was already in place. The purpose was clear to everyone, as was the definition of doing it right. It was also within everyone's technical competence to meet technical specifications. While each job has its own peculiarities, this job was not very different from all the others. It was right in the middle of what should have been the organization's strengths, just another game that should have been doable within the company's repertoire of plays. The only thing needed was all of these resources being used properly.

Human interaction is often called the soft stuff in training circles, while technical training is called the hard stuff. Using technical resources properly, of course, is what the quality movement is all about and why, for managers, the soft stuff is really the hard stuff. The work of the construction company's problem-analysis team was much like viewing game films to see what and how things went wrong. Starting with a new organization was not an option, nor was it desirable. Incremental improvements in the project management process created a new level or organizational quality without disruption, turmoil, or hard feelings. Quality improvement works best when it is an ordinary part of management.

Incremental advantage

When pursued with an effective change strategy, incremental change or organizational learning has several advantages over radical change. Specifically, strategic incrementalism:

1. Avoids the turmoil and pain of large-scale, uncontrolled change
2. Avoids costs of false starts and clean-up of large-scale change
3. Affords control of process to ensure success at each step
4. Does not disrupt production processes
5. Builds upon existing strengths
6. Develops, as part of the improvement process, internal capabilities to sustain improvements once accomplished
7. Develops through learning rather than assuming all the answers
8. Provides a steady basis for specific, high-yield, fast-track efforts
9. Leads to system changes while keeping the focus on performance

An incremental change strategy allows management to consider the application of new techniques and technologies in ways that more fully utilize their potential in strengthening the existing operation. Technology in the right hands can bring an elegant capacity to an organization. For example, there are programs available to computerize or reengineer some personnel functions by putting information on a server, such as policies, job descriptions, and even individual records, to be accessed through on-site terminals throughout a company.[7] With security controls, employees could even input hours worked, allowing the company to automate both its database and payroll.

The savings in staff no longer required to answer these kinds of questions and of employee time off the job to ask them, not to mention the problems that come from getting wrong answers from supervisors or just assuming things, would likely bring a quick payback. This kind of system would also not disrupt the general human resource processes, but would provide a technological improvement that most would appreciate. This would be a considerable change but one which the organization could fit in comfortably, provided the change is strategically managed and properly translated.

A truly strategic incremental approach could also harvest greater value from opportunities that are available. For example, a computer program is available that was designed primarily for training workers in the chemical industry to comply with OSHA-required process safety management standards. The program allows an operation to make available pictures of the facilities, drawings of piping and circuits, safety information with text and pictures, or even video animations of processes, manuals, etc. A employee can interactively learn all about operating a piece of equipment safely at any suitable time when a computer is available.

If the program can train in the office, why can't it train in the field on-site and be a heckuva job aid? For example, a maintenance technician could be equipped with a notebook computer, connected to the server by modem or an on-site connection, and could repair most any piece of equipment with safety and quality assurance. The technician could not only access the repair manuals (which are often not available or are awkward in the field), pictures of the equipment in various stages of disassembly, a database of operations for this particular machine, an interactive analysis process to locate the most likely problem, a parts list, a procedures checklist, and so forth. The technical training requirements, the prospect of cross-training, the ability to respond to breakdowns, improvements in safety, the ability and flexibility of employees to respond — all are qualitatively changed.

The potential of this program for incremental improvement is profound provided the organization is postured to take advantage of it through a rich dialog about what is needed, what is available, and how best to match the two. In the case above, the home office acquired the program to deal with an immediate problem of OSHA requirements with no local involvement. There was little interest by management and little opportunity by others to explore the program's potential. There was also no champion for such an improvement effort because it only represented cost (any expenditure over what is necessary at the time) and more work (when we are so pressed by the urgency of the moment).

It may be impossible to start over, but one can start in a new direction at any time. The turning of the herd may not be quick or neat, but it can be done. The trick is to connect strategy and specific effort in a way that each makes sense in terms of the other. The grand purposes and strategies cascade down through an organization in the form of countless adjustments and negotiations through myriad arrays of interactions where intent and its common sense pursuit is determined. The case of the construction company is an object lesson of what often goes wrong in organizations when there is a lack of excellent knowledge.

While managers are expected to think globally, action is local, and effective global thinking requires good information and understanding about local situations and options. At the same time, those involved in the practical local application are expected to think globally, but that requires information at a more general level about what is being done and why. In the case of the construction company, neither was done. Management made several bad decisions because of a failure to appreciate the effects of these decisions, and the on-site staff got some bad surprises because they were not in good communication with management. The use of authority was such that dialog was not encouraged and communications were stifled. In critical areas of the enterprise, the organization was essentially absent. The translating connection between strategic and incremental is only as good as the dialog that occasions it.

Endnotes

1. Epley, Tom, Technology turnaround: how to win in today's explosive marketplace, *Inter@ctive Week,* December 9, 23, 1996.
2. Terry Ivany, quoted in Bemowski, Karen, VIA rail puts the brakes on runaway operations, *Quality Progress,* October, 37–42, 1996.
3. Epley, Tom, Technology turnaround: how to win in today's explosive marketplace, *Inter@ctive Week,* December 9, 23, 1996
4. Schaffer, Robert H., *The Breakthrough Strategy: Using Short-Term Performance To Build the High Performance Organization,* Ballinger, Cambridge, MA, 1988.
5. These authors have been variously cited throughout this book.
6. American Institute for Research, *Winning Competitive Advantage: A Blended Strategy Works Best,* Zenger-Miller, San Jose, CA, 1995.
7. Interestingly, this idea was offered in a proposal under the title *Reengineering HR: When RADICAL Rather Than Incremental Improvements Are Needed,* by Lyle M. Spencer, Jr., of McBer and Company at a meeting of the ASTD/Suncoast Chapter on March 4, 1994.

chapter seventeen

Quality and organizational rationality

How the things we already know, but often forget,
are the keys to organizational excellence

> *It is not the strongest of the species that*
> *survives, nor the most intelligent, but*
> *the one most responsive to change.*
> ∾Charles Darwin

Several years ago, I worked with a plant manager of a glass products manufacturing company. He was a nice guy who wore a uniform with his name over the pocket just like the workers. Once while we were discussing employee relations he said, "You can't always be a nice guy." I replied that no one was paying him to be a nice guy. His job was to find ways to get the most work he could out of every person on the payroll. When I tell this story there is usually a gasp at such heresy. I go on to say that if making everyone in the plant unhappy, sullen, and resentful would do the job, he should take that approach, but that things don't really work that way. Everyone sits backs in their chairs.

Certainly, everyone should be nice. As Rocky the Squirrel, Bullwinkle's buddy, said, "Good is better than evil because its nicer." Precisely, but that is beside the point. The basic challenge remains not to be nice but to be effective and, all things being equal, nicer people are less threatening and can communicate better over time than blowhards, bullies, and bastards. But then who but the self-deluded does not know that. Smart managers understand that the reason you treat people decently is that they respond well to that but respond defensively to threats.

Management gets what it gives. When Malden Mills burned down, the owner, Aaron Feuerstein, announced that he would rebuild the mill in Lawrence, MA, rather than relocating in a cheap labor country. It was certainly a nice thing to do, but the reason was smart as well as heart. Feuerstein understood that loyal employees make the kinds of products and provide the kind of service that make for loyal customers. As Feuerstein explained:[1]

> "Once you break the workers' trust, I don't think you ever get it back. You'll never get the quality you need. Once you treat them like a cuttable expense, instead of your most important asset, you won't recover. I am firmly convinced the degree of loyalty our people have extended Malden Mills is equal to or greater than what we have done for them."

An unclear picture

It is a rare manager who sets out to be mean. The great truth about organizational life, one that is often forgotten, is that everyone is pretty much just trying to do his or her job, make some money, have some success and satisfaction, and go home at a decent time. It is true that organizations can be corrupting, often combining the worst fears of Lord Acton and Jean Jacques Rousseau.* Like all of human society, organizations can be ennobling as well, depending on how they are managed. They can also be as difficult to understand, predict, and control as the people in them. Most of the world's literature, including that about management, is about this very perplexity. Perhaps more than most literature, musings about management are often as confounding as enlightening.

It is no wonder that mangers are perplexed when they hear things such as, "Quality is excellence continually reinventing itself" or when they simply try to define the elusive "quality". The notion of reengineering conjures up a mechanical adjustment to what is essentially a social system, which, while it uses tools that can indeed be engineered, is in reality behaviorally adaptive. Moreover, it is difficult to know if quality improvement programs work or not. For example, in 1993, *Industrial Engineering* reported that there was "a lack of confidence in financial benefits of quality programs" and companies applying reengineering were worried about managing the changes. That same year the magazine reported that TQM was bringing about "positive changes" and proving to be a "long-term success."[2]

There is a constant stream of reports of quality program successes and failures, a mix of short-term surges of improvement that settle back into the old ways, or sometimes initially poor results but long-term improvements, or sometimes a little of both. For every failure there seems to be an explanatory book or article with suggestions about how to really do it right this time. It is difficult to pick up any trade or airline magazine without at least one article

---

* Rousseau, one may recall, was the proponent of the nobility of mankind in a primitive state that becomes corrupted by social institutions.

on quality improvement. Most of them talk about vision and focus, commitment of management, treating employees decently and empowering them, having good systems, and measuring progress. The problem, however, is not whether one should do these things, because most managers try to do them, think they already are, or have what seems to them compelling reasons not to. Everyone knows there is a need for improvement. It is how to bring it off that seems so confounding.

Search for a better way

In every nook and cranny of American enterprise, thousands of organizations of every stripe are trying some improvement program or other, and a number have achieved impressive success using a variety of these new techniques. For most others there is usually some organizational improvement whatever the approach, because almost any self-assessment and improved communication in an organization will help, at least short term. For many managers, however, the results are disappointing and they are left waiting for the Phoenix like the Pacific islanders waiting for the C-47s.* In many cases, managers are misusing such techniques as BPR to downsize and butcher their organizations. As a result they put more fear in the workplace and disable the workforce, becoming, ironically, not lean and mean but fat and mean.[3]

This kind of mindset favors, and such an environment requires, more supervision and hierarchy to drive the workforce. The result is less quality and efficiency, and less effective systems, but paradoxically more rewards for management. Sometimes management improvement is sought by exhorting people to achieve nonsense, such as giving 110%, another pitfall of our language. Sometimes it is a poor understanding of what one is about, such as ranking employees against each other rather than by their work expectations, a weird logic at best. And sometimes managers are just lost in academic and operationally irrelevant hairsplitting, such as defining the difference between productivity and quality.[4]

The choice facing management is not whether to pursue quality improvement. Competition and other environmental pressures will eventually demand a more optimized operation, and the question becomes when. Nor is the question one of continuous improvement or not, but whether the constant and unavoidable organizational adjustments serve to increase market goodness of fit and operational strength or to undermine them. Organizational capacity, in turn, is determined by organizational control and leadership,

---

* During World War II, natives of some Pacific islands watched American military planes bring in supplies and thought such "great birds" were sent by the gods. For years after the war, these "cargo cults" would keep fires lit and watch the skies for the return of the giant birds and their wonderful cargo.

either elegantly and systematically by its management or chaotically by whomever controls the response to whatever urgency is happening at any give time. The only choice for management is whether it wants to lead the organization and, if so, how to do what must be done.

Start where you are

Whatever might be said to please the boss or consultants, most managers really do not spend much time thinking about strategic operational improvement. What they want and need desperately are ways to deal with the urgent problems they face daily. When things are going well, managers are happy for the respite and do not want to disturb what seems to be working. When things are going badly, they do not have time for non-urgent activities. New programs only threaten them with more work and take away their staff and funds, and they are understandably resistant to waste any effort or resources. Everyday work pressures and a lack of understanding of new science concepts make it difficult for managers to appreciate the truth that only by improving their organization will they get any real relief from their immediate difficulties.

Most of their more frustrating and perplexing problems concern people. Much of these difficulties stem from having to do their work by overcoming poor or misdirected organizational systems or generating *ad hoc* improvisations in their absence, rather than having their efforts facilitated by these systems. The way to improvement is known, and, when done well, its value is indisputable.*[5] The troublesome questions for most change managers, however, are eminently practical ones, such as how to take the necessary steps without dropping the other balls they are trying to juggle or how to establish greater staff involvement and communications without losing control and accountability.

A given activity may not seem different on the surface, but the essence of any behavior is its purpose. Our understanding of a person's intentions not only guides our assessment of that person's efforts, but also determines how that person will perform that act. Bricklayers lay bricks, but they will attend their work differently depending on whether they are putting in their eight hours, laying a wall, or building a house. In a rational organization they are building a house. In a rational organization, they are not just loading trucks but are making sure the product gets to the customer in good condition. The street-sweepers at Disney World do not just sweep streets, they act as street sweepers in the total, make-believe environment that is Disney World.

---

* The qualifier "done well" is the critical characteristic. A poorly done quality improvement effort can be worse than none at all.

The radical change is an ideological adjustment that changes ruts to grooves by incorporating the guiding and elevating force of purpose into ordinary work. A rational ideology creates an organizational environment that moves every person's common sense actions to an efficient and quality-assured application of common organizational goals, a process we have called translation.

Establishing organizational rationality

A sound strategic approach to quality improvement achieves effective change without the remedy being more harmful than the disease. Strategic incrementalism seeks comprehensive change through an array of problem-solving actions that, on the whole, constitute strategic change. It has an end result in mind and uses the principles and power of the general change techniques, but in a strategically focused and controlled way. This allows management to facilitate system improvement without the disruption, turmoil, and production loss of radical surgery.

The guiding principle of organizational quality is organizational rationality, where each incremental action is guided and measured by its contribution to achieving the grand organizational purpose. This organizational rationality provides the foundation for harmony of each individual's situational, common sense determinations about his or her work. This harmony is generated through discussions among the participants that afford opportunities for them to gain an understanding of how they fit into particular work, and what is required to do that work while at the same time adjusting work assignments and organizational support to enhance success.

Seeking to establish rationality brings the entire organization along rather than setting up a foreign, intrusive, and disruptive hot-house flower that will not be supported nor long survive. While avoiding the giant leaps that are theoretically tempting but operational unrealistic, strategic incrementalism guided by common sense rationality acquires, on a more permanent basis, those extra margins of discriminatory performance that distinguish the excellent from the ordinary. There may be other priorities, more important than quality and efficiency, that could cause management to perform radical surgery on their operation. Cost control when an organization is in financial difficulty is perhaps the most common. Nonetheless, an organization in turmoil loses both quality and efficiency, because these can be achieved only to the degree that one optimizes organizational rationality. Indeed, one could define quality and efficiency as an optimally rational organization where all work practice serves the organizational purpose. Moreover, continuous improvement can be defined as the strategic incremental adjustment of work processes to establish and maintain a goodness of fit with the operating environment.

The rational, common sense strategy for quality might be summarized as follows:

> Quality
> ... is establishing and maintaining
> ... an optimal goodness of fit with the market
> ... gained through managerial leadership
> ... that achieves operational excellence
> ... by applying modern understandings of organizations and behavior
> ... and using appropriate modern tools and approaches
> ... to establish elegant and quality-assured rational systems
> ... that control hypercomplexity
> ... through open, free enterprising dialog
> ... to afford excellent knowledge and the translation
> ... of grand organizational purpose into practical situational applications.

Organizational rationality can be measured or, at least, assessed. While most organizational assessments are not of rationality *per se,* many provide some indication of rationality by exploring such areas as climate. Because of the holographic nature of organizations, its true level of rationality can be determined anywhere in the organization and at any time. In actuality, everyone in every organization makes such assessments all the time and, when the situation fails the rationality test, we have fodder for *Dilbert*.

Marks and measures of rationality

Optimal quality is an optimum state of rational management throughout the organization. This condition exists to the extent that an organization's policies and practices logically and reasonable serve to fulfill the organization's goals. Organizational rationality has six marks and measures:

1. There must be a clear purpose defined through specific goals by which all effort is guided and measured.
2. There must be a comprehensive plan for fulfilling that purpose by achieving these goals.
3. Decisions must be based on the best data and analysis.
4. There must be continued effort to have the best tools and craftsmanship.
5. Management must use performance-based systems.
6. There must be managerial control of the operation.

In reviewing the list of rational management requirements it is easy to think they are obvious and that everyone is doing these things. The requirements of rational management are not radical in any sense. Indeed, they are quite traditional concerns of management. Certainly, most managers are doing several or all of these things in some way or another. The measure, however, is not whether there is a chemical trace or some form of these elements to be found, but how truly these marks and measures characterize the organization. The primary difference in life is not whether one is doing something or not but whether one is doing it *well* or not. That is the difference between the chess novice and the chess master, between my tennis game and that of Andrè Agassi, and between an okay operation and an optimized one. Every organization has some rationality, but the issue is not okay but excellence.

Clear purpose

"Who are you and what are you doing here?" This is a seemingly obvious question that frequently gets lost among the "trees" of everyday activities. This question is answered to the extent that everyone in the organization can respond in terms that make strategic and situational sense. Many times corporate goals provide no guidance because they were written for purposes other than being a useful organizational tool. Sometimes they are political statements, sometimes public relations, and sometimes just overblown. A family-owned business was forced to increase its operation dramatically in order to support a growing number of family members.

Their statement of business purpose, however, was to provide our customers with the finest widgets, etc. While supplying quality products was their market niche, their real purpose was maintaining the family in a preferred lifestyle, a proper goal for the company. Because their actions were not aligned with their stated purpose, rationality became lost, and in a short while even the owners stopped pretending they were following the ostensible purpose.

Their corporate purpose could have been stated in terms of enduring financial success through a quality product niche. That would have been more honest, but more importantly, it would have been more clear, consistent with intended actions, and therefore more effective. Efforts to make a company goal sound noble beyond requirements are bound to be met with cynicism and, eventually, disappointment. Unless an organizational purpose is honest and true and can be defined in terms of operational achievement, it has little value.

Benefit of customer focus

A critical element in quality is focus on the customer. The power of this focus is primarily that the connection between a strategic view of market goodness of fit and the specific treatment of a given customer is perceivable to most anyone. In other words, customer focus has both strategic and specific situational definition, and these definitions are holographic. Customer focus not only allows for effective conceptual translation of purpose to practice, it provides both an implementation strategy and a basis for an internal organizational customer chain. Importantly, it provides a foundation for meaningful process management and free enterprise decision making.

How does one measure results such as customer satisfaction or, using a Deming term, customer enthusiasm? The traditional way is to wait until a customer complains and then try to make things right. This is the old detect-and-correct approach, with the customer having the job of detector. It may lead to some customer relief but is likely to garner very little customer enthusiasm. A better method is to form an employee team representing all organizational areas and levels to establish and maintain effective customer relations and continuous improvement, such as demonstrated by Hewlett-Packard. As this customer focus is incrementally established throughout an organization, the operation becomes strategically transformed.

Plan as translator

"How are you going to get where you want and how will you know when you get there?" While some companies have effective planning, most, perhaps the great majority, do not. Typical is an international company that called for unit goals and plans every year but allowed little time to prepare them. The result was that the units just got something on paper and forgot about it. Since the upper levels never really paid any attention to the unit plans or seemed to follow any plan itself, planning was just another hoop one had to jump through once a year.

Even for those who try to have effective plans, there are several reasons why their plans are not effectively used as a real guide and measure for its organizational efforts. Many plans are not used because they never really addressed the question of what success or progress would really look like. Perhaps the goals are off target or too vague and, therefore, planning to achieve such things becomes meaningless. Most plans fail, however, because they are never factored throughout the organization and are not based on present or needed organizational capacity. They may assume excellence but never really enable it. The only measures of interest are end results, such as ROI, total production, or the bottom line. But the idea of good management is not to wait to see how things turn out but to ensure how things turn out. That is, after all, what planning is for.

As Crosby noted, "Change ... should happen by plan, not by accident."[6] A plan should serve as a score card but not just for the final tally. It should provide progress reports that tell management what adjustments are needed during the game. This assumes, of course, a compelling purpose defined with clear goals and a system of gathering and utilizing appropriate measures. These are measures of performance as results not just activities. One reason for the disenchantment with such seemingly rational programs as management by objective (MBO) and the planned program budgeting system (PPBS) is that they became essentially activity counts rather than performance goals measures, i.e., the number of students per course per year rather than improvements in SAT scores.

"Planning," writes Farson, "may not be effective at assessing the future, but it can be a good way to assess the present. ...At its best, planning becomes a form of anticipatory, strategic thinking — the basis for organizational flexibility and readiness."[7] A plan lets everyone know what to do and when to do it by providing true organizational priorities. A plan has value beyond the final document because the work of planning itself is a critical part of improvement. Planning is the process of looking ahead and anticipating what will be required. It provides the vehicle for organizational conversations, the dialog that translates purpose to practice, the essential process in generating organizational common sense. For this reason, the entire organization must in some way be involved if a plan is to provide for effective proactivity.

When a plan is dictated and forced on the organization through a cascade of authority, it basically self-destructs for all the reasons discussed earlier. The plan becomes irrelevant as people become boss-oriented, and the war against the urgencies intensifies. When a plan is introduced through dialog, however, it is self-creating and becomes the organizational intent. The value is not so much in the plan, although a written document is essential for common reference, but in the act of planning in a way that translates purpose to rational action.

It is not necessary to have an annual plan, especially if it is a ridiculous *pro forma* exercise. It is much better to plan year around through conversations about goals and activities to achieve those goals, and it must be a multi-level, multi-functional process. This is not to say that the CEO must listen to the part-time sales clerk about market plans, but planning should involve several organizational levels feeding each other information and insights, as in the Harley-Davidson "circles" model. The Soviet model is instructive for those who feel that centralized planning at the top is preferable to organization-wide planning. One year Gosplan, the Soviet central planning agency, set the quota for chandeliers in tons. As a result, Russia produced the heaviest chandeliers in the world. Unfortunately, no ceiling could support them. It would be more laughable were it not for the "chandelier plans" in most every American organization.

The biggest problem with plans may be that management frequently chooses to ignore them. An example that seems typical is a major corporation that established an extensive and detailed plan. A major consulting company was used to assist management in developing a plan (which was factored throughout the organization) that included even the number of contacts to be made with existing customers, new customers, potential customers, and the like by the sales staff. The consulting firm's fee for this effort was more than $250,000. Shortly after the plan was implemented for the year, management established a sales incentive program that focused on different products and customer development, which essentially killed the carefully developed comprehensive plan.

Unfortunately, management did not make appropriate adjustments in the other parts of the organization so that production and others kept to the new goals and incentives. As a result, the organization did not really operate on the basis of any plan, but just winged it as it went along. The organizational fit with the market was less than good. Everyone tried to adjust to each new change of direction that came from on high and from various departmental chiefs, providing Scott Adams with a steady stream of material for his cartoons.

The internal plan essentially establishes the organization's customer service needs and expectations. When this is thrown into disarray, quality falls off quickly. Unless there are some binding commitments by management and employees at all levels to a common purpose and rational effort, no plan will stick. The result is not free enterprisers but mercenaries and buccaneers. A detailed model for planning is beyond this book, but, in general, the strategy should not be to plan then act, but to plan/act, an integral part of that being constant review. That way, the organization is continually adjusting the decisional downstream to maximize the organization's odds of success and market goodness of fit.

Best available data and analysis

"Are decisions based on good information?" Most managers will argue that they make decisions based on the best information available, and that is almost true. The situation is more likely that they use the most politically correct and easily available information. In many cases, a great deal of information could be available but is not gathered or, even worse, much is readily available but not used. There are a number of reasons for this, most centering around an organization's being highly driven by authority, urgencies, and cost-cutting, three conditions that are usually found together.

Managers will lack good information and, therefore, good decisions if they do not develop the data and do the analysis required. Information has a cost like everything else, which management often views as overhead to be reduced. For example, a large insurance company tried to focus on high-yield marketing opportunities. Support staff were seen as overhead, while commission sales staff were viewed as producers. The support staff, however, were the very people who could have collected and analyzed sales contact data and identified those customers who had the highest sales and profit potential. Had management fully appreciated these "overhead" operations, everyone would have made more money.

Another example is an industrial plant with a history of expensive capital projects to unbottleneck the facility. There had not been, however, any analysis of what equipment, suppliers, times, operators, material feeds, etc. were most associated with equipment or process failures. After years of *ad hoc* solutions, the plant was so particularized that there was no real model of how the plant as a whole could be optimized. While these things are easier to determine when there is equipment involved, patching in other kinds of work processes is more typical than data gathering and analysis for process optimization.

Without good data and analysis each problem has equal weight and its priority is often established by the clout of its sponsor, which is to say it becomes another urgency. Millions of capital dollars can be spent on marginal problems, while the major causes of productivity loss are neglected. Worse, large capital outlays may be invested for improvements that could have been achieved almost immediately and for much smaller costs, such as operator training, job aids, or process improvement.

Managers do not have to develop all of their data. As mentioned earlier, there is a great deal of information and analysis already available to them. An organization that acquires good data, uses sound analysis, and bases its decisions upon them, however, will find itself a learning organization, provided there is a dialog that validates and shares this information. It will also find itself using the techniques of quality management, such as statistical controls and Pareto analysis, as a matter of course. It will use these techniques as tools in the craft of management, not as procedures they must go through to satisfy the latest management program.

Best tools and craftsmanship

The question is: "What is the most critical factor in performance quality?" In a simpler environment where one can more directly observe the relationship between skill and quality of work, one can appreciate that the difference in quality of work is in the craftsmanship, not the tools. A less able person may use the same tools but with inferior results. When the tools get big and complex, however, this perspective is turned on its head and many people now see the tool as the critical element, with the operators as mere appendices. However, quality *is* as the worker *does*.

Companies invest in equipment but try to cut labor costs, often by denying proper training and other steps that develop higher levels of craftsmanship. The difference between investment and costs reflects the low regard many managers have for their workforce, a perspective that does not go unnoticed by employees. The lower the level of employee, the less regard and consideration they are given, even though it is these people who most often perform critical customer-related functions. The technical system should be modern and competitive, but primarily it should provide the human operating system the best chance to use its craftsmanship to the company's best advantage.

Managers, especially those in technical enterprises, often talk of making their plants "idiot-proof" to lessen the impact of the operators. The need for idiot-proofing comes from a failure to prepare people properly for their jobs. The value of Microsoft's Windows operating system is not that it idiot-proofs computers; rather, it does what technology is supposed to do, i.e., facilitates user learning and expands the range of ordinary abilities. It does not replace the craftsmanship of writing, designing, and communicating; it merely provides better tools for it.

Managers who try to replace craftsmanship with equipment will find quality assurance and efficiency quite elusive. An excellent example of what can happen is the newest plant of a major bottle manufacturer that was initially the company's most technically advanced and productive, but became the least productive within 5 years. During those years, the journeyman program had become so neglected and abused that hardly anyone in the plant could maintain the equipment properly. Indeed, many journeymen could not even operate the equipment. As a result, the factory deteriorated into a mess of barely operating machinery and nearly helpless operators.

When the craftsmanship is poor, both product and equipment suffer. One sign that managers have failed to understand the importance of their human system and the craftsmanship of the people is a failure to provide adequate technical/operator interfaces or control systems. In one chemical plant, an area that suffered the greatest understaffing was that of instrumentation and controls in their engineering department and among the maintenance and repair technicians. As a result, operators were less able to control their equipment, making it difficult to process material to specifications. As a result, the fastest growing part of the plant was the blending facility, where the already processed products were finally adjusted to meet customer specifications. Even there, blending operators spent a great deal of time guessing or taking hand samples.

Using new equipment with new technologies can provide an operation with a step increase in productivity, assuming that the operators and maintenance technicians are properly trained, etc. Developing the craftsmanship of the employees and a system that supports the continued strengthening of that craftsmanship, however, is the only strategy that provides continuous improvement and, by its nature, sustains its own growth and development. No one has better technology in their arena than Disney, but the focus of Disney management is not just on the gee-whiz stuff. Repeating what Walt Disney said, "You can dream, create, design, and build the most wonderful place in the world ... but it requires people to make the dream a reality."

According to company studies, Disney World in Florida enjoys a 70% visitor return rate, of which 90% is because of service "directly attributed to the cast members." Turnover has been reduced from 30 to 16%, which is remarkable considering that most of the 42,000 people are part time, and Disney operates 24 hours a day, 365 days a year. Shift work and, especially, part-time work are two of the major areas of turnover. Contrast this with the national average where even 69% of management personnel reportedly have sent out resumes in the past year.[8]

Performance-based systems

Quality and efficiency are often lost because management strategies and values are not aligned with organizational goals. The question that keeps management properly focused is, "Are decisions and actions based upon their value-add to the desired organizational results?" Actions that contribute to achieving organizational goals are performance based, those that are intended to meet other criteria (e.g., keep the boss happy) are not. As has been previously discussed, managers often think their actions are performance based, but often they are based on managerial authority or its offspring cost-basing, rule-basing, and preferential indulgence.

The logic of authority is that managers are appointed based on their qualifications and are expected to know what they are doing. If they don't, then they are replaced. It sounds good on paper, but it often does not work out that way for a variety of reasons:

1. *Those appointed are not always excellent.* People are selected from those available, not from a list of ideal candidates, and often times for their technical success rather than leadership promise. One of the most telling findings on employee surveys is the negative response to the statement, "The best people are promoted." The Peter Principle notwithstanding, many appointments come from a system that does not consciously develop its people for promotion before or after appointment.

2. *Managers are always, or should always be, on a steep learning curve.* Even when excellent people are appointed to management they are often moved every two years or so, especially if the company is growing. Even when positions are more stable, the situations every organization faces today are constantly changing and require different ways of dealing with them. The push for quality improvement is not to reach some particular steady-state of operation but to maintain an ability to constantly deal with new challenges.

3. *The real world is too complex for the traditional management role.* For every complex, difficult problem there is an answer that is simple, easy, and wrong. The rule of commensurability requires that the management or human operating system be of a complexity to fit the nature of the technical system and environment of operation.

4. *The real work of the organization does not follow the organizational chart.*
   There are built-in problems when organizations try to manage:

this: with this:

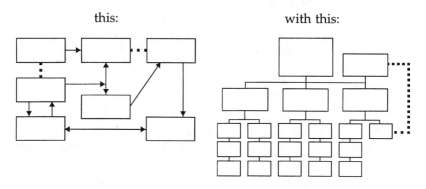

5. *Management systems may be performance based in initial design or intent,
   but they rarely stay that way.* Many examples have been discussed, but
   one of the best is the typical performance appraisal program that starts
   off talking about development and ends up dealing with performance
   problems, or, worse, *not* dealing with them. Because such systems are
   so flawed, there is generally a disconnection between performance
   and reward, and most raises seem designed to placate rather than
   reward. Most performance appraisals serve only to create bad feeling
   rather than good work, and supervisors dread them more than the
   subordinates do.
6. *Managers try to manage people rather than systems.* For all the foregoing
   reasons, this is the dominant mode of management, and the result is
   the undermining of whatever systems may have been attempted.

One could probably think of other reasons why operations are not performance based, but the above give the general idea.

Managerial control

When the first five "marks and measures of rationality" have been satisfied,
management can acquire the one thing it must to be successful: control.
Control here does not refer to the ability to stop action, for that is within the
power of most every bureaucrat or autocrat; rather, control means the ability
to cause the right actions, to ensure that all resources are used optimally to
achieve organizational goals. Control exists when there is a high level of
rationality, when systems are responsive and efficacious, and when people
employ that margin of discretionary effort that makes the difference between
okay and excellent.

If orders would do the job, then control would stem from commands. The only effective avenue of control for quality improvement, however, is through dialog, the conversations of Senge's learning organization. Management control comes not from the power to order actions but from understanding the effects of actions. For example, the executive who denied clerical assistance to his staff essentially lost control of much of their activities, turning them from productive professionals into expensive amateur clericals. When an effective plan is lacking, when the craftsmanship or human operating system is deficient, and when decisions and actions are not based upon sound data and analysis, control is only illusionary. Managing becomes much like driving a bumper car and thinking you are on a trip.

Many managers confuse technical or parochial control with managerial control. Parochial and technical control here refer to a situation where a decision about a particular aspect of the total operation is tantamount to a strategic decision. Managerial control refers to the strategic processes which define the context for technical and situational matters. Most managers were at one time professionals or technicians of one kind or another and can easily make the mistake of using that perspective in dealing with system problems.

Authority-based systems invite parochial and technical controls. Since many system problems are manifest as technical problems, a different perspective beyond a given incremental situation is required to understand its strategic significance. In recent years, technology and process sophistication have created a much more complex environment in which a variety of specialties, wide geographic operations, and critical coordination and delivery times have created a far more complex world. In this new world, maintaining managerial, rather than technical or parochial, control of an organization will be increasingly difficult unless one's management approach is as sophisticated as the problems.

Endnotes

1. See Uchitelle, Louis, In becoming an icon a mill owner bets his company, *The New York Times*, D-1, July 4, 1996.
2. See, for example, "Lack of confidence in financial benefits of quality program" in *Industrial Engineering*, June, 12, 1993; "Companies applying reengineering worried about managing change" in *Industrial Engineering*, June, 11, 1993; "TQM programs making positive changes" in *Industrial Engineering*, December, 7, 1993.
3. Gordon, David M., *Fat and Mean: The Corporate Squeeze of Working Americans and the Myth of Managerial "Downsizing"*, The Free Press, New York, 1996. The author argues that management in many companies is treating employees worse, requiring more supervision and management hierarchies and rewarding themselves at the expense of those who actually do the work.

4. The point is not that precision in definitions is not important but that operating managers generally find such discussions outside the realm of real value. See Huff, Lenard, Claes Fornell, and Eugene Anderson, Quality and productivity: contradictory and complementary, *Quality Management Journal*, 4(1), 22–39, 1996.

5. Evidence of the value of a quality program is the record of the General Securities Fund, which began investing only in companies practicing TQM after noticing that their stocks did comparatively well over the long term. See "Investing in quality pays off for General Securities" in *Quality Progress*, December, 10–11, 1996.

6. Crosby, Philip, *Let's Talk Quality*, McGraw-Hill, New York, 1989, p. 7.

7. Farson, Richard, *Management of the Absurd: Paradoxes in Leadership*, Touchstone New York, 1996, p. 125.

8. The Disney information is found in Smith, Vernita C., Spreading the magic, *Human Resource Executive*, December, 28–31, 1996. See also "Avoiding execs who abandon ship" in *HR Focus*, April, 14, 1996.

chapter eighteen

The quest for quality

*How management improvement is looking
at ordinary things in a more rational way*

> *There are many fine things which you mean to do someday,*
> *under what you think will be more favorable circumstances.*
> *But the only time that is surely yours is the present.*
>   ∾Grenville Kleiser

Quality is not something you *have* but something you *do*. More accurately, it
is how you think about what you are doing. The difference between a fake
and a replica is how it is represented — that is, what one is supposed to think
about it. The difference between someone cutting wood and someone building a house is also in the mind, but the difference is profound both for the
quality of work and indeed the nature of the work itself. The human enterprise is essentially conceptual, so when you think differently about what you
are doing, you are in effect doing something different. As the Japanese have
amply demonstrated, doing things right and doing the right things are really
no different.

Making it happen

Rational managers understand that their job is to accomplish organizational
purpose and, therefore, seek ways to get others to perform at their best. They
establish an open-door policy in which they go out the door into the workplace to learn what is required to ensure that what the company needs will
be done. They will seek ways to enable employees for optimum performance.
They will not try to manage by "walking around" but by "working around",
by joining their own team and working with them rather than just issuing
orders and placing blame. The impact of these changes could be tremendous.
Not only would managers be more informed and the employees supercharged,

but managers will find that they have options of which they had never dreamed.

For example, a study of why people were resistant to, even undermining, change programs found one of the key things the people wanted was for management to get to know the employees and to encourage and trust them.[1] We do, indeed, have more trust in those we know can do the job. A manager working around, moreover, is more likely to spot a person who cannot do the job and take appropriate and timely action. The idea is not for managers to become less engaged, one perversion of empowerment, but to become *more* engaged. The key to success in change programs is not more employee participation (they have little choice) but more *management* participation. With that, employee participation is a given. Without it, employee participation is a sham.

Managers would save themselves a lot of grief by not making a big deal about their new efforts and by just starting to operate differently. Everyone will notice, and not only will the expectations be more reasonable but the progress will also be more appreciated. As one manager said about a change effort, "Why *call* it anything; let's just *do* it!" Sage advice. Don't make a big deal about open communications; just ask people what they think and share your thoughts with them. The CEO could start a marvelous cascade of improvement interests simply by asking at the end of each staff meeting, "What have you done today in your area to improve our operation?" After that, it will be a rare supervisor who responds to a suggestion with, "We're not paying you to think, Jones."

Managers can also ask people who have worked on a problem what they have done to prevent these kinds of problems in the future, thereby letting them know that patching is no longer the acceptable response. If things are not done well at first, coach people on how to do them properly. The idea is not to tolerate or merely allow improvement efforts, but to demand them, pay off on them, and make them an integral part of work.

Actions and reactions

Management actions, like all other actions, have multiple effects that either reinforce or change behaviors and structures. Sometimes, those things that a manager thinks of as being the least significant can have the most profound effect, such as failing to recognize good effort. Everything impacts an organization at four levels:

- The substantive or technical area, such as safety, sales, etc.
- The individual in ways that are often interactive with work groups
- The work group, a work or socially related cluster that people identify as such
- The system, which can refer to the organization as a whole or a major component

A number of examples of this aspect of hypercomplexity have been discussed. A common experience is setting up work teams but not adjusting the organization to support team efforts. This creates more work and risk for the team members and possibly weakens the departments that provide team staff. Usually, in such circumstances, the team has been given no authority or means to do anything, so the employee's feeling of powerlessness is reaffirmed. There are other examples, however, that have equally harmful effects; one is simply by not responding to staff who bring questions. No decision, of course, *is* a decision. That management does not maintain certain work priorities or have respect for staff concerns can reach far beyond a particular issue. People leave a meeting and say nothing happened, but indeed something did happen and it was not good. People feel their time was wasted and, therefore, they have been trivialized. They both resent it and have less confidence in management, who does not seem to know any better.

Invariably, when an improvement program is underway people will complain about having too many meetings or not getting anything done in the meetings. Yet, when trying to improve communications, staff invariably sees the need for meetings. Organizations spend hundreds of thousands of dollars on meetings and much more than that as a result of them. Teams, one might say the organization itself, exist largely through meetings. Meetings are, therefore, a key leadership venue. Still, conducting meetings is not only a neglected art but one that has virtually no standing. Few things are more critical in organizational communications than meetings or the absence of them, because that is where people are informed, reestablish their relationships, negotiate deals, make collective decisions, and get trained. When these things are done outside of meetings, it is generally to the detriment of the operation as a whole.[2]

The being of doing

It may be a bit existential but, like quality, management is not what one *is* but what one *does*. That there are people called "managers", some of whom may have no management responsibility, tends to confuse us. Management as a set of people rather than a process loses sight of the essence of control and creates a privileged class of employees who enjoy various organizational duchies and fiefdoms, the perquisites therefrom, and punitive authority over subordinates.* Similarly, management tools and techniques are not merely what management does; they are, like management style, what management is. Teams, for example, are not a tool or management but a form of it.

---

* That characterization may seem extreme at first, but almost everyone can remember the organizational supervisor or manager who was a virtual bully or tyrant, used authority badly, and enjoyed the fear of subordinates. While these may be unusual and extreme, threat is ever present in most organizations in one form or another. For example, one can observe a casual joking threat about a person's job by the boss. People laugh, but only the boss is really amused.

Management as a "thing" gets one into such awkward concepts as *self-managed* teams when such is rarely the actual case. That they have been seen in the past as somehow separate from management, meaning the hierarchical authority structure, is perhaps the primary reason they have often done so poorly. It is inconceivable that an organization can have any sort of successful quality program without multi-functional and multi-level collective effort at solving problems or even ongoing management of many systems.

Teams are an elegant form of management in that they bring control to complexity by more tightly binding the organization through improved communication and translation. When done properly, the requirements and agreements for team enablement have been worked out in advance. Decisions, coordination, and information are all available among the players either in real time or with minimum delays.

There is no lack of available tools for the enterprising manager. It is more likely that a person will be overwhelmed with options than be without them. There are entire subdisciplines of improvement techniques and tools, often organized into professional associations such as the International Society for Performance Improvement (performance technologies), American Society for Quality Control (TQM and ISO 9000), and training (American Society for Training and Development). The difference, however, in ordinary *ad hoc* use of such tools and a strategy of rational management is the difference between authority-based dabbling and rational, performance-based strategic incrementalism. Table 1 is a comparison.

The purpose of this book has not been to lay out a specific program for establishing organizational quality, but rather to explore the oftentimes hidden factors that thwart managers as they try to optimize their operations. I have attempted to explore the nature and causes of these problems, and suggest some general strategies for dealing with them. As noted in the introduction, each of the elements of organizational behavior is profound in itself, such as motivation, paradigmatic thinking, decisional processes, budgeting, organizational design, or technology.

As you have no doubt found, to put all of these together and explore their relationships is not for the manager who is looking for an easy answer to the challenges he or she faces. Any "easy" solution should be viewed with deep suspicion. Simplism is not elegance, and actions based on simplistic thinking are invitations for adverse unintended consequences. All of the factors, which I have attempted to explore as chapters, have a convoluted integrity and complexity and cannot be ignored with impunity. On the other hand, like other hypercomplex things, such as fingerprints, traffic, and even weather, the complexity of organizational behavior can be effectively understood with the proper paradigms and effectively used with the proper elegant tools.

Once one understands the factors that must be dealt with to put the odds in your favor, one can then look at the key system in any organizational effort

Table 1   Comparing Quality Conditions of Rational/Performance-Based and
Traditional/Authority-Based Organizations

Characteristic	Rational/performance-based	Traditional/authority-based
Organizational design	Organization forming itself around work processes	Rigid hierarchies/ departments
Organizational structure	Open communications around work process	Hierarchical/departmental silos
Organizational sizing strategy	Seeks market goodness of fit	Looks for head-count reductions, minimal capability, cost-cutting
Management style	Managerial leadership	Management by authority/ threat
Management ideology	Applied modern science concepts	Traditional/mechanical perspective
Management role	Translation of purpose to common sense practice	Give orders backed by threat
Quality standards	Operational excellence	Okay, parochial control
Decision strategy	Enable and facilitate performance	Reliance on authority, boss knows best
Utilization of technology	Use of modern tools and approaches	Failure to use tools to best advantage
Change strategy	Transformation through creative adaptation	Rigidity, change when problems require it
Characteristics of control	Elegant controls of hypercomplexity	Miss complex implications, driven by *ad hoc* and urgent problems; control by yanking and wrenching

and outline how they might be fashioned to engender an optimized organization. The key control systems in an organization are those that control information and assign resources. Unless these systems are effective, it is hard to imagine achieving any high degree of rationality. Perhaps the key system, and the one that is most often found inadequate, is that which tells people what they should do and how they are doing, enables and enhances their performance, and assigns rewards.

The keystone system

An associate of mine specializes in human resource management. Recently, while assessing the personnel practices of a new client, he learned that three workers had just been terminated. These men had been, the client explained, long-term performance problems. When my associate looked at the files of the terminated employees, each had received a letter from the company's CEO announcing their raise for the year and commending them on their "outstanding work". The letter was dated less than two months ago.

A person getting fired for cause and having a file full of laudatory reviews and raises is so common that we often overlook just how profound a problem this is. Such letters are often seen as the problem, principally when there is litigation, but they are only symptoms of the real problem. First, when everyone gets an across-the-board raise, we know that people are not being rewarded for performance. Second, because everyone gets a good performance rating regardless of their work, we know that management either does not know or does not care about what about performance. Third, we can be fairly confident that minimum performance (compliance) is the acceptable quality standard. One would anticipate further that people are poorly trained and that management is not being held accountable for its performance. It is unlikely that anyone really knows the organization's real capability for productivity and profitability.

The keystone system of any organization is a performance management system. While performance management has been used to denote a variety of things, ranging from disciplinary processes to behavior modification, it properly encompasses all those activities that directly affect an individual's performance. It is the system that lets people know what is expected of them and how they are doing at any given time, provides suitable rewards for proper performance, and, in general, guides, facilitates, and supports employee effort. This system begins with establishing performance expectations and qualifications, i.e., providing the appropriate information to recruiting services, and continues through orientation, training and development, performance review, and incentives.

There is ample evidence that quality failures stem largely from poor performance management. One typical example is a county government that has had a quality program for 5 years. Recently, when I talked with the person responsible for coordinating that effort, she noted that managers were not really using the quality techniques and did not seem too concerned about the quality program. When I inquired about their incentives, she noted that "human resources is working on a new incentive program now;" however, she was not working with them to ensure quality was being one of the things rewarded. Indeed, neither the quality program nor the new incentive program were tied into the so-called performance management system.

No wonder quality ends up in the management closet, out of the way of the "real" work of the organization. If what gets rewarded is what gets done, common sense should tell us that quality must be rewarded and that there must be an effective, credible system for determining those rewards. A graphic representation of a quality-oriented performance management system might look like Figure 1.

```
┌─────────────────────────────────────────────────────┐
│  Quality  ←  Performance expectations                │
│              Performance feedback                    │
│              Performance support                     │
│              Performance rewards  ←  Incentives      │
└─────────────────────────────────────────────────────┘
```

Figure 1   Quality-oriented performance management system

Effective performance management

Organizational management cannot be better than the performance management system affords. And, while this area, or parts of it, are often the most cussed by management, it is also the most neglected and poorly done. At a national workshop, I watched a pair of internal consultants to a Fortune 100 company present their performance management system and crow about how modern it was. When the fancy wrapper was removed, it was nothing but a gussied up version the old personnel evaluation.

When a person talks about how to handle the annual appraisal interview, it is a bad sign that reflects that they are thinking of personnel evaluations, not performance management. In an effective performance management system, the formal annual interview, if there is one, should be solely for the purpose of documenting what has transpired during the past year. If anything significant happens there that surprises the employee, the system has already failed. The only reason employees should get a poor evaluation on anything is because they have not improved in a specific area despite the efforts of their coach.

True performance management strives to ensure that everyone earns a good rating through good work. When the year is over, it is too late for managing. Engendering high performance is the only interest an organization should have in performance review. Certainly there is little profit in just finding ways to "gig" employees, especially months after the person's supposed poor performance was observed. Indeed, if supervisors have no responsibility for the performance of their direct reports, one must wonder what they have been doing for the past year.

While a downward review is appropriate and probably necessary, a downward review *alone* fails the test of rationality. Customers, i.e., those who rely on a person's performance, should be involved. Every performance management system should include some upward review, focusing on the rationality of the working environment that management has been charged with creating. Appropriate questions include:

- "Do you know how your work fits into the overall mission of the company?"
- "Do you have the equipment and materials you need to do your best work?"
- "Does your department have good relations with others?"

To reiterate, performance management is perhaps the most critical system in any organization. But there is an interconnectivity of all actions and systems. For example, performance would seem the only rational basis for rewards in an organization. To truly have pay for performance, however, there must be some real control by employees over their ability to perform. Without reviewing all the aspects of that covered in this book, reward for performance and control over effort comprise a good definition of internal free enterprise.

If a free enterprise environment is necessary for true pay for performance, an effective performance management system is necessary for true quality improvement. The object of quality can never be just to turn out better widgets or cut costs. It must have the more strategic goal of transforming the organization, and that is done through employee performance. The role of management in optimizing employee performance is in providing effective, rational work systems that guide and enable such performance.

Preparing for modern management

At first glance, the six elements of the rational management model may not seem too different from the many other ideas about ways to develop an effective and sustained quality improvement program. There are some differences, however, and they are critical. For example, John Kotter's reasons for quality program failures, outlined in his popular article in the *Harvard Business Review*, are typical. Most such analyses are essentially on target because the immediate reasons for quality program disappointments are pretty well known. What is not so evident, however, are the causes of these reasons. Table 2 modifies Kotter's eight steps for transforming an organization to fit with the six elements of rational management and is not intended as a criticism but rather a demonstration of how a different formulation can make implementation more practicable.

Perhaps the most difficult thing about understanding our world is stepping back to see it in proper perspective. That is much of what Henry Kissinger meant when he said reality is the hardest thing to see. It is also what is meant by the observation that the obvious is where the search for understanding begins, not ends. Kotter is correct in his call for a sense of urgency by management, but the urgency is for management's development into leadership through understanding and enlightened practice. Perhaps management can more fully appreciate the urgency for organizational improvement with an Organizational Rationality Audit (Table 3), which can give management a clear picture of where irrationalities are wasting corporate resources.

Organizational Rationality Audit Syllabus

In mathematics, the Goedel Theorem of Incompleteness states that a system cannot be understood from the inside only but must be observed from the

Table 2 Kotter's Eight Transformation Steps in Rational Management Terms

Kotter's transformation steps	Rational management approach
Establish a sense of urgency	Establish priorities — managers are overwhelmed with urgencies due to a lack of effective priorities. Priorities are based on purpose, plan, and analysis; urgency is based on immediate pressure.
Form a powerful guiding coalition	Form the organization through rational systems — when performance management, for example, makes clear what is expected, assesses performance, and rewards on that basis, everyone is a part of the coalition.
Create a vision	Statement of worthwhile purpose, with specific goals — seek to optimize goodness of fit as a formulation of that vision.
Communicate the vision	Establish management systems that enable and promote dialog to translate purposes into practical applications.
Empower others to act on the vision	Enable and require others to act on organizational purpose.
Plan and create short-term wins	Strategic incrementalism is a strategy of short-term improvements in goodness of fit.
Consolidate improvements and produce still more change	Strategic incrementalism is a strategy of organizational development with minimum disruption of work processes.
Institutionalize new approaches	Strategic incrementalism is a strategy of focused, continuous development.

Source: Adapted from Kotter, John, Why transformation fails, *Harvard Business Review*, March/April, 59–67, 1995.

outside as well. The prosaic statement of that is that fish will be the last to understand water. It is equally true that understanding our organization and ourselves requires that we find ways to give ourselves new perspectives on old practices. Fortunately, this is the unique quality of human beings — i.e., the ability to envision ourselves in another state and then making it so.

To step away for the simpler, easier, and more comfortable mechanical notions of management and into the somewhat blinding light of modern thinking based on relations and dynamics is not easy. Douglas Hofstadter wrote a marvelous book exploring the understanding of reality, and its complexities and elusiveness called *Goedel, Escher, Bach: An Eternal Gold Braid*, in which he observed:[3]

Table 3 Organizational Rationality Audit Syllabus

Rationality mark and measure	Documents/artifacts review	Workplace assessment methods	Important questions
Purpose	Overall statement Departmental statements, other statements regarding purpose mission, goals, values, etc.	Survey all employees Interviews with managers, supervisors, and selected employees Workplace observations Do they find it viable? Is it being pursued? Is the customer focus clear?	Is there a clear statement of purpose? Who knows what it is? Who understands it? What do they understand?
Plan	Written strategic plan Written operating plans at each level and for every function (to fit the business strategy, performance measures, etc.)	Survey all employees Interviews with managers, supervisors and selected employees	Is there a strategic plan? Is it viable, up to date? Are there supportive operating plans? Is work done according to plan? Is there a plan for change and adjustment?
Use of data and analysis	Strategic plan Operating plans Monitoring systems and practices Response systems and practices	Interviews with managers, supervisors, and selected employees Is the information management system rational?	Is there a clear set of business goals? Are there operating goals for all critical processes? Are there goals and measures for desired customer response?

Best tools and craftsmanship	Technical system optimization plan Work performance mastery standards Quality standards Training plan and program Problem-solving methods Best practices program	Survey all employees Interviews with managers, supervisors, and selected employees Workplace observations Is there a performance optimization plan and is it being followed?	Is there a technology optimization plan and is it being followed? Are there standards for performance expectations? What is the status of training? What are the criteria for promotions? Is there a plan to ensure qualified people are in and are available for every position?
Performance-based systems	Performance-management system Information-management system Budgeting structure Business and organizational performance score-carding Problem-response systems and practices	Survey all employees Interviews with managers, supervisors, and selected employees Are people paid for performance? Workplace observations	Are performance expectations clear? Are they related to business strategy? Is necessary information available in the right place, at the right time, and in the right form? Are budgeting and cost decisions linked to benefits and results? Are people customer focused?
Managerial control	All documents noted above	Survey all employees Interviews with managers, supervisors, and selected employees Workplace observations	Are decisions based on business goals or parochial or technical goals? Are departments customer focused? How are decisions made?

> "In most systems that we know, the parts retain their
> identities during the interaction, so that we still see the
> parts inside the system. For example, when a team of
> football players assembles, the individual players re-
> tain their separateness — they do not melt into some
> composite entity, in which their individuality is lost.
> Still — and this is important — some processes are
> going on in their brains which are evoked by the team
> context, and which would not go on otherwise. ...[T]he
> players change identity when they become part of the
> larger system, the team."

That insight well describes the dynamic phenomena of organizational formation. The traditional view sees the players, but the modern view sees the team whose interactions transform a collection of individuals into something quite different. The effort for mastery in organizational management (leadership is the usual term) requires study, thought, and work. More than any other part of an organization, management learns by doing. It achieves excellence, to paraphrase Vince Lombardi, through excellent practices.

Mastery is typified by a gentle touch, of deep engagement with the enterprise, of a profound understanding that anticipates what is needed and what will happen when actions are taken. When there is understanding, when things are done for different reasons, when the ideology is modern and efficacious, and when the striving is for rationality, then quality is within the grasp. Preachments about pain are suspect, although one should certainly anticipate discomfort with any change. But when the organization has been understood properly and the full potential of every employee is being utilized in a common sense way, there is no need for conflagration. The Phoenix is already yours.

Endnotes

1. American Institute for Research, *Winning Competitive Advantage: A Blended Strategy Works Best*, Zenger-Miller, San Jose, CA, 1995.
2. For more on meetings as a leadership function, see English, Gary, How about a good word for meetings?, *Management Review*, June, 58–60, 1990.
3. Hofstadter, Douglas, *Goedel, Escher, Bach: An Eternal Golden Braid*, Basic Books, New York, 1979.

Index

Index

A

acceptable, as okay, 65–66
across-the-board raises, 128, 129
action
    basis of, 188
    orientation, 81
activity trap, 96
activity-based costing, 126–127
American Airlines, 179
American Society for Quality Control
    (ASQC), 50, 63, 244
American Society for Training and
    Development, 244
American vs. Japanese views, 65, 80–81,
    82
analysis, of data, 234–239
Analytical Pragmatists, 175
Aquinas, Thomas, 86
Aristotle, 86, 149
AT&T, 5
authority, 91–102
    and failure of quality control, 102
    as power to punish, 101
    unchecked, 94
    use of, 93

B

Baldridge, Malcolm, 11, 12, 13, 14, 67,
    74, 198
    core values of awards, 198
banking operations, 5

beehive, as self-managed team, 195
behavior, population vs. individual, 23
best practice, 8
Blackstone, Sir William, 86
blame, as privilege of authority, 93
blind faith, 93–94
blind hope, 123
bossism, 93–94
    bad habits of, 94–95
BPR, *See* business process
    reengineering
brain, illustration of, 24
budget, and control, 125–126
budgeting, 119–132
    as knowledge, 131–132
    discrete element, 126, 127
    integrative, 127–128
    process, 127, 128
bureaucracy
    and rule-basing, 99–100
    creation of, 97
    product of authority-based
        management, 99
bureaupathology, 136
business process reengineering (BPR),
    6, 14, 15, 74, 227

C

Canadian Airlines, 4
categories of events, 203
centrifugal force, 201
centripetal force, 201

chance, gaining favor of, 110
change, 59
  incremental approach, 218–219
  inherent dynamic of, 154
  organizational, and translation,
      166–168
  pressure for, 4–6
  providing time for, 153–154
  radical, as threat to work stream, 152
  resistance to, 148–149, 152–153
  strategies for, 213–224
  vs. stability, 154
chaos, 35–36
  control of as purpose, 152
clean slate, fallacy of, 7–8
clerical staff reductions, 120
coaching, 175–186
  to win, 180–181
Coca-Cola, 50
common sense, 42, 92, 203–204
  and aspects of enterprise, 204–206
  and translation, 190–191
  applying to real-life situations, 166
  assessment of being on time, 191
  challenged by high complexity, 84
  components of, 24–25
  contours of, 23–24
  defining, 21
  faculties, 58, 109
  ideology as framework of, 82
  individual styles of, 29
  management, 199–209
  measures of, 27–28
  organizational, 47–49, 193–194
  organizational excellence and, 21–31
  organizations as collective form of, 141
  rationality, and purpose, 196–197
  relationships, as human system, 152
  situational, 27
  strategy for quality, 230
  undermining, 64–65
communications, 45, 143
  lack of, 56–57
  open, 245
competence, in managerial skills, 177
complexity
  challenge of, 33–40
  control and, 37

compliance, 66
conceptual learning, 43–44
conformance, 66
confusion, 8–9
consultants, hiring workers back as,
      123
context, rational, 194
control, 91–102, 238–239
  and budget, 125–126
  and leadership, 100–102
  confusing technical or parochial
          control with management, 239
  elegant, 39–40, 203
  management failures, 93
  modern, need for, 95–96
  paradox of, 96–98
  parochial vs. management, 52–53
  under rational circumstances, 100
core business, identifying, 80
cost control, 120
cost vs. waste management, 120–121
cost-basing, irrationality of, 121–123
cost-cutting, 121
  and cost-basing, 122
  mentality, results of, 126
cost-to-benefit ratio, 122
costing, activity-based, 126–127
costs, non-value-adding, 127
Covey, Stephen, 13, 14, 15, 23, 26, 136,
      142, 204
craftsmanship, 235–239
  replacing with equipment, 236
Crandall, Robert, 179
Crosby, Philip, 83, 135, 155, 163, 205,
      221
cultures, low vs. high, 80–81
customer enthusiasm, 232
customer focus, benefit of, 231–239
customer relations
  external, 68
  internal, 67–68
cycle-time reduction, 128

D

Darwinism, 86
data, using best available, 234–239
debriefing, 181

decision
    -related activities, 114
    as discrete act vs. ongoing stream, 105
    beginning and end of, 110
    good, definition of, 109
    stream, 104
    vs. command, 104
decision making, 103–115
    as choice of potentials, 108
    as creative process, 107–108
    logic vs. values, 109
decisional circles, 112
decisions
    as adjustments of ongoing activities,
        115
    as choice among alternatives, 166
    as translations, 105
    inadequate, 106
    intuitive, 108
    rational, 112–113
demands, honest, 179–180
Deming, W. Edwards, 5, 6, 9, 10, 12, 13,
        15, 73, 77, 81, 83, 97, 142, 163, 184,
        204, 207, 232
dialog, 109
    of reality, 111–112
    open, necessity of, 54–55
    organizational, forums for, 170
    thwarted, 96
Dilbert, 11, 57, 58–59
disagreement, as search for common
        sense, 100
DISC, 176
discipline, true, 196
Disney, 110, 178, 228, 236
    Contemporary Hotel, 92
Driver-Expressives, 175
Drucker, Peter, 16, 27, 50, 83, 126, 150,
        160, 166, 179
DuPont safety program, 8

E

Eastman Chemical, 138
easy answers, search for, 16–17
effort
    as element of enterprise, 100, 131
    judging of, 49

Eisner, Michael, 130
elegance
    natural, 202–203
    search for, 37–38
    vs. simplism, 38–39
elegant control, 39–40
emotion, and rationality, 207–209
employee
    involvement, 56–57
        as source of control, 204
        reason for, 54
    meetings, 56
    newsletters, 69
    suggestions, 51
    training, 67
employees
    rewarding of, 128
    treating all as worst, 184
empowering, 101
    vs. enabling, 72
empowerment, 70, 71–72
    failure of, 181
enabling, 72
    vs. empowering, 72
enterprise, basics of, 189, 219
errors
    pressure to prevent, 92–93
    three basic, 141–143
excellent knowledge, 41–60, 132, 190
    lack of, 106–107
exhortation, as nemesis of good
        management, 204
experience, 28–29
    lessons from, 43
expertise
    business, 135
    misplaced, 135–136
    technology, 135

F

farmer and mule, 119
Fidelity, 181
finding the organization, 138–139
fitness, as model for change, 7
flexibility, 216–217
    good vs. bad, 217
Florida Power & Light, 73

folk knowledge, 41, 42, 43, 44, 51
follow-through, 105
Ford, Henry, 86, 138
frame of reference, 160–161
framing the organization, 133–143
free enterprise, 129–130
    internal, 248
frugality, as function of ownership,
        130–131
Fujitsu, 111

G

Galbraith, John Kenneth, 83
GE Business Information Center
        (GEBIC), 130
General Electric, 56
General Motors, 55, 82
goal inversion, 67
goals, translating into action, 160
Goedel Theorem of Incompleteness,
        248
goodness of fit, 213–215, 245
    maintaining, 215–216
gripe sessions, 56
groove vs. rut, 154
gut
    as decision maker, 111
    feelings, 28

H

Hammer, Michael, 6, 13, 14, 145
Harley-Davidson, 79, 112, 127, 233
Herzberg's satisfier-motivator model of
        motivation, 188
Hewlett-Packard, 57, 59, 111, 112, 184,
        232
hierarchy, 157–171
    as a problem, 161–162
    as organizational feature, 157
    new, 158
    new concepts of, 168–169
    of knowledge, 158–160
    performance-based design, 169–170
high vs. low context, defined, 81
Holiday Inn, 84
honesty, as leadership trait, 178–179

Howard Johnson, 84
hubris, 82, 83
human faculties, unique, 17
hypercomplexity, 36, 107, 154, 202, 243,
        245

I

Iaccoca, Lee, 159
idealism vs. realism, 64
ideology, 82
    as a system, 76–77
    free enterprise, 129–130
    vs. science, 134
impatience, 82
improvement advice, range of, 218
incentives, irrational, 124–125
incremental
    advantage, 222–224
    approach to change, 218–219, 222
    holographs, 220
incrementalism, *See also* incremental
        approach to change
    strategic, 219
inference, 28–29
information-based workplace, 158
innovative vs. adaptive, 52
instruction, 28–29
integrative budgeting, 127–128
Intel, 49, 51
intellect, 29, 58
    defined, 24
intelligence, strategic, 50
intent, as measure of acceptability, 28
intentionality, as standard of judgment,
        106
International Society for Performance
        Improvement, 244
intuition, 29, 58, 113
    defined, 24
Intuitive Thinkers, 175
Investigative Realists, 175
irony of success, 83–84
irrational incentives, 124–125
irrationality
    of cost-basing, 121–123
    organizational, 47
ISO 9000, 5, 6, 13, 14, 26, 66, 67, 244

J

Jung, Karl, 24

K

Keillor, Garrison, 10
Kelleher, Herb, 179
Kepner-Tregoe, 26
keystone system, 245–246
Kirton Scale, 176
knowledge
    conceptual, 190
    conceptual vs. folk, 42
    creating blend of, 163–164
    excellent, 41–60, 132, 190
        lack of, 106–107
    folk knowledge, 41, 42, 43, 44, 51
    growth of, 84
    industries, 84
    managing, 50–51
    organizational, 44–45
    particular, 43, 44, 45, 190
    particular vs. conceptual, 159
    technical, 190
    workers, 95–96, 201
Kotter, John, 248
Kotter's Eight Transformation Steps,
    249
Kroc, Ray, 105

L

labor costs, minimizing, 69
labor unions, 68
language
    and thought, 63–64
    paradox of, 63–74
leaders, four qualities of, 177
leadership, 100–102, 175–186
    and motivation, 187–198
    components of, 189
    defined, 17, 45, 187
    managerial, model of, 198
    style, 175–176
learning
    organizational, 157–171
Lewin, Kurt, 149

Locke, John, 86
looking vs. seeing, 133–135

M

Malden Mills, 225
management
    actions, 242–243
    activity-based, 127
    activity-centered, 151
    American ideology of, 75–89
    and leadership, 189–190
    as chess, 88
    authoritarian, 167
    authority- vs. performance-based,
        244, 245
    authority-based, 97, 99, 111, 125, 154,
        155, 170, 239, 244, 245
        prevention of problems, 220
    by objective (MBO), 233
    change, focus on, 168
    command, 129
    common sense, 199–209
    compared to chess, 106
    control, 52–53
        converting parochial, 53–54
    cost vs. waste, 120–121
    craft of, 183
    cycle-time, 5, 6, 14, 26
    defined, 17, 45, 135
    detect-and-correct, 94, 105, 120, 232
    focus, 141
        on technical system, 142
    hard-nosed vs. hard-headed, 47
    improvement
        as not a passing phase, 10–11
        comparison or approaches, 14
        promises and pitfalls, 13–14
    knowledge vs. accounting, 120
    lack of information from, 55
    maintenance, 52
    middle, *See* middle management
    models and, 137–138
    modern
        preparing for, 248
        making sense of, 3–20
    of knowledge, 50–51
    performance-based, 170

effective, 247–248
primitive models of, 136–137
quality-oriented performance
    system, 247
reactions, 242–243
science, 22
    scope, 22
    vs. common sense, 22
scientific, 106
sense, 22
shade tree, 42–43
sheep-dog, 94
styles, 24–25, 175–176
    defined, 113
    vs. substance, 29
symmetrical fit of leadership and
    motivation, 190
system-oriented, 5
traditional, real world too complex
    for, 237
vs. labor, dichotomy, 68
vs. labor, price of, 69–70
vs. parochial decisional drivers, 201
whole-minded approach, 25–27
managerial control, 238–239
managers
    as professionals, 134
    managing people rather than
        systems, 238
    modern, 4, 5
    not always being excellent, 237
    steep learning curve of, 237
Marx, Karl, 84
Maslow's hierarchy of needs, 188
Matsushita Electronics, 70
medication errors, 5
meetings, 243
merit pay, 129
metaphors, 85
Microsoft, 49, 181
middle management
    alternatives, 164
    as locus of organizational coherence,
        162
    attacks on, 157, 161
    muddle, 161
    role of, 162
Mill, John Stuart, 86

Milliken Company, 79, 176
minimum acceptable level, 67
mission statement, 194
motivation, 187–198
    elements of, 188–189
Motorola, 4
Myers-Briggs, 24, 176

N

Naisbet, John, 84
Newton, Sir Isaac, 85, 86
    vs. Einstein, 84–85
Newton Vineyards, 181

O

OJT, *See* on-the-job training
"okay" becoming "excellent", 66–67
on-the-job training (OJT), 149–150
opinions, inherent diversity of, 165–166
optimism, 81
organization
    amoeba-like, 49–50, 51–52
    as black box, 142
    as orchestra, 37, 140
    as routine, 145
    charts, 137
    defined, 30
    description of, 138
    enablement of, 71–72
    framing, 133–143
    function of, 48
    natural unity among components, 202
    purpose as cohesive force, 192
organizational
    being, essence of, 45–47
    bloat, 153
    change, and translation, 166–168
    chart, real work not always
        following, 238
    classes, 68–69
    common sense, 47–49, 193–194
    irrationality, 47
    knowledge, 29–30, 44–45
    learning, 50, 157–171
    quality as discipline, 194–196
    rank, defined, 113

rationality, 41–60, 119–132, 225–240
  as strategic model, 203
  establishing, 57–58, 229–230
  marks and measures of, 230–231
Organizational Rationality Audit, 248, 250–251
organizations
  as tangles of routines, 149
  flat, 157–158, 168–169
organizing and managing personnel, 135
Ouchi, William, 65
outcomes, multiple, inevitability of, 105–106
overcontrol, 203
  paradox of, 96–98
ownership and frugality, 130–131

P

paradigm, the invisible, 149–151
paradigms, 76
  clash of, 160–161
paradox of overcontrol, 96–98
Pareto analysis, 235
passion, 29, 58
pay, based on the number of subordinates and size of budget, 124
paying for performance, 128–129
Penn Central Railroad, 80, 83
Pepsi-Cola, 138
performance, paying for, 128–129
performance-based design of hierarchies, 169–170
performance-based systems, 237–239
personnel evaluations, 247
Peter Principle, 86–89, 237
  defined, 88
Peters, Tom, 5, 6, 49, 84, 85, 86, 87, 145, 163, 204
phlogiston, 22
plan, as translator, 232–239
planned program budgeting system (PPBS), 233
Polaroid, 50
power
  and responsibility, 183–185
  diminished when shared, 98

price of, 182
pressure
  to prevent, 92–93
  to produce, 93
pride, 150
principle-centered leadership, 26
priorities, and urgencies, 200–201
priority vs. urgency, 200
probabilities vs. absolutes, 106
problems, equal weighting of, 235
process analysis, 127
productivity, 70, 72
Protestant ethic, 86
purpose, 203–204
  and common sense rationality, 196–197
  and discipline, as inseparable, 195
  and priorities, 192–193
  as element of enterprise, 100, 131
  centrality of, 191–192
  clear, 231
  losing sight of, 200
  vs. practice, 49

Q

quality
  and leadership, 175–186
  and managerial leadership, 197–198
  and organizational rationality, 225–240
  as a term, 70
  as organizational excellence, 30–31
  as reduced variation in process and product, 155
  circles, 14, 15
  common sense strategy for, 230
  defined, 30, 213
  logic of, 4
  making it happen, 241–242
  problems, cause of, 148
  programs, mixed reviews of, 11–13
  quest for, 241–252
  vs. quantity, 73
  vs. volume, 26
quantity vs. quality, 73
quantum thinking, 85
questions, asking the right ones, 79–80

R

rational reframing, 78–79
rational systems, 182
rationality, 113, 196–197, 203–204
    and emotion, 207–209
    as test of common sense, 100
    ideology as framework of, 82
    organizational, 41–60, 119–132
        establishing, 57–58
        maximizing, 106
    purpose as beginning of, 191
    search for, 15–16
    situational, 27
    strategic, 17–18
    work-process, 103
rationalization, 207
"rawhidin'", 94
realities, creating, 108–110
reality, dialog of, 111–112
realm of desirability, 66
reasoning, 63
reliability, 57
responsibility, and power, 183–185
rewards, as reflection of efforts, 129
risk, 16
routine
    as a bad thing, 145
    as not a problem, 146
    as organization, 145
    as profound management choices, 148
    as rut and groove, 145–156
    paradox of, 146–147
    purpose of, 151
    when good ones go bad, 151–152

S

safety management, 205
Saturn, 130
science
    ambitions of, 22–23
    vs. common sense, 22–23
Sears, 112
Second Law of Thermodynamics, 154
second-guessers, 92
self-directed work teams, 9
self-discipline, 39

self-esteem, 39
Senge, Peter, 50, 77, 199, 204
Shapiro, Eileen, 26
silver bullets, 9–10
simplism, 38, 85
Skandia, 50
Smith, Adam, 86
smoking, process of quitting, 153
snake oil, 9–10
sophistication, 202
Southwest Airlines, 179
Soviet model, 98–99
Sputnik, 82, 98
St. Augustine, 86
stability, 216–217
staffing needs, appropriate, 120
Starbucks, 129
statistical controls, 235
Sterling Chemical, 130
strategic rudder, need for, 14–15
strategies for change, 213–224
strength as weakness, 81–83
style, as management, 175–176
success, irony of, 83
swamp vapors, 22
syllogistic reasoning, 64
system, as element of enterprise, 100,
    131
systems
    as categories of events, 203
    human, characteristics of, 140
    keystone, 245–246
    levels of, 35
    performance-based, 237–239
    social, 139–141
    technical, 139–141, 141
        characteristics of, 140
        vs. human, 138–139

T

Taco Bell, 74
Taylor, Frederick, 5, 86, 136
team management, 164
teams, 101, 243, 244
    as collective manager, 164
    establishment of, 164
textile industry, of Dalton, Georgia, 34

Theory X, 65, 68, 69
Theory Y, 65
Theory Z, 65
thinking
    adaptive, 77–78
    mechanistic, 85
Thomas, Dave, 146, 178
thought, illogical vs. logical, 64
threshold acceptability, 66
tools, using best, 235–239
Total Quality Management (TQM), 6, 9,
        12, 14, 74, 136, 226
    failures of, 12
TQM, *See* Total Quality Management
training, purpose vs. activity oriented, 150
translation of change, 167
trust, in organizations, 178
truth, search for, 91–92

U

Union Carbide, 92
urgencies, 200–201, 233

V

valuation, 26, 29, 58
    defined, 24

value, concept of, 71
value-add, 120
    analysis, 127
    goals, 132
    loss of, 155
    optimizing employee, 168
value-adding, 15, 70–71
    initial cost of, 121
    investments vs. waste, 127
    knowledge, 95
Velcro, 4
vocational unhappiness, 176

W

Wallace Company, 74
Weber, Max, 86
Wheatley, Margaret, 138, 204
winning performance, 72–73
workplace, information-based, 158
World War II, 82

Y

Yoshida, Kosaku, 66
Young & Rubicam, 50